Pygmalion and Galatea

For Richard

Pygmalion and Galatea
The history of a narrative in English literature

Essaka Joshua

LONDON AND NEW YORK

First published 2001 by Ashgate Publishing

Reissued 2019 by Routledge
2 Park Square, Milton Park, Abingdon, Oxon, OX14 4RN
52 Vanderbilt Avenue, New York, NY 10017

Routledge is an imprint of the Taylor & Francis Group, an informa business

Copyright © Essaka Joshua, 2001

The author has asserted her moral right under the Copyright, Designs and Patents Act, 1988, to be identified as the author of this work.

All rights reserved. No part of this book may be reprinted or reproduced or utilised in any form or by any electronic, mechanical, or other means, now known or hereafter invented, including photocopying and recording, or in any information storage or retrieval system, without permission in writing from the publishers.

Notice:
Product or corporate names may be trademarks or registered trademarks, and are used only for identification and explanation without intent to infringe.

Publisher's Note
The publisher has gone to great lengths to ensure the quality of this reprint but points out that some imperfections in the original copies may be apparent.

Disclaimer
The publisher has made every effort to trace copyright holders and welcomes correspondence from those they have been unable to contact.

A Library of Congress record exists under LC control number:

ISBN 13: 978-1-138-72880-6 (hbk)
ISBN 13: 978-1-138-72878-3 (pbk)
ISBN 13: 978-1-315-19035-8 (ebk)

Contents

List of Plates		vi
Acknowledgements		ix
Introduction		xi
1	Beginnings to the Nineteenth Century	1
2	'Don't look at J. J. Rousseau': Pygmalion and the Romantics	37
3	Adam's Dream: Post-Romantic Renarrations	53
4	The Pre-Raphaelite Pygmalion and Mid-Victorian Hellenism	81
5	Nineteenth-Century Pygmalion Plays: The Context of Shaw's *Pygmalion*	97
6	The Twentieth Century: Towards a Conclusion	135
Appendix 1	The Pygmalion Story in Dictionaries and Handbooks of Classical Literature	157
Appendix 2	Bibliography of Pygmalion References	161
Bibliography		193
Index		209

List of Plates

1. Edward Burne-Jones, *Pygmalion and the Image – IV, The Soul Attains* (1878). Reproduced by kind permission of Birmingham Museums and Art Gallery   89

2. George Frederic Watts, *The Wife of Pygmalion: A Translation from the Greek* (1868). Reproduced by kind permission of the Faringdon Collection Trust   90

3. William Bell Scott, 'Pygmalion' (1875). Reproduced by kind permission of the Bodleian Library, Oxford   92

4. Marion Terry as Galatea (1877). Reproduced by kind permission of the Victoria and Albert Museum   109

5. Mary Anderson as Galatea (1883). Reproduced by kind permission of the Victoria and Albert Museum   112

General Editors' Preface

The aim of this series is to reflect, develop and extend the great burgeoning of interest in the nineteenth century that has been an inevitable feature of recent decades, as that former epoch has come more sharply into focus as a locus for our understanding not only of the past, but also of the contours of our modernity. Though it is dedicated principally to the publication of original monographs and symposia in literature, history, cultural analysis, and associated fields, there will be a salient role for reprints of significant texts from, or about, the period. This, we believe, distinguishes our project from comparable ones, and means, for example, that in relevant areas of scholarship we both recognize and cut innovatively across such parameters as those suggested by the designations 'Romantic' and 'Victorian'. We welcome new ideas, while valuing tradition. It is hoped that the world which predates yet so forcibly predicts and engages our own will emerge in parts, as a whole, and in the lively currents of debate and change that are so manifest an aspect of its intellectual, artistic and social landscape.

Vincent Newey
Joanne Shattock

University of Leicester

Acknowledgements

This book is a revised version of my doctoral thesis, 'The Pygmalion Story in British Literature until 1900, With Special Reference to the Nineteenth Century' (University of Birmingham,1995). I am indebted to my supervisor, Professor Kelsey Thornton, for his inspiration and support, to Professor Tony Davies, and to my colleagues and students at Birmingham University. I should like to thank Erika Gaffney and Ellen Keeling at Ashgate, the staff of the Bodleian Library, the British Library, Birmingham University Library, and the Theatre Museum Library, Covent Garden. My thanks also go to the Pierpont Morgan Library, New York for granting permission for a quotation from a manuscript in the Gilbert and Sullivan Collection and to the editor of *Nineteenth Century Theatre* for permission to reproduce parts of my article, 'The Mythographic Context of Shaw's *Pygmalion*', which appears in volume 26 (1998) of that journal. The School of Humanities at Birmingham University gave me a generous grant for photographic reproduction. I should also like to thank Richard Cross, Tim Jones, Robert Vilain, and my sister, Eleoma Joshua, all of whom helped me in various ways. My mother, Sue Beardmore, provided moral and financial support during my time as a doctoral student and as a fledgling academic: *sine qua non*.

Introduction

The story of Pygmalion and his statue is one of the most enduring tales in Ovid's *Metamorphoses*. It tells of a sculptor who, rejecting the women of his island, creates a beautiful woman from ivory. The statue, who in later literature comes to be known as Galatea, is brought to life when Pygmalion prays to Venus. *Pygmalion and Galatea* traces the development of the Pygmalion story in English literature from the Middle Ages to the present, following it through a wide variety of versions ranging from tales of love and ideal beauty to vehicles for philosophical, religious, political and aesthetic ideas. Retold for centuries, the Pygmalion story acquires its own distinctive stylistic and thematic marks in each age. It is the aim of this study to bring together these renarrations and examine the interaction between them.

Tracing the history of such a tale is problematized by its classification as a myth, though it is common to refer to it as such. Calling a narrative a 'myth' implies much about how it functions. Myth is associated with social and cultural practices, and has, therefore, been of great interest to anthropologists and psychologists. Indeed, whether one can meaningfully divorce myth (as narrative) from its societal function is a problem. The definition and usage of the word 'myth' has changed so much that it is impossible to give a universal explanation which does justice to all of its connotations. It is more practical to ask, rather, what is the status of a story from Ovid's collection? Most writers on myth concur that there is a difference between an artistic tale such as Ovid's and the story on which it is based. Martin Day suggests dividing the tale types into 'archaic', 'intermediate' and 'derivative' myths.[1] The pre-Ovidian Pygmalion story, as an 'archaic myth', functions only in the society to which it is indigenous. Only fragments remain of the Pygmalion story of this type. Ovid's *Metamorphoses* belongs to the category of 'intermediate myth'; it is the work of a 'highly conscious artist, dominated by aesthetic impulses and intent upon neat, attractive telling of a good story' (Day, p. 5). *Metamorphoses* contains many culturally important versions of myths.

Post-classical renarrations, such as are discussed here, are 'derivative' myths, and are distinguished from intermediate myths by their variety and flexibility. As a derivative myth, the Pygmalion story has undergone numerous changes over the years, and, like many classical tales, for much of its history it has been most often retold by men. In the past, male writers have had better access to classical education and have found it easier to connect with a story which describes the male artist's definition of the ideal female body and the role of that body as a

---

[1] Martin Day, *The Many Meanings of Myth* (Lanham, Maryland, 1984), p. 5.

perfect wife. Women writers show an interest in the story from the late nineteenth century onwards, often giving it a feminist gloss. Re-readings of classical myths have come to the fore in feminist and psychoanalytical criticism (and in combinations of the two).[2] Both schools use myth as an archetypal or metaphorical narrative with which to explain human behaviour. Feminist critics argue that myths perpetuate masculine misogynistic constructs of gender, but that they can nevertheless be reinterpreted:

> At first glance traditional myths seem remarkably anti-woman. [...] Feminist critics argue that Graeco-Roman myths are often masculine constructs whose narratives only reflect the anxieties of male psyches. The main project of feminist myth-critics is to move away from these constructs, perhaps to find that myths are originally feminine or at least to discover the outlines of some earlier, more specifically female, mythologies (Humm, pp. 16–17).

In this type of criticism, the study of the overt renarration of the myth (i.e. a particular named version of the story) is passed over in favour of locating it as a general pattern in other narratives. This involves an '*overlay* [of] meanings *from* myths on to texts, forming filters of critical explanations' (Humm, p. 26). Mythic filtration of narratives necessitates an acceptance of the social function of myth (as an archetypal narrative with enduring significance within a community) and a willingness to combine this acceptance with the methods of literary criticism.

Myth as archetype is quite distinct from myth as (named or unnamed) text. Archetypes are by no means easily defined, but critics concur that there is a universal quality in archetypal narrative which leads to its transmission through the ages, and generates its applicability to texts that may or may not be intentionally alluding to it. Such narrative is 'perennial and recurring'.[3] When used as an archetype, a myth is extracted from its historical context and grafted onto another period. Northrop Frye sees archetype as an enlightening critical tool for understanding narratives:

> Rousseau says that the original society of nature and reason has been overlaid by the corruptions of civilization, and that a sufficiently

---

[2] See Marina Warner, *Monuments and Maidens: The Allegory of the Female Form* (London, 1985), Adrienne Auslander Munich, *Andromeda's Chains: Gender and Interpretation in Victorian Literature and Art* (New York, 1989), Katherine Heinrichs, *The Myths of Love: Classical Lovers in Medieval Literature* (Pennsylvania, 1990), Maggie Humm, *Practising Feminist Criticism: An Introduction* (London, 1995) and *The Woman's Companion to Mythology*, ed. by Caroline Larryngton (London, 1997).

[3] Alvin A Lee, 'Archetype', in *Encyclopedia of Contemporary Literary Theory: Approaches, Scholars, Terms*, ed. by Irena R. Makaryk (Toronto, 1993), p. 508.

courageous revolutionary act could reestablish it. It is nothing either for or against this argument to say that it is informed by the myth of the Sleeping Beauty. But we cannot agree or disagree with Rousseau until we fully understand what he does say, and while of course we can understand him well enough without extracting the myth, there is much to be gained by extracting the myth if the myth is, in fact, as we are suggesting here, the source of the coherence of his argument.[4]

Identifying the historical origin of the archetype and examining its method of transmission is less significant, for Frye, than the analysis of the archetype's effect on critical analysis. These effects are profound: 'all commentary is allegorical interpretation' (Frye, p. 89). Frye's archetypes impose a logic on the text, integrating it into a systematic framework, but they leave him open to criticism. The format of an archetypal story is never scrutinized, with the echoes of the myth being more important than its original instances.

The whole process of using archetypes has been seen as reductive: the reader prunes the narrative until it is recognizable as a version of an archetype.[5] This is often an unintentional attempt to universalize literature. Elizabeth Hayes reads Toni Morrison's *The Bluest Eye*, Zora Neale Hurston's *Their Eyes Were Watching God* and Alice Walker's *The Color Purple* in terms of the Persephone myth.[6] Arguing that feminist versions of the Persephone archetype can be read as positive for women, the study implies that the African-American text needs to be somehow legitimized by filtration through a classical pattern valued by a predominantly white middle-class culture. Hayes observes that all three writers were aware of the Persephone story, and participated, to varying degrees, in the culture of the establishment through their academic interests. Morrison, however, denies that she 'consciously set out to write a reenactment of the Persephone story' (Hayes, p. 173), and Hayes falls back on the assumption that the myth must have affected the writer subliminally. In effect, Morrison's mind is colonized by this implicitly superior culture: 'Archetypes [...] can operate subliminally, through the unconscious, as well as through rational thought: that is precisely what gives them their astounding resonance, their numinosity' (Hayes, p. 173). While a case could be made for the cultural hybridity of these authors, this kind of approach appropriates the work to such a degree as to abrogate the cultural identity of the author. Furthermore, to read using an archetypal filter is to make a teleological imposition on a text: the text is only of value if it can be identified as, and perhaps

---

[4] Northrop Frye, *Anatomy of Criticism: Four Essays* (London, 1957), pp. 353–354.
[5] See Thomas Willard, 'Archetypes of the Imagination' in *The Legacy of Northrop Frye*, ed. by Alvin A. Lee and Robert D. Denham (Toronto, 1994), p. 20.
[6] Elizabeth T. Hayes, '"Like Seeing You Buried": Persephone in *The Bluest Eye*, *Their Eyes Were Watching God*, and *The Color Purple*', in *Images of Persephone: Feminist Readings in Western Literature*, ed. by Elizabeth T. Hayes (Gainesville, Florida, 1994), pp. 170–194.

moulded into, a predetermined pattern. Difficulty arises with the selection of archetypes. If one is to fix a classical story as an archetype, then a reason is needed for choosing the version deemed relevant to the narratives which supposedly echo it. Should this be the urtext (if there is one), or the most influential version (if this is different from the urtext), or a composite of different versions (such as the frequent association of Pygmalion's statue with the name 'Galatea' suggests)? When a version is agreed upon, we encounter further problems with the interpretation of the archetype which, like any narrative, is polysemic.

In the case of the Pygmalion story, Ovid's version is most often used by critics as an archetype. A variety of interpretations of Ovid's text, however, has lead to diverse emphases in the archetype. The Pygmalion archetype is often applied to stories about people being created (e.g. *Frankenstein* or *The Winter's Tale*) and it is also widely employed as an archetype for women being educated or socially improved by men (e.g. *Educating Rita*).[7] Analyses of the Pygmalion story as archetype have thus taken different routes. Gerald Gresseth, for example, strips away Ovid's literary expansions to reformulate the story as a Formalist paradigm based on Vladimir Propp's *Morphology of the Folktale*:

1. There is a young man without a wife
2. He makes a statue of a woman
3. He goes to the temple (or the like) to seek divine aid to bring this statue to life
4. After returning home the statue miraculously comes to life
5. There is a happy ending; they become man and wife.

Gresseth's analysis reduces the tale even further to identify it as a combination of abstract event-types which form part of Propp's finite list: '1. Lack [...] 2. Consent to counter-action [...] 3. Departure [...] 4. Liquidation of lack [...] 5. Return of hero [...] 6. Wedding'.[8] The Pygmalion story, unrecognizable from this second list, is construed as part of a greater set of abstract archetypal patterns.

Stephen Butler's construction of the Pygmalion archetype, in 'The Pygmalion Motif and the Crisis of the Creative Process in Modern Fiction' (1984), retains more of the character of the myth. Butler argues that the Pygmalion archetype (based on Ovid's version) has been reinterpreted by modern authors to reflect the

---

[7] There are several studies of educational methods which discuss the "Pygmalion effect". See for example, Robert Rosenthal and Lenore Jacobson, *Pygmalion in the Classroom: Teacher Expectation and Pupils' Intellectual Development* (New York, 1968) and John Honey, *Does Accent Matter? The Pygmalion Factor* (London, 1991).

[8] Gerald K. Gresseth, 'The Pygmalion Tale', *Journal of the Pacific Northwest Council on Foreign Languages*, 2 (1981), 15–19 (p. 15 and p. 18).

artistic struggle or crisis in the modern period.[9] He examines, as is usual in archetypal studies, texts which do not mention Pygmalion by name, such as Oscar Wilde's *The Picture of Dorian Gray*, Thomas Mann's *Death in Venice* and Vladimir Nabokov's *Lolita*. J. Hillis Miller's *Versions of Pygmalion* (1990), on the other hand, postulates that the Pygmalion story is the 'literalising allegory' of prosopopoeia (the ascription of 'a face, a name, or a voice to the absent, the inanimate, or the dead').[10] Here, Pygmalion's desire to bring the statue to life is akin to the 'fundamental generative linguistic act making a given story possible' (p. 13). Echoes of it are found in Heinrich von Kleist's *Der Findling*, Thomas Hardy's *Barbara of the House of Grebe* and Henry James's *The Last of the Valerii*. Gail Marshall offers a convincing refutation of Miller's argument on the grounds that the name Galatea is a late addition to the myth:

> Pygmalion's desire to 'animate' his statue, which has only subsequently come to be known as Galatea, falls short of what Hillis Miller defines as the full narrativizing implications of prosopopoeia, that is, the ascription to entities that are not really alive first of a *name*, then of a face, and finally, in a return to language, of a voice. Galatea's name appears not to have been coined until 1770, and in the Ovidian legend she lacks her own voice.[11]

For both Butler and Hillis Miller, the Pygmalion story functions as an archetype based on an interpretation of Ovid's text; it acts as an organizational, associative device linking texts together for critical comment. In the same vein, Catherine Maxwell's 'Browning's Pygmalion and the Revenge of Galatea' (1993) filters Robert Browning's poetry through the Pygmalion story:

---

[9] Stephen Henry Butler, 'The Pygmalion Motif and Crisis of the Creative Process in Modern Fiction' (unpublished doctoral dissertation, University of Brandeis, 1984).

[10] J. Hillis Miller, *Versions of Pygmalion* (Cambridge, Massachusetts, 1990), p. 4.

[11] Marshall's dating of the first use of the name 'Galatea' for the statue is, however, incorrect. Walter Buske and Meyer Reinhold both conclude that the earliest use of this name for the statue is in a French novel, *Pygmalion*, by Thémiseul de Sainte Hyacinthe Cordonnier (1741). Reinhold's article is a refutation of Helen H. Law's suggestion that Rousseau was the first to give the statue this name. Walter Buske had, however, already settled this question some years before. Richard Jenkyns assumes incorrectly that Law was right in her suppositions. Both Reinhold and Buske agree that although Cordonnier's was the first use, Rousseau's play is likely to have been the most influential, and can therefore be regarded as the most likely source for subsequent uses of the name. Gail S. Marshall, 'Artful Galateas: Gender and the Arts of Writing and Acting in Novels, 1876–1900' (unpublished doctoral thesis, University of Cambridge, 1992), p. 2, Walter Buske, 'Pygmaliondichtungen des 18. Jahrhunderts', *Germanisch-Romanische Monatschrift*, 7 (1915), 345–354, Meyer Reinhold, 'The Naming of Pygmalion's Animated Statue', *Classical Journal*, 66 (1979), 316–319, Helen H. Law, 'The Name of Galatea in the Pygmalion Myth', *Classical Journal*, 27 (1932), 337–342, Richard Jenkyns, *Dignity and Decadence: Victorian Art and the Classical Inheritance* (London, 1991), p. 115.

> Browning's real compulsion is Ovid's story of Pygmalion. [...] Browning lays bare the misogyny of Ovid's Pygmalion, for whom no living woman is good enough. His poems show how male subjects, threatened by woman's independent spirit, replace her with statues, pictures, prostheses, corpses, which seem to them more than acceptable substitutes for the real thing. Browning's male subjects typically invert Ovid's myth, reducing woman, even through her death, to a composition of their own creating.[12]

Browning, however, never mentions the Pygmalion story, and there is no hard evidence to suggest that he actively intended to invert Ovid's version. Maxwell reads Browning's poetry through an interpretation of Ovid's Pygmalion story as archetype.

Gail Marshall's use of the Pygmalion myth is more subtle: she employs it as a metaphor for an aesthetic (the 'Galatea-aesthetic') that defines the visual and sexual personae of the Victorian actress, both on the stage and in her personal life.[13] The 'Galatea-aesthetic' positions actresses as the objects of male control, rendering them passive, statuesque and fundamentally heteronomous. Stressing the attraction of the timelessness, silence and beauty of the female statue-form for Victorian writers, Marshall locates an aesthetic of statue-simulation which points at both innocence and overt but unselfconscious sexuality. I explore some of these issues in my article 'The Mythographic Context of Shaw's *Pygmalion*', published in the same year as Marshall's book, and which now forms the basis for Chapter 5.[14] Marshall's point is that, on the stage, actresses began as the demure Galatea, shaped by Pygmalion, but developed into self-determining individuals, whether through autobiography, theatre-management, or interpreting their own roles. Marshall suggests that the Pygmalion myth 'operated both practically and metaphorically to shape and define women's theatrical lives' (p. 6). Marshall's aim is to draw on a nineteenth-century understanding of the story in order to illustrate her conception of the statuesque aesthetic at work on the English stage in that period.

Marshall's study is, however, marred by a few assumptions about the nineteenth-century version of the Pygmalion story which do not stand up to scrutiny given a more extensive exploration of the morphology of the tale. Marshall attempts to give the Galatea-aesthetic historical authenticity by identifying it as a generalized account of the Pygmalion story as it existed in

---

[12] Catherine Maxwell, 'Browning's Pygmalion and the Revenge of Galatea', *English Literary History*, 60 (1993), 989–1013 (p. 990).

[13] Gail Marshall, *Actresses on the Victorian Stage: Feminine Performance and the Galatea Myth* (Cambridge, 1998).

[14] Essaka Joshua, 'The Mythographic Context of Shaw's *Pygmalion*' in *Nineteenth Century Theatre*, 26 (1998), 112–137.

English poetry of the period. Her claim that most nineteenth-century poets return Galatea to stone at the end of the narrative is factually incorrect:

> Most of the nineteenth-century poets [...] deviate from their Ovidian source in one particular which serves to confirm their sense of the greater desirability of the statue: with few exceptions, modern Galateas are returned to stone at the end of their narrative. This makes of the statue's 'life' rather a fleeting episode than the miraculous metamorphosis which is the climax of Ovid's story, and renders the marble state both the ultimate as well as the initial site of desire (Marshall, p. 23).

The majority of nineteenth-century poets, as I will later show, retain a human Galatea at the end of the narrative. (The exceptions are confined to a few dramas and a small quirky minority of poems in which either the narrative concludes before the statue changes or Pygmalion falls in love with someone else; occasionally Galatea is abandoned precisely because she is too human.) Marshall's understanding of the Pygmalion metaphor is tainted by her assumption that nineteenth-century poets privilege 'closure' (in the form of a symmetry embodied in a return to stone) over 'living form' (p. 24). Focusing on prosopopoeia, and on closure over transformation (pp. 23–24), Marshall overlooks more significant ways in which the story is used to explore questions of artistic creativity. I explore these issues in Chapter 3 below. Marshall omits to mention, too, something that reinforces her general argument: that, during the 1880s, feminist poets reclaim Galatea, giving her a voice with which to express her individuality and to protest against her yoke. It seems likely that feminist writers are drawing on the stage interpretations of Galatea's character which often conceive her, at least for a time, as contrary to conventional notions of femininity. Marshall's view of the Pygmalion poems is at odds with her thesis; just as Galatea as actress 'comes to life' and finds a voice at the end of the century, so it can be argued that in late nineteenth-century poetry Galatea likewise challenges the gaze of Pygmalion. Marshall's construction of the Victorian Pygmalion poem as a tale which has a 'greater concentration on, and frequent return to, the statue-state' (p. 25) is not backed by discussion of any examples, and it is difficult to see from where it originates.[15]

While Marshall's study is illuminating on the rhetoric of the statuesque on the English stage, her account of the nineteenth-century Pygmalion story is ultimately secondary. Marshall in effect constructs her own archetype of the Pygmalion story

---

[15] The short list of nineteenth-century Pygmalion poems Marshall cites in her notes does not contain a single version in which the statue changes back at the end of the narrative (Marshall, p. 193, n. 45).

in the same way that Butler and Hillis Miller do. The Pygmalion story's archetypal status is perhaps obscured in Marshall's study by its (supposed) derivation from texts belonging to the nineteenth century. Marshall's difficulty is that a narrative which acts as a text and as an archetype, supposedly revealing something universally significant for the nineteenth century, has to be confined to a single meaning. Once we expose to scrutiny the nature of the Pygmalion text in the nineteenth century, we see that to speak of a 'nineteenth-century Pygmalion' is to gloss over much, and that to define it in the way that Marshall does is misleading.

Butler, Hillis Miller, and Maxwell employ distinctive interpretations of the Pygmalion archetype, stressing creative crisis, the act of story-telling and the suppression of women's independence. Butler and Maxwell argue that the writers they discuss reject the Ovidian archetype, yet it is these critics themselves who have selected this version of the tale as an overlay. We may well question the relevance of an archetype that is rejected – especially if it is employed on the grounds that it is superficially similar to the stories studied; another interpretation of the archetype, or even a different archetype, would result in a different conclusion. Furthermore, the authors these critics discuss may have understood the Pygmalion story in a particular way that an archetype cannot reveal; nineteenth and twentieth-century writers may have been surrounded by other renarrations with different emphases. With the exception of Marshall's account, it is, nevertheless, assumed in these studies that Ovid's archetype has a direct relevance for the people of any time, and that writers react exclusively to Ovid's version. Whilst Ovid's Pygmalion is of great importance, only a study of the interaction of the many and various renarrations of the story can show us which version writers are responding to, and how they make a Pygmalion narrative that is appropriate for their age. If we are to claim a relevance for an archetype which is anything more than ephemeral, then we need to be sensitive to the historical circumstances which surround and inform each author.

In what follows, I will focus on myth as text and aim to show how the Pygmalion story has developed.[16] Writers do not necessarily respond to Ovid's myth directly. There are significant versions which redefine the myth, directing writers into diverse directions. Adrienne Munich asserts, in *Andromeda's Chains*, that

> by identifying momentarily with a classical myth, an artist leaps backward into the womb of civilization when the origins of the gender arrangements in the western world were being mythologized,

---

[16] Some of the texts I examine here are briefly discussed in *Classical Mythology in English Literature: A Critical Anthology*, ed. by Geoffrey Miles (London, 1999), pp. 332–345. *Classical Mythology in English Literature* includes a number of useful Pygmalion and Pygmalion-like texts and is well worth consulting in conjunction with the analysis I provide here.

reconceiving the importance of that binary arrangement of the sexes for his own times (Munich, pp. 5–6).

I argue, on the other hand, that in some cases writers may not be leaping back very far, but are reacting, instead, to other versions of the myth and to contemporary issues. The use of Ovid as an archetype obscures this, not merely because different critics interpret his work in different ways, but because archetypal criticism of this kind encourages us to stop at Ovid and to gloss over other versions. To focus exclusively on the Ovidian archetype is to deny what is at the heart of mythic stories: evolution. Myths are retold and redefined by their narrators, reflecting changes in culture and literary tradition. The Pygmalion story is not static; it is an evolving tale with a rich history. Consequently 'Pygmalion' does not signify one context but many. In this I echo Lévi-Strauss's comment on the Oedipus myth:

> It cannot be too strongly emphasized that all available variants [of a myth] should be taken into account. [...] There is no true version of which all the others are but copies or distortions. Every version belongs to the myth.[17]

To accept this view of myth is to accept that contextualizing a version of the Pygmalion story is not as simple as placing it within a classical context, viewing it as a pure and direct development from an intermediate myth. Rather, versions should be seen as part of a network of 'Pygmalion' contexts. For example, I read George Bernard Shaw's *Pygmalion* not in the context of Ovid, as many prior critics have done, but in the context of nineteenth-century plays on the Pygmalion story. To exclude all versions of the myth except Ovid's has a significant effect on the way we view the play. Pygmalion stories are often contexts for each other. Freezing the Pygmalion myth in its Ovidian form and automatically bestowing a universal significance on Ovid is misleading. Rather, we should understand the Pygmalion story as an historically situated and changing narrative. If we were to suppose that the story could work as an archetype, then we would still have, nevertheless, to find out what form the archetype should take ostensively and empirically, by looking at all the cases there are.

This book looks at how writers treat the Pygmalion story when they are explicitly directing their readers to its tradition: they do this by using the name 'Pygmalion'. I am not arguing for, or even against, the identification of the story as a reflection of something universal in the minds of writers and readers, but rather that, irrespective of its (problematic) archetypal status, the Pygmalion story is a polysemic narrative which works within a literary tradition, and that this

---

[17] Claude Lévi-Strauss, 'The Structural Study of Myth', in *Myth: A Symposium*, ed. by Thomas A. Sebeok (Bloomington, Indiana, 1965), pp. 81–106, p. 94.

tradition needs to be explored fully. My main aim is to scrutinize the changes in the meaning of the Pygmalion story by examining its principal renarrations. My intention is not as such to produce a theoretical work, but to discover how each age has redefined the Pygmalion story. I will be asking: what does the Pygmalion story mean? Which versions of the story are writers reacting to? Why does the Pygmalion story interest the writers who use it? What changes do the writers make?

My approach, not a new one, resembles that outlined by Theodore Ziolkowski in *Varieties of Literary Thematics* (1983).[18] 'Literary thematics', he argues, 'offers many possible varieties' of organization (Ziolkowski, p. 220). Ziolkowski advises that selectivity is the key to a successful thematic study. Much as the collector obsesses about including every version of the tale, ultimately she has to leave much out of the final analysis. The shaping of the material is the hardest task. In my case, I have found that the stories fall naturally into clusters of texts which share either generic or thematic affinity, or are otherwise similar in their outlook. As Ziolkowski points out, certain 'themes and motifs sometimes display an affinity for certain genres; periods and epochs in turn display a pronounced affinity for certain themes, motifs, and images' (p. 221). I have also found that, although all periods show some interest in the Pygmalion story, its heyday is the nineteenth century, and its favoured genre is poetry. The Pygmalion story was retold and reworked during the nineteenth century more times than in any other; and it is for this reason that I write at length on this period, whilst providing less-detailed sketches of the story before and after this time. The diachronic study of a story has an advantage in that the process can easily reveal precedents and authorial influences. These may escape those who study texts solely from the perspective of an individual writer's works or his or her socio-political situation. My chapter on Bernard Shaw is a case in point. This chapter overturns a mistaken belief that the Pygmalion story is an irrelevant context for Shaw's play *Pygmalion* – a context which has been dismissed by critics because the myth is assumed to be significant solely in its Ovidian form. Through the context of nineteenth-century renarrations of the Pygmalion story it is possible to understand why Shaw chose to write the play as an account of Eliza's social education.

The first chapter will establish the history of the Pygmalion story from its origins in early Greek myth until the end of the eighteenth century. At that point Jean-Jacques Rousseau grasped the importance of the myth for expressing his view of the relationship of the artist to the art-work. His depiction of the statue as an ideal, attractive to him because it is part of him, was admired by the English Romantics; but it was not fully accepted. Thomas Lovell Beddoes and J. H. Leigh Hunt reject Rousseau's Pygmalion's narcissistic egotism for a different kind of

---

[18] Theodore Ziolkowski, *Varieties of Literary Thematics* (Princeton, 1983).

Romantic epiphanic moment (Chapter 2). Post-Romantic versions of the story emphasize the art-life debate by inserting a new episode into the story in which Pygmalion is given a vision of the statue in a creative dream (Chapter 3). By mid-Victorian times, this inspired vision is not enough, and moral questions begin to arise about the nature of Pygmalion's art: does his art represent the spiritual or the sensual (fleshly)? In this crisis of representation, known as the 'Fleshly Controversy', the Pygmalion story is a battle-ground for Victorian Hellenism's clash with moral obsession. Writers ask: does the animated statue possess a soul? Is she a beautiful body designed to tempt Pygmalion? (Chapter 4). These questions are also unavoidable in the physical art of the stage, where the tensions between naivety and sophistication, between intrinsic worth and cultural overlay, are debated by Gilbert and Shaw (Chapter 5). On the stage, Galatea, formerly a woman of few words, gains a voice and by the end of the century, the emphasis has moved from the sculptor to his creation. The voice which the playwrights gave to Galatea is now used to question Pygmalion's right to control her, a question which establishes the note for the twentieth century (Chapter 6). The metamorphosis of the Pygmalion myth involves a change from a 'patriarchal' interest in Pygmalion to the 'feminist' development of Galatea's character. Feminist revisionism, however, does not saturate the modern period, and the Pygmalion story is here connected with the theme of artistic crisis. Twentieth-century writers demonstrate a new-found interest in Pygmalion's frustration with his unfulfilled idealism.

This book will demonstrate the flexibility and dynamism of the Pygmalion story, a narrative which can tell us much about the representation of women and about the changing role of the artist. Like the stories of the Lady of Shalott, Mariana, and Andromeda, the Pygmalion story represents women as controlled, trapped, rescued, idealized, defined and owned by men, but it also communicates much about the aesthetics and psychology of the artist, and the relationship between the artist and his work. The experimentation with this story continues even today.

Chapter 1

Beginnings to the Nineteenth Century

Classical Origins

> His mind, his soul, the light of his reason and his judgement were blinded, and in his madness, as if it were his wife, he would lift up the divinity to the couch.[1]

As is the case for many tales which begin as myths, the urtext for the Pygmalion story is no longer extant. Though Ovid's is the most important classical version of the tale, stories similar to his tale have been recorded by several classical mythographers and early Christian apologists, and there are good grounds for thinking that the story was a local legend of Cyprus.[2] The earliest written version of the Pygmalion story formed part of the no longer extant *History of Cyprus* or *Cypriaca* written by the Hellenistic writer Philostephanus – a poet and collector of myths, who flourished in the third century BC. Philostephanus's version is only available to us through the later works of Clement of Alexandria (c. AD 150–c. AD 211) and Arnobius of Sicca (d. 330), who recount it in slightly different forms.[3] Both mythographers use the story as a parable to justify religious polemic: Clement warns that pagan statue-worship is wrong; Arnobius argues that it is impossible for gods to dwell in statues.

Clement, an Athenian and a Christian, records Philostephanus's story in *Protrepticus* or *The Exhortation to the Greeks* (4, 51).[4] He tells of Pygmalion, a 'well-known' man of Cyprus, who falls in love with a sacred ivory statue of naked Aphrodite and embraces it. Arnobius's account, in *Adversus Nationes* (4, 22), contains more detail than Clement's. He elevates Pygmalion's status to king of Cyprus, changes the holy statue from the Greek Aphrodite to the Roman Venus, suggests that Pygmalion is mad, and is the first writer (that we know of) to imply a sexual violation of the statue: '[Pygmalion's] mind, his soul, the light of his reason and his judgement were blinded, and in his madness, as if it were his wife, he would lift up the divinity to the couch'. The writers connect Philostephanus's Pygmalion with a similar story, from Poseidippus's book on Cnidus, of an

---

[1] Arnobius of Sicca, *The Case Against the Pagans*, trans. by George E. McCracken, 2 vols, Ancient Christian Writers, 7–8 (Westminster, Maryland and London, 1949), II, 475.

[2] See Helen H. Law, pp. 338–339.

[3] *Fragmenta Historicorum Graecorum*, ed. by Karl Müller, 5 vols (Paris, 1841–1870) III (1849), 31.

[4] Clement of Alexandria, *The Exhortation to the Greeks*, trans. by G. W. Butterworth, The Loeb Classical Library (London, and Cambridge, Massachusetts, 1960), pp. 130–133.

unknown man's amorous liaison with a marble statue of Aphrodite. The man from Cnidus is also elevated by Arnobius, who describes him as young and of noble birth. He suggests further, that the Cnidian's love for the goddess caused him to perform 'lewd' acts with it; according to Clement, it is, rather, the craftsmanship of statue itself which beguiles the man.

There is also a reference to a Pygmalion in Hyginus's *Fabulae* (written before AD 207).[5] It is not clear, however, whether this is the Pygmalion of Ovid's story. Hyginus writes that 'In Egypt in the land of Busiris, son of Neptune, when there was a famine, and Egypt had been parched for nine years, the king summoned the augurs from Greece. Thrasius, his brother Pygmalion's son, announced that rains would come if a foreigner were sacrificed, and proved his words when he himself was sacrificed'.[6] Hellanicus also includes a very brief reference to Pygmalion in his *Cypriaca*: 'Carpasia [was] a city of Cyprus, which Pygmalion founded' (Müller, I [1841], 65).

Ovid's story of Pygmalion, in *Metamorphoses* (composed between AD 1–8), is the earliest version of cultural importance.[7] According to Meyer Reinhold, it was Ovid's account 'that remained the canonical form of the myth until the end of the seventeenth century' (Reinhold, p. 316). It is certainly canonical, but it is by no means the only version to which writers reacted. Ovid's sources have not been identified, but his story is similar to those of Philostephanus and Poseidippus. The similarity is noted by Joseph Solodow.[8] Though Philostephanus's is the earliest known written version of the story, only Solodow infers a direct connection between Ovid and Philostephanus:

> Comparison of this [Ovid's] version with its Greek source shows how, in making it over, the poet gave it a new subject and reconceived it so powerfully that it became a paradigm for later ages. Philostephanus of Cyrene, a pupil or friend of Callimachus, wrote what appears to be the original account; Philostephanus' work is lost, but two later writers have preserved notice of it (pp. 215–216).

He is, however, only able to support his case by comparing the two versions. There is no other evidence that Ovid knew this work.

Ovid's Pygmalion, a sculptor of Cyprus, scorns the libertine women of his nation and creates his own perfect woman in ivory. He falls passionately in love

---

[5] Hyginus, *Fabulae*, ed. by P. K. Marshall (Stuttgart, 1993), p. 60.
[6] Hyginus, *The Myths of Hyginus*, trans. by Mary Grant (Kansas, 1960), p. 60.
[7] This date is given by E. J. Kenny in *Ovid's Metamorphoses*, trans. A. D. Melville (Oxford and New York, 1986), p. x.
[8] Joseph B. Solodow, *The World of Ovid's Metamorphoses* (Chapel Hill, North Carolina and London, 1988).

with the statue, dresses it, showers it with gifts, and takes it to bed with him. At the festival of Venus, Pygmalion prays to the goddess to give him a woman like his ivory maiden. When he returns home from the temple, he kisses and embraces the statue, which warms to life in his arms. They marry and produce a child called Paphos.[9] The sex of the child is not conclusive owing to manuscript difficulties. Pygmalion is said to be an ancestor of Adonis, with whom Venus later falls in love.

Aside from being just a simple sketch of Ovid's artful and poetic tale, the story, as it is here, has been taken out of the context of the larger narrative of the *Metamorphoses*. It is important to acknowledge, that post-Ovidian renarrations of the Pygmalion story usually divorce the story from the significant place it has in the *Metamorphoses*. The story, however, has one set of interpretations when it is separated from the *Metamorphoses*, and another when it is left in its context. Perhaps the most striking result of removing the Pygmalion story from the *Metamorphoses* is seen in the implications of Pygmalion's actions. When divorced from its context, the story ends happily with Venus answering Pygmalion's prayers. As part of the *Metamorphoses*, it ends tragically, with Pygmalion's descendants being punished for his marriage to his own creation. Myrrha falls in love with her own father, Cinyras, and tricks him into sleeping with her. Venus is punished for her part in the transformation of the statue, as the son whom Myrrha conceives is Adonis. The goddess falls in love with the beautiful Adonis and mourns his loss when he is killed by a wild boar in a hunting accident.

Various other aspects of the Pygmalion story take on special significance when it is placed within the context of the stories in the *Metamorphoses*. For example, the story tells of an inanimate object becoming animate, whereas the reverse is more usual in Ovid's collection. The story immediately preceding that of Pygmalion tells of the punishment of the Propoetides, who have denied Venus's divinity. The goddess makes them the first prostitutes and turns them into stone, a reversal of the Pygmalion situation. The blood of their faces hardens, contrasting with the blushing innocence of Pygmalion's awakened statue. Pygmalion, we are told, sculpts his statue because he is disgusted by the Propoetides. This point, requiring the distinctive Ovidian context of the tale, is often omitted in later renarrations. On one reading, Ovid appears to be stressing Pygmalion's piety, but this is not universal. Through close scrutiny of the nuances of the language, Jane Miller concludes that Ovid uses sexual innuendo in his description of the statue, implying that Pygmalion is less than pious:

> Once the statue is finished, Pygmalion falls in love with it: 'operisque sui concepit amorem' ('and he falls in love with his own work'. The

---

[9] See Franz Bömer, *P. Ovidius Naso. Metamorphosen. Kommentar* (Heidelberg, 1980), pp. 109–110.

word 'concepit' is a sexual metaphor, already hinted at by the use of 'nasci' in the previous line').[10]

Miller argues that there is a sexual sub-text which tells against the view of the story as one of piety rewarded. Douglas Bauer suggests that the Pygmalion story has further significance within the framework of the *Metamorphoses*:

> Of all the themes in the *Metamorphoses*, none recurs either as frequently or as patently as that of stone. The variety of its manifestations – now functioning literally and at the same time symbolically as the subject-matter in the account of a bizarre petrification or its inverse, now as the metaphor of physical or moral insensibility, and now as a complementary simile or verbal echo – warrants its distinction as the dominant image.[11]

The story forms a striking connection between two of the major themes in the collection: love and stone, and is located in the golden section of the *Metamorphoses*. Bauer concludes that the ratio between the number of lines which precede the Pygmalion story and the number of lines which 'divide it from the cognate epilogue is exactly 0. 618, the Golden Section' (p. 20). This, he claims, shows both the premeditation of the poet in constructing the *Metamorphoses*, and his 'familiarity with the mystical Pythagoreans' (p. 20). If the golden section theory is correct, it means that Ovid has emphasized the Pygmalion episode. Bauer speculates that this could be because the stone, love and art themes are all interwoven in the story. Other explanations have been proposed to explain the significance of the metamorphosis of the statue. Jane Miller suggests that the metamorphosis of the statue is an archetypal birth-myth: 'This birth-image reinforces the view that the statue is, in a sense, the child of Pygmalion, a notion which would have an obvious bearing on the Myrrha story' (Miller, p. 208). The idea that Pygmalion was the father or creator of the statue-maiden, and therefore should not marry her, connects it with the sexual guilt and punishment of Myrrha. Errol Durbach suggests a third interpretation, arguing that the Pygmalion story contains within it the germ of its anti-myth: that form of Romantic idealism that stands in danger of changing living flesh into stone. Pygmalion wants a living doll,

---

[10] Jane M. Miller, 'Some Versions of Pygmalion', in *Ovid Renewed. Ovidian Influences on Literature and Art From the Middle Ages to the Twentieth Century*, ed. by Charles Martindale (Cambridge, 1988), pp. 205–214 and p. 281, note 19 (p. 206).

[11] Douglas Bauer, 'The Function of Pygmalion in the *Metamorphoses* of Ovid', *Transactions of the American Philological Association*, 93 (1962), 1–21 (p. 2).

like Hoffman's Coppelia.¹²

Later classical accounts of Pygmalion can be found in fragments of mythographic and historical writings. These, like those which preceded Ovid, are unsophisticated and divergent. *Bibliotheca* or *The Library* (first or second century AD), a collection wrongly attributed to Apollodorus, refers to a Pygmalion, though his relationship with a statue is not mentioned. The text merely records his genealogy, and the account differs from that given by Ovid.¹³

> This Cinyras in Cyprus, whither he had come with some people, founded Paphos; and having there married Metharme, daughter of Pygmalion, king of Cyprus, he begat Oxyporus and Adonis, and besides them daughters Orsedice, Laogore and Braesia (Apollodorus, II, 84–85).

Ovid's Pygmalion is Cinyras's grandfather, rather than his son-in-law; and Pygmalion's child is Paphos rather than Metharme. A Pygmalion, described as a Phoenician who became king of Cyprus, is alluded to in the fourth book of *De Abstinentia* by Porphyry (c. AD 270).¹⁴ Here Pygmalion is connected with priests who break their rule of vegetarianism by eating sacrificial flesh.

> The Cyzicenean and Asclepiades the Cyprian say, about the era of Pygmalion, who was by birth a Phoenician, but reigned over the Cyprians. [...] On one occasion a priest touched cooked flesh, burnt his fingers and put them in his mouth. Having tasted the flesh, he wanted more, ate some and gave it to his wife. Pygmalion, however, becoming acquainted with this circumstance, ordered both the priest and his wife to be hurled headlong from a steep rock, and gave the priesthood to another person, who not long after performing the same sacrifice, and eating the flesh of the victim, fell into the same calamities as his predecessor. The thing, however, proceeding still farther, and men using the same kind of sacrifice, and through yielding to desire, not abstaining from, but feeding on flesh, the deed was no longer punished (pp. 152–153).

There are two prominent Pygmalions in classical history: Pygmalion, the king of Cyprus who fell in love with a statue, and Pygmalion of Tyre (in Phoenicia)

---

¹² Errol Durbach, 'Pygmalion: Myth and Anti-Myth in the Plays of Ibsen and Shaw', in *George Bernard Shaw's 'Pygmalion'*, ed. by Harold Bloom (New Haven, 1988), pp. 87–98 (p. 90).

¹³ Apollodorus, *The Library*, trans. by Sir James George Frazer, The Loeb Classical Library, 2 vols (London, 1921), II, 84–85.

¹⁴ Porphyry, *Selected Works*, trans. by Thomas Taylor (London, 1823), pp. 152–153. Porphyry notes that Pygmalion is mentioned by Neanthes Cyzicenus and Asclepiades Cyprius. See Müller, III (1849), 10 and 306.

who was the brother of Dido, queen of Carthage. Though Tyre and Cyprus are geographically close, it is generally thought that these were two different men. Porphyry's Pygmalion is, however, connected with both of these places and it is not possible to say for certain which Pygmalion this is. Occasionally, later writers have confused Pygmalion of Cyprus with Pygmalion of Tyre. Finally, Nonnos Panopolitanus's *Dionysiaca*, from the fifth century, connects Pygmalion, king of Cyprus, with a story about his longevity.

> Echelaos lad, you have belied your birth as a Cyprian! You are not sprung from Pygmalion, to whom Cypris gave a long course of life and many years. Ares the bridegroom of your Paphian did not save you.[15]

Pygmalion is connected with both Tyre and Cyprus in this text.

The classical versions of the myth all differ in their accounts. The three main stories of Pygmalion – those of Clement, Arnobius and Ovid – share only the common element of a Pygmalion falling love with a statue. They do not agree on Pygmalion's status in Cyprus, on whether he sculpted the statue himself, or on whether the statue was brought to life. The statue is made from ivory in the stories of both Clement and Ovid. The medium for Arnobius's statue is not specified. The fragmentary nature of what remains of the work of the Greek mythographers means that it is impossible to establish a clear history for Pygmalion in this period. Ovid's version is, however, the most important of these, though its influence was not felt immediately. Post-Ovidian accounts by Greek mythographers show no obvious signs of having been influenced by Ovid. Wilmon Brewer confirms, in *Ovid's 'Metamorphoses' in European Culture*, that neither Nonnos nor Apollodorus 'showed any acquaintance with Ovid'.[16]

The Medieval Pygmalion (1200–1500)

> To þis fable may be sette many exposicions, and in liche wise to othir such fables; and the poetis made them because that mennys vnderstandynge schulde be the more scharpe and subtill to finde dyvers exposicions.[17]

During the Middle Ages, the English Pygmalion story developed closer associations with theology through the moralizing tradition. Ovid's tales were

---

[15] Nonnos, *Dionysiaca*, trans. by W. H. D. Rouse, notes by H. J. Rose, 3 vols (London and Cambridge, Massachusetts, 1940), II, 459.

[16] Wilmon Brewer, *Ovid's 'Metamorphoses' in European Culture* (Boston, 1941), p. 19.

[17] *The Epistle of Othea: Translated From The French Text of Christine de Pisan by Stephen Scrope*, ed. by Curt Ferdinand Bühler, Early English Text Society, 264 (Oxford, 1970).

retold with glosses which interpret them as moral stories. Though, at first, rarely found separately from the moralizations of the *Metamorphoses*, it is during this period that we see the beginnings of the detachment of the Pygmalion story from the larger poem.[18] The period from the eleventh to the thirteenth century has been described as an *aetas Ovidiana*, during which Ovid 'had a more wide-ranging impact on the art and culture of the West than any other classical poet' (Martindale, p. 1). Little is known of Ovid before the twelfth century. In the latter part of the eleventh, and in the twelfth century, however, 'the circulation and influence of Ovid's poetry increased dramatically'.[19] Despite this activity, the *Metamorphoses* 'is remarkable for the total absence of extant complete manuscripts before the second half of the eleventh century' (Reynolds, p. 276). The *editio princeps* of the *Metamorphoses* was published in 1471 (Vinge, p. 128).

As the Pygmalion story evolved, its significance changed over the years, under influences from many directions. Just as art had to justify itself in the relationship between God and people, so pagan stories had to be reinterpreted according to Christian teaching. The principal literary reaction to the *Metamorphoses*, at this time, is to retell its stories in such a way as to bring out a Christian moral allegorical meaning. Medieval writers condensed Ovid's tales and added a separate allegorical section (either at the end or in the margin) which acted as a Christian interpretation. The story's popularity during the medieval period has much to do with its easy incorporation into the moralizing tradition: 'To the fourteenth century, the *Metamorphoses* was the key example of fabulous material that could be demystified to produce Christian Doctrine, and commentaries [...] abounded' (Martindale, p. 74). Stories from the *Metamorphoses* were also used as a basis for the practice of rhetorical exercises in Latin, although there is not a Pygmalion story of this type.[20] Some of these renditions are highly condensed: for example, the story of Phaethon is reduced to an elaborate couplet. The use of Ovid's *Metamorphoses* for such practices must have undoubtedly made the work more well known and more likely to be retold and reinterpreted.

In the Middle Ages, the Pygmalion story is incorporated into two distinct mythographic conventions: the theological convention and the classical convention. As part of the theological-mythographic convention, the story is given new interpretations in the form of didactic *exempla*. Classical stories or *fabulae*

---

[18] See *Ovid Renewed*, Louise Vinge, *The Narcissus Theme in Western Literature up to the Early Nineteenth Century* (Lund, 1967), Ann Moss, *Ovid in Renaissance France*, Warburg Institute Surveys, 8, (London, 1982), *Texts and Transmission*, ed. by L. D. Reynolds (Oxford, 1983), Jane Chance, *The Mythographic Art* (Gainesville, Florida, 1990).

[19] R. J. Tarrant, 'Ovid', in L. D. Reynolds, *Texts and Transmission*, pp. 257–284 (p. 258).

[20] Bruce Harbert, 'Lessons From the Great Clerk: Ovid and John Gower', in *Ovid Renewed*, pp. 83–97.

were used as a shell for the pearl of moral or theological teachings: 'Writers and thinkers of this time looked upon myths primarily as stories; if the stories could yield a moral, so much the better. [...] Myths offer a multi-faceted, multi-layered view of the world'.[21] There are many Christian interpretations of Ovid's stories, and it is often the case that single texts provide multiple expositions on the same story. The main hermeneutic methods by which individual authors in this period derive their understanding of the tale are allegorical and typological. The allegorical interpretations of the Pygmalion story possess common features, though it is evident that the story acquired multiple allegorical referents in the medieval period. Some texts give both allegorical and typological interpretations of the story: 'The polysemantic or multilevel approach was [...] characteristic of medieval exegesis in its interpretation of sacred or profane authors'.[22]

One might expect medieval authors to be interested in the central motif of the story, the transformation of the statue, and its obvious associations with the creation myth. Instead, the texts concentrate on the nature of the relationship between the statue and the artist. Representations of the Pygmalion story in this period are essentially about contrasting opposites, for example, good and bad, active and passive, strong and weak. Pygmalion is usually portrayed as the superior figure, and the statue as an inferior and dependent figure. The renarrations are allegories about dominance and the importance of hierarchy, whether it be between God and a person or between a man and a woman. Pierre Bersuire's allegory in *Ovidius Moralizatus* (c.1340), for example, is about the love which can arise between a nun and a monk.[23] *Ovide Moralisé* (1316–1328) describes a beautiful, untaught servant-girl who is educated by a lord until she is fit to be his wife.[24] Pygmalion, as a character, claims authority and dominance for men; the statue affirms an acquiescent, self-effacing role for women. Pygmalion is experienced and active; the statue is new-born and passive. The contrast is emphasized at every level.

The earliest of these theological glosses is by Arnulf of Orléans. His work, *Allegoriae super Ovidii Metamorphosin* (c.1200), interpreted Ovid's stories 'morally, historically, and allegorically' and is the earliest moralization of the whole of the *Metamorphoses*.[25] Arnulf reduces the Pygmalion story to a tale of lust:

---

[21] Kathleen Wall, *The Callisto Myth From Ovid to Atwood* (Kingston, 1988), pp. 27–28.

[22] John M. Steadman, *Nature Into Myth: Medieval and Renaissance Moral Symbols* (Pittsburgh, 1980), p. 16.

[23] W. D. Reynolds, 'The *Ovidius Moralizatus* of Petrus Berchorius: An Introduction and Translation' (unpublished doctoral dissertation, University of Illinois, 1971).

[24] See Wilmon Brewer, I, 20, and W. D. Reynolds (1971), p. 12.

[25] Frank T. Coulson, *Vulgate Commentary on Ovid's Metamorphoses Book 10* (Toronto, 1991), p. 5.

Pygmalion's statue [was changed] from ivory into a living woman. Truly, Pygmalion, the wonderful artist, made an ivory statue, fostering the love of which, he began to abuse her after the manner of a true woman ('Statua Pigmalionis de eburnea in vivam mulierem. Re vera Pigmalion mirabilis artifex eburneam fecit statuam cuius amorem concipiens ea cepit abuti ad modum vere mulieris').[26]

Although he begins the gloss with information about the statue's transformation from ivory to living woman, Arnulf ends with the idea that Pygmalion abused the ivory statue.[27] He leaps, in a few lines, from Ovid's tale of successful love to a story of a strange sculptor with a statue fetish. Though I cannot determine whether Arnulf could have known the work of Clement and Arnobius, it is clear that Arnulf reacted to the story of Pygmalion in a similar way.

The major French moralization of the *Metamorphoses* in this period is the *Ovide Moralisé* (c.1316–1328). This '70,000-line French octosyllabic version of the *Metamorphoses* [...] brings the task of Christianizing Ovid to its culmination'.[28] Its allegory is summarized by Jane Miller as follows:

[In] the first interpretation put forward in the *Ovide Moralisé* [...] Pygmalion is interpreted as a great lord who has in his household a serving girl, dirty and uneducated perhaps but nonetheless beautiful. Such a lord might take this girl and groom her until finally she is fit to be his wife. The second interpretation sees the story as a Christian allegory of the relationship between God and his Creation, humanity (Miller, p. 208).

These two interpretations are quite distinct. In the first interpretation we see the beginning of the story's association with the education of a woman of a lower class by a man of a higher class – the theme of George Bernard Shaw's *Pygmalion* (1912); the second is more in keeping with other Christian allegories. Louise Vinge suggests that the moralizations of the *Ovide Moralisé* are primarily based on Arnulf of Orléans's *Allegoriae super Ovidii Metamophosin* and John of Garland's *Integumenta Ovidii* (Vinge, p. 96). *Ovide Moralisé* could also have been influenced by Jean de Meun's part of the *Roman de la Rose* (c.1277):

---

[26] Quoted in Fausto Ghisalberti, 'Arnulfo d'Orléans, un cultore di Ovidio nel secolo XII', in *Memorie del Reale Istituto Lombardo di Scienze e Lettere*, 24 (1932), 157–234 (p. 223).

[27] Thomas D. Hill, in 'Narcissus, Pygmalion, and the Castration of Saturn: Two Mythographic Themes in the *Roman de la Rose*', *Studies in Philology*, 71 (1974), 404–426, notes that Giovanni del Virgilio discusses the story of Pygmalion in his exposition of the *Metamorphoses*. Giovanni rejects Arnulf's exposition on the grounds that Ovid says that Pygmalion and his transformed statue had a child (p. 411).

[28] Helen Cooper, 'Chaucer and Ovid: A Question of Authority', in *Ovid Renewed*, pp. 71–81 (p. 74).

> To cite a few details which are common to the *Roman* and to the *Ovide Moralisé* but which are not found in Ovid, both French poets remark that love seized Pygmalion, they both call him a fool and both say that Pygmalion claimed his statue as his *espouse* before her transformation. Jean de Meun apparently misconstrued the Ovidian phrase 'similis mea [...] eburnae', and the *Ovide Moralisé* resembles the *Roman* rather than the Latin poem in this respect. [...] Ovid does not emphasize the folly of Pygmalion, but Jean de Meun and, to a lesser extent, the anonymous author of the *Ovide Moralisé*, deliberately exploit the comic potential of Pygmalion's *fol amour* (Thomas Hill, p. 412).

The most important English version of the *Metamorphoses*, in this period, is William Caxton's in 1480. It was a translation of *Ovide Moralisé*, following it closely, and includes the same allegory of the great lord who grooms a servant girl to be his wife:

> This is to saye that some grete lord myghte have a mayde or a servant in hys hows. Whiche was pouer nacked and coude no good. but she was gent and of fayr fourme. but she was Drye and lene as an ymage. This ryche man that saw he[r] fayr Clothyd. norysshyd and taughte her so moche, that she was wel endoctyned. And whan he sawe her drawynge to good maneres he lovyd her so moche that it plesed him tespowse her and take her to hys wyf. of whom he hade after a fayre sone. prudent. wyse and of grete renomee. Whiche was named Cynaras whome hys doughter deceyved afterward and laye with hyme.[29]

Elizabeth Story Donno asserts that 'Caxton had used a text enriched with the moralizings of Berchorius'.[30] Clarke Hulse suggests, however, that Caxton's work is 'a translation combining Bersuire and *Ovide Moralisé*'.[31] Geoffrey Miles suggests that Caxton's text is the seed of Shaw's *Pygmalion*, but as the allegory on educating the servant-girl is a translation from *Ovide Moralisé*, then the French text claims this credit (Miles, p. 353).

Ovide Moralisé also influenced the allegorical work of Pierre Bersuire. Bersuire's *Ovidius Moralizatus* (c.1340), which was part of the *Reductiorum Morale*, though it circulated independently from it (Reynolds [1971], p. 17), compares the sculptor to a preacher. The preacher's art is to sculpt or influence another person for the better. Pygmalion, the monk, proposes to desire neither

---

[29] William Caxton, *Ovyde, Hys Booke of Metamorphose*, ed. by S. Gaseles and H. F. B. Brett-Smith (Oxford, 1924), p. 26. Geoffrey Miles implies incorrectly that this is a prose paraphrase of Ovid (Miles, p. 352).

[30] Elizabeth Story Donno, *Elizabethan Minor Epics* (London, 1963), p. 3.

[31] Clarke Hulse, *Metamorphic Verse: The Elizabeth Minor Epic* (New Jersey, 1981), p. 245.

woman nor 'carnal embraces' turning away from the temptations of life to the society of his chaste image (a nun). Bersuire describes the process of animation as the gradual awareness of concupiscence in the relationship between the monk and the nun. The monk desires this change from Venus.

> Through this ivory girl I perceive a holy woman who is said to be ivory because she is said to be chaste, cold, weighty, and honest. It often happens that some good Pygmalion – that is some good religious – promises not to desire a woman or carnal embraces and converts himself to making ivory images – that is forming holy women and matrons in chastity and sanctity and fashioning them in spiritual habits. It sometimes happens that he selects one of them whom he calls sister or daughter and touches her with a good and chaste spirit and love. But at last it happens that Venus the goddess of wantonness – that is concupiscence of the flesh – interposes herself and changes this dead image into a living woman. She causes that chaste woman to feel the goads of the flesh and changes her from a good person into a foolish one. Pygmalion – the preacher – himself seeks and desires this alteration from Venus. When they return in the customary manner to their colloquies they find themselves so changed that she who had been ivory becomes flesh and he who abhorred women begins to desire the filth of the flesh. These carnal people then take one another and sometimes produce sons. It is not safe for male religious to contract too much familiarity with women or vice versa (Reynolds [1971], pp. 355–356).

This danger, caused by the woman's beauty, is a frequent subject for moralistic glossators and other medieval writers. Bersuire cites Ecclesiasticus 9. 8–9 in his argument: "'Turn away your face from a woman dressed up and gaze not about upon another's beauty. For many have perished by the beauty of a woman and by it lust is enkindled as a fire". A little earlier in 9.5 it is said: "Do not look upon a maiden lest her beauty be a stumbling-block to you"' (Reynolds [1971], pp. 355–356).[32] As in the exposition of Arnulf of Orléans, Bersuire's Pygmalion story is an emblem for cupidinous desire. Here the excessive love of female beauty is a sign of a strong interest in earthly things, an interest which can rival the contemplation of God.

The foil to the lust-inspiring woman is the 'good woman'. The 'good woman' plays a part in the portrayal of women in the medieval Pygmalion story. Kathleen Wall argues that 'women in medieval literature are pictured either as sex objects or as noble and virtuous wives and mothers nursing their children. [...] If they dared confront a male in any other role, they were resented and vilified' (Wall, p.

---

[32] D. W. Robertson notes that Robert Holcot, in his *Super Librum Sapientiae*, links idolatry with the doctrine of Ecclesiasticus 9. 8–9 (p. 99).

33). The statue-like nun, before her transformation, is a good woman: 'chaste, cold, weighty, and honest' (Reynolds [1971], p. 355). In Bersuire's allegory, both Pygmalion and the statue (monk and nun) become aware of earthly love. The outcome is that 'these carnal people then take one another and sometimes produce sons'. (In the summary of Ovid's narrative, Bersuire gives the sex of Paphos as male.) Bersuire concludes that it is not safe for a monk to occasion too much familiarity with a woman. Even the good woman is not safe from cupidinous desire. He lays particular stress on the dangers of beauty. Although the story has been Christianized, Venus retains her pagan identity because of her significance as the goddess of love.

Though there is evidence that John Gower used both *Ovide Moralisé* and *Ovidius Moralizatus* as inspiration for the *Confessio Amantis*, he does not interpret the Pygmalion story in terms of the Matthew 5. 28 / Ecclesiasticus 9. 8–9 doctrine, nor the stereotype of the 'good woman'.[33] Gower's representation of the Pygmalion story evens the balance between these contrasting perceptions of women. Gower's statue is not the blushing and timid girl whose modesty contrasts with the brashness of the Propoetides; she is a 'lusti wif' (Macaulay, p. 312). Gower renders Ovid's *Metamorphoses* freely in his *Confessio* and his statue-woman is given more positive and active qualities. Importantly, Gower develops the character of Pygmalion. His Pygmalion has only one characteristic in common with Ovid's: he is a sculptor. Gower's Pygmalion is a young man ('a lusti man of yowthe') with no dislike of women (Macaulay, p. 311); he is also more vociferous than his Ovidian counterpart. Ovid's Pygmalion offers a timid and short prayer to the goddess; Gower's 'made such continuance / Fro dai to nyht, and preith so longe' (Macaulay, p. 312). The role of Venus is diminished, and there is no mention of her festival. Gower interprets the story as evidence for the importance of articulate prayer. He suggests that good prayers will help you get what you desire: 'if that thou spare / To speke, lost is al thi fare, / For Slowthe bringth in alle wo' (Macaulay, p. 313). The 'confessor' sums up, saying that words work better than deeds, and that the god of love is favourable to those whose love is stable. Like Ovid, Gower moulds the story to fit his own purpose within the structure of the larger poem. Ray gives a further interpretation of Gower's story, emphasizing the melancholy nature of Pygmalion in order to prove her point that idolatry and melancholy are connected in this story.[34] In the light of Gower's assertion that his story is about the efficacy of prayer, Ray's reading of the story seems rather

---

[33] G. C. Macaulay, *The English Works of John Gower*, Early English Text Society, 81, 2 vols (London, 1900), I, 311–313; John Gower, *Confessio Amantis*, trans. by Terence Tiller (Baltimore, Maryland, 1963), pp. 151–153.

[34] Bonnie MacDougall Ray, 'The Metamorphoses of Pygmalion: A Study of the Treatment of the Myth from the Third Century BC to the Early Seventeenth Century' (unpublished doctoral dissertation, University of Columbia, 1981).

forced. Rightly, however, Ray also sees a similarity between the portrayal of Pygmalion in the *Confessio* and Chaucer's 'The Knight's Tale'.

The only extant account of the tale by a woman in this period is Christine de Pisan's *Épître d'Othéa*. This, as the title suggests, takes the form of a letter and is a fictional epistle from Othea, the goddess of prudence, to a young Hector, son of the Trojan king and queen, Priam and Hecuba. Edith Yenal describes Christine's method of drawing an exposition from a tale:

> The Texte tells a story about a mythographic character or legend from which the reader is supposed to draw a moral concerning a particular virtue or vice. The Glose comments and expands on the Texte, reinforcing its meaning with a saying by an ancient philosopher. The Allegorie forms the concluding part of each chapter. It deals with the spiritual message contained in the two preceding sections. Its function is to enlarge upon them with quotations from a theological source like the Church Fathers and a verse from the Bible.[35]

Like the rest of the *Épître*, the Pygmalion story divides into three sections: the 'texte', the 'glose' and the 'allegorie'. The texte reduces the story to a four line poem:

> Pymalyones ymage for to fele,
> If that thou be wise sette therbi no dele,
> For of such an ymage so wel wroughte
> The beaute therof was to dere boughte (Pisan, p. 33).

In the narrative of the gloss, Pygmalion is a chaste sculptor who shies away from 'the gret lewdenes that he sawe in the women of Cidoyne' (Pisan, p. 34). 'Cidoyne' probably stands for Sidon; this town was traditionally associated with Tyre, the place from which Pygmalion, the brother of Dido, came. This is a divergence from Ovid's story. In view of its Biblical associations with Sidon, it is an appropriate one. Pygmalion is motivated by a wish to create a beautiful woman 'where-in there schulde be nothing for to blame' (p. 34). He prays to Venus for the statue to come to life and the statue does so as he warms her in his arms. Then Pygmalion marries her. The allegory, like Bersuire's, links the statue with the sin of lechery: a good knight should not be besotted with the statue which 'we schal take for the synne of lecherye' (p. 35). Christine cites an epistle of St Jerome on hell fire and gluttony, and ends with a Latin quotation from II Peter 2.13: 'They count it a pleasure to revel in the daytime. They are blots and

---

[35] Edith Yenal, *Christine de Pisan. A Bibliography of Writings By Her And About Her* (Metuchen, New Jersey, and London, 1982), p. 42.

blemishes, revelling in their dissipation, carousing with you' (p. 35).

Thomas Walsingham's *De Archana Deorum* (fl. 1360-1420) paraphrases and explicates the Pygmalion story in Latin prose.[36] Reduced to a few lines, the story is accompanied by a short exposition: Pygmalion forms an ivory statue of a woman more beautiful than any living woman and which is so realistic that

> it is truly the face of a virgin whom you believe to live, and, if reverence were not an obstacle you would wish to move. Therefore Pygmalion, moved by illicit love of his statue, obtained from Venus that it might be turned into a real woman. Exposition: Pygmalion, the great artist made an ivory statue, fostering the love of which he began to abuse her, truly after the manner of a woman (p. 145).

Walsingham's exposition is almost identical to Arnulf's gloss; both writers accentuate Pygmalion's lasciviousness.

Although Ovid's Pygmalion story is kept alive through paraphrase and quotation of the *Metamorphoses*, it is also given new meaning through the theological tradition. Allegorical interpretations influence each other. The story, as it is copied out by these writers, however, remains more or less the same. As their popularity grew, Ovid's stories began to assert their independence from the *Metamorphoses*. In particular, allusions to Ovid's lovers appear in narratives independent of the *Metamorphoses*, and it is no surprise that Pygmalion's role as lover is significant here. This classical-mythographic convention uses the story quite differently from the religious-mythographic. There is no separation of interpretation and text and instead we observe a gradual development of the text. In this convention, Pygmalion has two distinct characteristics: he is the classical lover (with his statue as the beloved), and the classical artist (where the statue is usually important for its beauty and its transformation). Pygmalion is most often cited for his skill as an artist.

The classical lover and the classical artist are alluded to for a variety of reasons. English authors were influenced in their classical conventions by continental love poetry, suggesting that when English poets comment upon classical lovers, 'they do so within the same rhetorical environments [...] [as those] constructed by their contemporaries on the continent' (Heinrichs, p. 98). Allusions to Pygmalion, the artist-lover, appear alongside references to other lovers, such as Narcissus and Orpheus:

> In making use of the allusion he [the medieval poet] has taken it out of the Ovidian or mythographic context and placed it into the context of a

---

[36] Thomas Walsingham, *De Archana Deorum*, ed. by Robert A. Van Kluyve (Durham, North Carolina, 1968), p. 145.

medieval love poem, within which we must try to understand it. In most instances, medieval writers do not interpret for us their allusions to the Ovidian lovers (Heinrichs, p. 54).

Pygmalion, the artist, is linked with such great names as Zeuxes and Apelles. Naming Zeuxes or Apelles, in a comparison, was a shorthand way of creating an impression of a great artist. In brief allusions such as these, it seems that the precise name of the classical artist was not important – the names were interchangeable. The artists' personal histories do not add much to the allusions, and in the case of one reference to Pygmalion by Lydgate, knowledge of the sculptor's personal history would undermine the purpose of the analogy.

Pygmalion is identified both as a lover and a sculptor (as he is in Ovid) in the *Roman de la Rose* (c.1277), the principal French renarration of the period.[37] The first 4,266 lines of this French poem were written by Guillaume de Lorris between the years 1225 and 1230, and the last 22,700 lines, containing the Pygmalion story, were written by Jean de Meun in 1270. The Pygmalion story is used (in its entirety) here because the poet is interested in the story and not because it is part of the *Metamorphoses*. Pygmalion is also referred to in other parts of the *Roman*, where his name is listed alongside those of Zeuxes and Apelles (Dahlberg, p. 226 and p. 274). There are major differences between Guillaume de Lorris and Jean de Meun, both in approach and emphasis. The story of Pygmalion is retold at the end of the *Roman* by Jean de Meun:

> The *exemplum* of Narcissus is narrated just before the lover begins his quest for the rose, and the *exemplum* of Pygmalion just before he consummates it. The relevance of these fables to the lover's [the main character's] situation is emphasized by the fact that he falls in love in the fountain of Narcissus, and the image which Venus wins for him is explicitly compared to the statue of Pygmalion (Hill, p. 407).

The Pygmalion story is selected because of the transformation element. The renarration draws much on Ovid. Sterile love (like that of Narcissus) is contrasted with sexual love, which produces children. Jean de Meun fleshes out Ovid's story with lists, descriptions and direct speech. For instance, the poet elaborates on Pygmalion's ability as a sculptor by cataloguing the number of materials with which he can work, talks at length on the genius of the sculptor and the beauty of the statue. Although the *Roman de la Rose* specifies that Pygmalion's statue was made of ivory, the manuscripts depict Pygmalion carving a stone statue: 'They undoubtedly wanted to make the metamorphosis more plausible by depicting a

---

[37] Guillaume de Lorris and Jean de Meun, *The Romance of the Rose*, trans. by Charles Dahlberg (Hanover and London, 1983), pp. 340–346.

life-size figure, and so rejected ivory which in medieval times was used only for small statuettes'.[38] Pygmalion gives his statue the clothes and presents appropriate for a lady of the era. The setting is medieval rather than classical. Ovid's other details, that Pygmalion lived in Cyprus, was single and that he despised the Propoetides, fall by the wayside. The sculpting and falling in love scene is significantly longer than Ovid's, and involves a description of Pygmalion's thoughts on being in love with an inanimate statue, and his apparent loss of reason. Ovid gives this section of the story twelve lines; the *Roman* gives it approximately sixty-five. Unlike Ovid's sculptor, the *Roman* Pygmalion questions his love for the statue:

> 'How did the idea of such a love come about? I love an image that is deaf and mute, that neither stirs or moves nor will ever show me grace. How did such a love wound me? There is no one who heard of it who should not be thunderstruck. I am the greatest fool in the world. What am I to do in this situation?' (Dahlberg, p. 341).

The sanity of those who love ideal and unattainable women is at issue, and the poet suggests that a one-sided sterile love is pointless. Pygmalion prays to the statue, but praying to an idol is seen to be as fruitless as loving an idol: 'She neither heard him nor understood anything' (p. 342). Pygmalion later prays to the 'true' deity (Venus), and admits to worshipping chastity (in the form of the ivory statue) and resolves to follow Saint Venus instead if she grants his request of transforming the ivory maiden. This scene is presented comically:

> 'I repent and beg that you pardon me and, by your pity, your sweetness, and your friendship, grant me, on my promise to flee into banishment if I do not avoid Chastity from now on, that the beautiful one who has stolen my heart, who so truly resembles ivory, may become my loyal friend and may have the body, the soul, and the life of a woman. And if you hasten to grant this request and if I am ever found chaste, I consent that I may be hanged or chopped up into pieces, or that Cerberus, the porter of hell-gate, may swallow me alive' (p. 344).

Pygmalion does as much as he can to bring his statue to life by creating a visual picture of her as a real woman rather than an aloof statue. He begins by worshipping her as an idol, and ends by wanting to live with a real woman. When Pygmalion's love is sterile and idolatrous, he is irrational or mad; when he embraces human sexuality and banishes chastity, he is rational. The statue is transformed from an idol of chastity to a child of Venus. Not blushing like her

---

[38] Virginia Wylie Egbert, 'Pygmalion as Sculptor', *Princeton University Library Chronicle*, 28 (1966), 20–33 (p. 21).

Ovidian counterpart, her first words are of love, not modesty: "'I am neither demon nor phantasm, sweet friend, but your sweetheart, ready to receive your companionship and to offer you my love if it please you to receive such an offer'" (p. 345).

There is some disagreement amongst scholars over the significance of the Pygmalion story in the *Roman de la Rose*. Thomas Hill examines some of the major interpretations in detail. Alan Gunn's *The Mirror of Love*, is the 'first modern study to argue seriously for the literary merit and intellectual coherence' of the text, though, Hill says, Gunn's 'interpretation of the *exemplum* of Pygmalion cannot [...] be seriously maintained' (Hill, p. 408). Gunn sees Pygmalion as exemplifying 'the attainment of maturity, which involves and requires the overcoming of selfishness'.[39] Pygmalion's love, Gunn says, has elements of chivalry in it. Hill suggests that D. W. Robertson interprets the story in a similar way to Gunn, emphasizing the chivalrous nature of Pygmalion's relationship with the statue. Robertson writes: 'The sculptor seeks to palliate the element of sensuality in the story by means of tenderness and refinement, qualities which have the power to stimulate the warmest compassion' (Robertson, p. 103). Although this description of the Pygmalion story is clearly the opposite of Hill's, it must be added that Hill's assessment of Robertson is, perhaps, a little ungenerous. Robertson is aware of the sexual connotations of the story. He writes a few lines earlier that Venus represents 'the pleasure of sexual intercourse' and that she is not just a 'fairy godmother' (Robertson, p. 102). Hill argues that 'Pygmalion's behaviour is ludicrous and verges on the obscene [...] in comparison with the *Metamorphoses*' (p. 408). Hill's interpretation is convincing: Pygmalion, after all, undresses his statue and takes it to bed with him. But Hill misses the irony of the poem. Pygmalion is foolish, and his fear of committing the sin of chastity is deliberately comical. As the story is about a progression from one way of thinking to another, in this case from chastity to concupiscence, it would seem reasonable that both Pygmalion's chivalry and his lechery are portrayed to some degree. The problem of interpretation is, then, whether or not the story is meant to be ironic. Perhaps it is best read as a tale which warns us of the sin of concupiscence by describing the ludicrous situation of a lecherous man who dare not commit the 'sin' of chastity.

Where Pygmalion is identified solely as an artist, rather than an artist and lover, his story poses fundamental questions about the nature and status of art. How, and using what criteria, should we create a work of art? Should art be the imitation of divine beauty or a product of the imagination? What is the relationship between art and nature? In both its secular and theological contexts the myth also generates

---

[39] Alan Gunn, *The Mirror of Love: A Reinterpretation of the Romance of the Rose* (Lubbock, Texas, 1952), p. 288.

discussions about the artistic representation of women's beauty. Ovid's Pygmalion did not base his statue on the features of a live model, but created an ideal woman. The story thus explores the possibility that art does not imitate nature, but the artist's own idea. We see nature imitating art as the statue comes to life. As one critic writes, the 'conventional praise of Nature produces the inevitable citations of Zeuxes and Pygmalion and all the usual commonplaces about "imitation"'.[40]

The allusion to Pygmalion in *Pearl* (c.1375) is unusual in that it describes Pygmalion as a painter. This happened occasionally in short references to Pygmalion in later years. For example, Thomas Churchyard's 'Painter thought to please his owne dilite, / With pictures faire, as poore *Pigmalion* did' and George Wither sings of the 'Chastitie, / Old *Pigmalions* picture had'.[41] *Pearl* tells the story of a jeweller whose young daughter has died. The daughter, Pearl, appears in his dream as a beautiful woman. Her appearance is described at length:

> He who made your clothes was very wise. Your beauty was never natural; Pygmalion never painted your face, nor Aristotle neither in his letters discoursed the nature of these properties. Your colour surpasses the fleur-de-lys; your angelic demeanour is so brightly courteous. Tell me, brightness, what kind of office do you have, pearl so immaculate?[42]

Pygmalion's talent as a painter is compared with the powers of nature. In this context, the beauty of the Pearl-maiden surpasses both the beauty of nature and the beauty of the sculpture. The influence of the Pygmalion story may go beyond the allusion. There are some striking similarities between the structure of the Pygmalion story and that of *Pearl*. The pearl-maiden shares some of the important characteristics of Pygmalion's statue. Both, for example, are innocent and beyond the reach of the protagonist: the pearl-maiden is dead, the statue-maiden is inanimate. Both stories share the idea of a man talking to the inanimate beloved. The jeweller, like Pygmalion, is both the creator and the lover of the statue. Also, the transfiguration of the pearl-maiden is analogous to the metamorphosis of the statue-maiden.

Pygmalion is characterized by Chaucer (and later by John Lydgate) as a counterfeiter, someone who imitates. Chaucer was influenced by Ovid via the *Roman de la Rose* and Guillaume de Machaut's *Jugement dou Roy de Navarre*,

---

[40] Edward William Taylor, 'The Medieval Contribution', *Nature and Art in Renaissance Literature* (New York and London, 1964), p. 76.

[41] Thomas Churchyard, *A Pleasant Conceite Penned in Verse* (London, 1593) lines 1–2, no page numbers; George Wither, *Faire Virtue* (London, 1622), no page numbers.

[42] *The Poems of the Pearl Manuscript*, ed. by Malcolm Andrew and Ronald Waldron (Exeter, 1989), p. 89.

Dit de la Fonteine Amoureuse and *Livre du Voir*.⁴³ There is not much evidence that Chaucer knew *Ovide Moralisé*, though he may have been influenced by this text via Machaut.⁴⁴ Chaucer refers to Pygmalion in the description of a knight's daughter at the beginning of 'The Physician's Tale' (c.1387).

> For Nature hath with sovereyn diligence
> Yformed hire in so greet excellence,
> As though she wolde seyn, 'Lo! I, Nature,
> Thus kan I forme and peynte a creature,
> Whan that me list; who kan me countrefete?
> Pigmalion noght, though he ay forge, and bete,
> Or grave, or peynte; for I dar wel seyn
> Apelles, Zanzis, sholde werche in veyn
> Outher to grave, or peynte, or forge, or bete,
> If they presumed me to countrefete'.⁴⁵

Although he is once more the famous sculptor who made a statue of a beautiful, life-like woman, Pygmalion is downgraded to the status of an imitator whose art is inferior to the works of nature.⁴⁶

Lydgate's Pygmalion, in *Reson and Sensuallyte* (c.1412), is a crafty sculptor who is driven mad by his love for the beautiful statue.⁴⁷ Lydgate acknowledges the influence of Jean de Meun's version: 'For, as it is trewly to suppose, / Pigmalyon, remembrid in þe Rose'.⁴⁸ Like de Meun, he suggests that Pygmalion treated the statue as if she were a real woman and that for this reason his actions were those of a fool. Lydgate refers again to Pygmalion in the *Troy Book* (1412-1420). Here, Priam calls for artists, who could imitate Pygmalion or Apollo, to help him build a new Troy:

---

⁴³ Richard Hoffman suggests in 'Pygmalion in the "Physician's Tale"', *American Notes and Queries*, 5 (1967), 83–84, that the *Roman de la Rose* probably influenced these lines. See also Edward Rand, *Ovid and his Influence* (New York, 1928), p. 145.

⁴⁴ Helen Cooper, 'Chaucer and Ovid', in *Ovid Renewed*, pp. 71–81 (pp. 74–75 and p. 264, note 7).

⁴⁵ Geoffrey Chaucer, *The Riverside Chaucer*, ed. by Larry D. Benson (Oxford, 1988), p. 190.

⁴⁶ F. N. Robinson suggests that Chaucer followed the *Roman de la Rose* here, as Pygmalion's name also appears there alongside that of the sculptors, Apelles and Zeuxes, in a similar argument. Geoffrey Chaucer, *The Complete Works*, ed. by F. N. Robinson (Oxford, 1933), p. 832, note 14.

⁴⁷ John Lydgate, *Reson and Sensuallyte*, ed. by Ernest Sieper, Early English Text Society, 2 vols (London, 1901–1903), I (1901), 112.

⁴⁸ John Lydgate, *Troy Book*, ed. by Henry Bergen, Early English Text Society, 97, 103 and 106, 3 vols (London, 1906–1910), I (1906), 159.

> And swiche as coude with countenances glade
> Make an ymage þat wil neuere fade:
> To counterfet in metal, tre, or ston
> Þe sotil werke of Pigmaleoun.[49]

Pygmalion's identity as a sculptor is preferred to his identity as a lover. The everlasting or immortal qualities of sculpture are relevant for a new Troy which would not fall. The fact that Pygmalion precipitated the change of the immortal statue into the mortal woman is not mentioned, and indeed would make his position as an immortalizer untenable. In the fourth book, Pygmalion is likened to a divine sculptor. This pious Pygmalion contrasts with the foolish lover of *Reson and Sensuallyte*.

The depiction of Pygmalion as a mere copier of nature is the result of the reception of his story via the *Roman de la Rose*, rather than through the moralizing tradition. Pygmalion is on occasion, though, a great artist, a subtle workman and even a pious man (as evidenced in the work of Gower). J. A. W. Bennett suggests that 'the Ovidian story of the sculptor who brought marble beauty to very life was disparaged in an age that put Nature above Art' (Bennett, p. 250).[50] Broadly, however, there are two views of the Pygmalion story in this period. Though Pygmalion is largely condemned by theologians, his character is moulded to suit exposition as both a hero and a villain. To Arnulf of Orléans he is a lecher; Bersuire characterizes him as a monk who has strayed from the path of chastity; to Christine de Pisan he is both a man kept chaste because of his love of something he cannot have, and a knight who wastes his love and is tempted by lechery. Pygmalion's love is, predominantly, though not entirely, condemned in the moralizing convention; and, while often referred to as a great artist in the classical convention, his talent is sometimes questioned to serve the purposes of poetic hyperbole.

The Sixteenth Century

Sixteenth-century Europe saw a great increase in the number of vernacular prose and verse translations of the *Metamorphoses*. The most influential in Britain was Arthur Golding's verse translation (1565–1567). Though Golding attaches allegories to most of the tales, the Pygmalion story escapes moralization.[51] The story of Myrrha, which follows that of Pygmalion, begins with the unequivocal

---

[49] Lydgate, III (1910), 727.

[50] J. A. W. Bennett, *Middle English Literature*, ed. by Douglas Gray (Oxford, 1986), p. 250. Bennett is incorrect in stating that Ovid's statue was made of marble.

[51] Arthur Golding, *The XV Books of P. Ovidius Naso* (London, 1567), fol. 127^r–127^v.

statement: 'Of wicked and most cursed things to speak I now commence. / Yee daughters and yee parents all go get yee farre from hence'(p. 38). Golding's is hailed as 'the standard English translation during the greatest period of our literature, and it holds a special place as "Shakespeare's Ovid"'.[52]

Theological commentaries on the *Metamorphoses* continued to be written during this century, and were, as before, in Latin. Of these, the most significant are George Sabinus's *Fabularum Ovidii Interpretatio* (1555), written 'for the benefit of youthful students', and Johannes Sprengius's 1563 translation of Ovid.[53] Ann Moss notes that 'many of the points that Sabinus makes were to be repeated in almost identical phrases by Sprengius. Both have at the back of their minds the old ways of reading the text allegorically' (Moss, p. 48). Sabinus's moral suggests that a chaste and modest wife is a gift from God and should be asked for from God. He links the story with a similar episode which he says was told about St Francis, who, like Pygmalion, shrank from the company of women. In order to curb his desires, a wife and child were made for St Francis out of snow. Both the snow-woman and the ivory-woman are admired for their chastity. Like many later users of the story Sabinus shows concern about the statue's medium. Sabinus justifies the use of ivory for the statue in Ovid's Pygmalion story: either because of the brightness of her body, or 'on account of the likeness of the name, because she was perhaps called Ivory or Ivory-like' (p. 398). Sprengius's commentary draws out a similar theological message: that those who desire a happy marriage cannot succeed without divine help. These interpretations are nearer to those of Gower than to the medieval commentators.

There is a question mark over the extent to which the commentary tradition (still alive in the sixteenth century) influenced the Elizabethan poets: Elizabethan consumption of Ovid 'involved detaching the stories at least partly from the heavy weight of moralizing they had generally carried in the Middle Ages. How far this was done is a disputed question'.[54] With regard to the Pygmalion story there is some evidence that the commentary tradition affected Elizabethan interpretations. The poets are drawn to the statue as a symbol of the inconsistency and falseness of women. In sixteenth-century verse, Pygmalion's reputation as an artist-lover grew considerably. Whereas medieval theologians had branded him a lecher and a madman, this period saw a rise in Pygmalion's importance as a lover. Miles's

---

[52] Niall Rudd, 'Daedalus and Icarus (ii): From the Renaissance to the Present Day', in *Ovid Renewed*, pp. 37–53 (p. 38). Rudd notes that the translation was reprinted six times during Shakespeare's lifetime.

[53] George Sabinus, *Fabularum Ovidii Interpretatio Ethica, Physica, et Historica* (Cambridge, 1584), pp. 396–398. Johannes Sprengius, *Metamorphoses Ovidii* (Frankfurt am Main, 1563), p. 124.

[54] Laurence Lerner 'Ovid and the Elizabethans', in *Ovid Renewed*, ed. by Charles Martindale, pp. 121–135 (p. 121).

comment that when we move from the Middle Ages to the renaissance 'there is a striking change of tone' whereby 'Renaissance writers take a harshly unsympathetic, satirical view of Pygmalion' (pp. 334–335) underestimates the continuity and influence of the theological tradition in both periods, and it is noticeable that he regards Pygmalion as merely 'a flickering presence in the Middle Ages' (p. 334).

An old criticism is revived in the sixteenth century: Pygmalion is once again an idolator. Renarrations of the Pygmalion story in this period fall broadly into two groups, reflecting the medieval theological and classical traditions. Some concentrate on the theme of love, and often associate the feelings of an anonymous lover with those of Pygmalion; others relate the story to the theme of idolatry. The exception to this is a short poem by Bernard Garter called 'A strife Betweene Appelles and Pigmalion' (1566) which, rather than retelling the usual story of Pygmalion, invents a new narrative in which Pygmalion competes with Apelles to create the perfect woman and wins. Nature brings her to life.[55]

The earliest English poem exclusively on the subject of Pygmalion is 'The Tale of Pigmalion with Conclusion Vpon the Beautye of His Loue', in *Tottel's Miscellany* (1557–1587).[56] Here Pygmalion is a sculptor of great skill who has made several statues before going on to sculpt his 'woman fayre' (p. 126). The poet divorces the narrative from the main body of the *Metamorphoses*. There is no mention of the Propoetides, and Pygmalion is no misogynist. Pygmalion's motivation is to achieve an 'immortall name' for himself as a sculptor (p. 126). Emphasis is placed on his artistic skill, as is seen in the shorter references to Pygmalion of the previous century. With regard to the direct influences on this anonymous poem, little can be established other than that the poet was probably aware of Ovid's story. The poem, however, departs completely from the pattern of Ovid immediately after Pygmalion gives presents to the statue. Instead of the transformation scene, the narrator turns the story into a love address to a woman he loves:

> My dere, alas since I you loue, what wonder is it than?
> In whom hath nature set the glory of her name:
> And brake her mould, in great dispayre, your like she could not frame (p. 126).

Drawing, perhaps, on the techniques of the commentaries, the narrator compares Pygmalion's love for his ideal ivory statue with his own love for a uniquely beautiful woman. This dramatic switch from the classical past to the narrator's present suggests a metaphoric metamorphosis. Associations between Pygmalion

---

[55] Bernard Garter, *A Strife Betweene Appelles and Pigmalion* (London, 1566).
[56] *Tottel's Miscellany* (1557–1587), ed. by Hyder Edward Rollins, 2 vols (Cambridge, Massachusetts, 1965), I, pp. 125–126.

and the situation of the narrator are often seen in shorter references to Pygmalion in the sixteenth, seventeenth and eighteenth centuries.

William Fulwood's, 'A Secret Lover Writes His Will, By Story Of Pigmalion's Ill' in *The Enimie of Idlenesse* (1568) identifies Pygmalion as a skilled sculptor and counterfeiter of images.[57] This is the first English poem to use a marble statue. In the next few years it becomes the custom to refer to the statue as made of marble. From the sixteenth century to the twentieth century most renarrations describe the statue either as ivory, marble or stone. There are a few exceptions: Andrew Lang's is chryselephantine, and Gilbert Coleridge describes the statue as being made from clay, stone, marble and ivory.

Fulwood, like the medieval poets, places emphasis on Pygmalion's ability as a sculptor and counterfeiter. Pygmalion's ambition, as in *Tottel's Miscellany*, is to achieve immortal fame. Fulwood's poem departs from Ovid's structure at the same point as 'The Tale of Pigmalion', again relating the story to the narrator's own suffering in love rather than the transformation of the statue. He suggests that if Pygmalion 'pynde away' for his marble statue, it is no wonder that he, who is in love with a real woman, suffers 'with piteous plaint, and grevous grone' (p. 140). The narrator would like to play the part of Pygmalion as Pygmalion was able to embrace his beloved and place her in his bed. The poet hints that if his own beloved were in his bed, he 'should fynde better pastime sure, / Than poore Pigmalion could procure' (p. 141). The final lament of the poem is that the speaker cannot tell his lady that he loves her, in case she refuses him and his fantasy ends. He concludes with another classical reference linking stone and perpetual anguish: the punishment of Sisiphus.

The last two major renarrations of this century use the Pygmalion story as a vehicle for anti-Catholic polemic. Here Pygmalion is an idolator, as he occasionally is in the medieval period, and before that in the work of the Christian apologists. He is not a pagan idolator, however, but a Christian one. Renarrations of the story which dwell on Pygmalion's idolatry are also strongly misogynistic. George Pettie's 'Pygmalion's Friend, and his Image' in *A Petite Pallace of Pettie and his Pleasure* (1576) is no exception.[58] In this prose account of the story, Pygmalion is a gentleman from Piedmont who innocently loves and is loved by Penthea, the wife of Luciano. Penthea, however, rejects him in favour of another suitor. And so Pygmalion abandons the company of all women and carves a marble image of a woman. Falling in love with the image, he entreats Venus to transform it into a woman, whom he then marries. Unlike the previous two writers, Pettie adds to the beginning of the story. The poem is a diatribe on the inconstancy and 'imperfect nature' of women (p. 114) relieved only at certain

---

[57] William Fulwood, *The Enimie of Idlenesse* (London, 1568), pp. 139–141.
[58] George Pettie, *A Petite Pallace of Pettie and His Pleasure* (London, 1576), pp. 108–134.

points when the narrator divorces himself from the opinions of his misogynistic Pygmalion who commits 'bold blasphemy against your noble sex' (p. 127). At the end of the work, however, the narrator is persuaded to see women as fickle creatures, and advises them not to exchange old friends (as Pygmalion was to Penthea) for new ones.

A number of new reasons for Pygmalion's love for his statue are put forward by Pettie: Pygmalion, we are told, may have been possessed 'with melancholy passions', he may have thought himself to have been made of stone, and 'knowing that like agree best with their like' fell in love with the stone image (p. 129). Continuing this theme, Pettie suggests that Pygmalion may have fallen in love with the statue because he owned it, or because it was part of his religion to love images. This is not strange we are told:

> Neither is it any more to be marvelled at in him, than in an infinite number that live at this day, which love images right well, and verily persuade themselves that images have the power to pray for them, and help them to heaven (pp. 129–130).

The description of the statue's metamorphosis is likened to miracles purportedly occurring at the time of the poet's writing: 'The like miracles we have had many wrought within these few years, when images have been made to bow their heads, to hold out their hands, to weep, to speak' (p. 131). The work was published after Queen Elizabeth was well established on the throne and Pygmalion is condemned as a Catholic; though the story is in part an anti-pagan statement of the kind that we find in Clement and Arnobius.

John Marston's 'The Metamorphosis of Pigmalion's Image' (1598) has generated much critical discussion.[59] The debate largely focuses on the issue of whether the poem was intended to be satirical or whether it was 'a serious attempt in the Ovidian mode' and a lurid love poem (Finkelpearl, p. 334). Convincing arguments have been put forward on both sides. There is even evidence to suggest that Marston wrote it as a serious love poem, but revised it as a satirical poem once he had realized his talent for satire. Arnold Davenport notes that 'when Marston found his real vein in satire, he was drawn on to relate his earlier poem to his new mode, and so came to pretend that it was a parody' (p. 10). Marston's anti-Catholic jibes form part of a digression from the story:

---

[59] John Marston, *The Poems of John Marston*, ed. by Arnold Davenport (Liverpool, 1961), pp. 47–61. The issues are set out clearly in Philip J. Finkelpearl, 'From Petrarch to Ovid: Metamorphoses in John Marston's "Metamorphosis of Pigmalion's Image"', *A Journal of English Literary History*, 32 (1965), 333–348. See also Gustav Cross, 'Marston's "Metamorphoses of Pigmalion's Image": A Mock-Epyllion', *Études Anglaises*, 13 (1960), 331–336.

> Looke how the peeuish Papists crouch, and kneel
> To some dum Idoll with their offering,
> As if a senceles carued stone could feele
> The ardor of his bootles chattering (p. 55).

Like Pettie, Marston asserts the futility of worshipping images. Whatever the intention of the author, certain things pertaining to the development of the Pygmalion story can be established. The poem is about the frustration of the hero, Pygmalion. It is interspersed with cynical comments about the ease with which women are tempted by men, and it contains elements of the lover's complaint. The dedication to the narrator's 'Mistres' sets the tone: 'My wanton Muse lasciuiously doth sing / Of sportiue love, of lovely dallying' (p. 51). The narrator asks his mistress to behave like the statue in the story, 'take compassion' and not force him to 'enuie my Pigmalion' (p. 51). The mistress becomes a device to make the poem more salacious. When Pygmalion views his ivory-maiden naked, the narrator adds: 'O that my Mistres were an image too, / That I might blameles her perfections view' (p. 54). Marston sees Pygmalion as a man who hates women and love. There is no reason for him to sculpt a statue, other than that 'Loue at length forc'd him to know his fate, / And loue the shade, whose substance he did hate' (p. 52). The first part of the poem concerns the main conceit that all women are like relentless stone. The narrative sequence of the metamorphosis is abrupt: there is not a gradual coming to life, but a sudden one, deliberately devoid of feeling. 'The stonie substance of his Image feature, / Was straight transform'd into a liuing creature' (p. 58). When the statue finally yields and becomes a real woman, the poet remarks, 'Tut, women will relent / When as they finde such mouing blandishment' (p. 59). It seems that this Galatea is in a no-win situation.

Edward Guilpin's *Skialetheia* (1598) also identifies Pygmalion as a statue worshipper:

> Then how is man turnd all *Pygmalion*,
> That knowing these pictures, yet we doate upon
> The painted statues, or what fooles are we
> So grosly to commit idolatry?
> What are we Ethnicks that we honour beasts?
> (They are beasts which paint themselves) or els papists
> Whose over-fleeting brittle memories
> Right worshipfull intitle Images.[60]

Guilpin's satirical poem also makes a point about cosmetics, an association which is made for the first time in the Elizabethan period. Guilpin ridicules those who

---

[60] Edward Guilpin, *Skialetheia*, ed. by Alexander B. Grosart (Manchester, 1878), p. 42.

need to paint their faces in order to appear beautiful, suggesting that one must be as foolish as Pygmalion if one knows a woman to have a painted face and still love her. The statues of the time were painted. Pygmalion's relationship to his statue is again associated with Catholicism: admiring women who wear make-up is as wrong as being a Catholic, as both are attractive only on the surface. The poet talks of

> generall pardons, which speake gloriously,
> Yet keepe not touch: or a Popish *Iubily*.
> Thus altering natures stamp, they're altered,
> From their first purity, innate maidenhead:
> Of simple naked honesty, and truth,
> And given o're to seducing lust and youth (p. 43).

The sixteenth century is the earliest period in which characterization of the statue as anything other than modest and subservient becomes common practice. John Lyly's *Euphues* (1578) is an example of this.

> The Parthians, to cause their youth to loathe the alluring trains of women's wiles and deceitful enticements, had most curiously carved in their houses a young man blind; besides whom was adjoined a woman, so exquisite that in some men's judgement Pygmalion's image was not half so excellent, having one hand in his pocket as noting their theft, and holding a knife in the other hand to cut his throat.[61]

The idea of Pygmalion's image as a dangerous woman is taken up by Shakespeare in *Measure For Measure* (1604). Shakespeare's Lucio says: 'What, is there none of Pygmalion's images newly made women to be had now, for putting the hand in the pocket and extracting clutched?'[62] The similarity of Shakespeare's reference to that of Lyly has been noted by Lyly's editors (p. 16, n. 1). One edition of the play suggests that 'Pygmalion's images' were prostitutes.[63] The Arden edition provides a fuller gloss to these lines: 'because the Elizabethan statue was often painted, Pygmalion's beloved suggested the idea of a prostitute' (p. 84). This edition points to a further reference to Pygmalion's statue as a prostitute, in the fifth satire of Thomas Middleton's *Micro-Cynicon* (1599):

---

[61] John Lyly, *Euphues: The Anatomy of Wit*, ed. by Morris William-Croll and Harry Clemons (London, 1916), p. 16.

[62] William Shakespeare, *Measure for Measure*, The Arden Edition, ed. by J. W. Lever (London, 1965), I. 2. 49, p. 84.

[63] William Shakespeare, *Measure For Measure*, The Signet Classic Shakespeare, ed. by S. Nagarajan (New York and London, 1964), p. 88.

> Trust not a painted puppet, as I've done,
> Who far more doted than Pygmalion:
> The streets are full of juggling parasites,
> With the true shape of virgins' counterfeits.[64]

Middleton echoes Guilpin's satire with 'yet we doat Vpon / The painted statues' (p. 42).

The Pygmalion story appears in diverse forms in the sixteenth century. It occurs in many short references, and is interpreted allegorically in the mid-sixteenth-century, though not in Britain. During this period, we see, for the first time, the emergence of entire poems solely on the Pygmalion subject. As a result, the number of themes associated with the story increase. Many renarrations of this era talk of unrequited love, turning the story into an elaborate conceit for the lover who despairs of his 'stony-hearted' woman. The story describes both the woman who can resist male advances, and the inconstant woman who cannot; and the differences between natural and artificial beauty are highlighted. These developments are influenced by contemporary culture. In the reign of Elizabeth, when anti-catholic polemic was not unusual, the Pygmalion story, because of its association with the worship of images, becomes a medium for the condemnation of Catholicism. In a time when statues are painted in garish colours, the statue is seen as a painted lady or prostitute. Despite these divergences, Pygmalion continues to be a famous sculptor. There is little interest in the description of the transformation of the statue in this period.

The Seventeenth Century

The seventeenth century is 'another *aetas ovidiana*' in which the poet was an important source for themes in literature and painting (Vinge, p. 179). This period saw a tremendous increase in short references to the Pygmalion story; although there was not, however, a proportionate rise in the number of full renarrations of the story. Two Latin versions of the story were published by British writers: Richard Crashaw's poem 'In Pigmaliona' (1648) and an anonymously written verse playlet called *Pygmalion* (1630–50). The most important translation of the *Metamorphoses* in this period is a rendering in heroic couplets by George Sandys in 1626, the second edition of which contains a commentary (1632).

This century produced only one major English renarration and two short

---

[64] Thomas Middleton, *Works*, ed. by A. H. Bullen, 8 vols (London, 1886), VIII, 133.

epigrams on the Pygmalion theme.[65] The epigrams allude elaborately to the story without narrating it in any depth. Neither portrays Pygmalion in a favourable light and both epigrams refer to the statue as a 'picture'. The first is 'Against Pigmalion's Indiscretion' by John Davies:

> Pigmalion carves, and that with mickle heed,
> Dead stones like living men by *Cunnings* forces
> He makes Stones men; but he good men (in Deede)
> Himselfe makes like a stone by sencelesse courses:
> *If he makes men like Stones, and Stones like men,*
> Pigmalion's *Pictures are his Betters then.*[66]

Hugh Crompton's 'Pigmalion' (1657) asks:

> Why does *Pigmalion* on his picture doat?
> And to the worship of the same devote
> His purest thought? *Pigmalion*, dost thou see
> More value in thy image then in thee?
> That thou shouldst buckle, and incline thy wit
> To leave thy self, and fall in love with it?
> Alas *Pigmalion*, thou art but an Ape,
> That for the substance dost adore the shape.[67]

According to the *OED*, a picture is 'by extension, an artistic representation in the solid, especially a statue or a monumental effigy; an image'. As Pygmalion is still referred to as a sculptor, it is probably safe to conclude that the word 'picture' is being used in this sense. Examples of this usage date as far back as circa 1500, and are common in seventeenth-century references to Pygmalion.

Richard Brathwait's fifth satire, in *Nature's Embassie* (1621), takes for its subject the theme of love and vanity and likewise refers to the statue as a 'curious Image or *Picture* or an amiable woman'.[68] His Pygmalion is a skilful artist who has fallen in love with a painted ivory statue of his own making. Although, the statue is described as a 'faire saint' and an 'idle idoll', the idolatry theme is not entered into deeply. After explaining the pointlessness of Pygmalion's love, the narrator shows him praying to Venus for his statue to come to life. Venus responds positively, and Pygmalion marries his new woman. The story concludes with the

---

[65] I shall limit my reference to *The Winter's Tale* in this section, partly because it has already been studied in depth by Ray (pp. 128–170) and others, and partly because it does not contain a direct reference to the Pygmalion story.
[66] John Davies, *The Scourge of Folly* (London, 1611), p. 34.
[67] Hugh Crompton, *Poems* (London, 1657), p. 233.
[68] Richard Brathwait, *Natures Embassie* (London, 1621), pp. 98–106 (p. 98).

birth of a daughter, Paphos. There is little in the poem which marks it out as a satire, except that we are told that Pygmalion and his wife were constantly of one opinion, and that 'few wives be of her temper now adaies' (p. 105). Brathwait's

> Morall includeth the vaine and foolish *Loves* of such as are besotted on every idle picture or painted Image, whose selfe-conceited vanitie makes beauty their Idoll, becoming Creatures of their owne making, as if they dis-esteemed the creation of their Maker. The Satyre though compendious, compriseth such matter (Brathwait, p. 98).

A margin note to this introductory passage connects the 'painted image' with the user of cosmetics: 'Note this you painted faces, whose native Countrey (once white Albion) is become reddish, with blushing at your vanities' (Brathwait, p. 99). This looks back to the works of the previous century.

Pygmalion's reputation as an artist and lover is strong in this period and his name still frequently cited alongside those of artists like Apelles and Zeuxes. For example, Richard Johnson writes in 1612 that '*Pigmalion* with his gravers then could never worke so faire a peece: / Nor yet *Apelles* in his time, did never see the like in Greece'.[69] Richard Brathwait alludes to him in this fashion 1621: 'Zeuxes, Phydias, and Pigmalion, / Those native artists who indeed did strive / To make their curious statues seeme alive, / Reducing art to Nature' (*Natures Embassie*, p. 227). Pygmalion is rarely characterized solely as a lover in this period.

Whereas sixteenth-century poets castigated the statue, the seventeenth century saw a return to the practice of earlier years, attacking Pygmalion for his vices. This was not a universal practice in British literature, but it was a significant one. Several writers emphasize Pygmalion's lasciviousness: for example, John Davies in *Microcosmos* (1603): '*Pigmalion* / For his owne *Picture* did like *passion* prove / Damned *Lust* what pleasure provid'st thou in a Stone'.[70] Robert Gomersall writes in 1628 that 'the barreness is in' Pygmalion's love and 'this hath no other Motive then the Sinne'.[71] Abraham Cowley writes in 1647: 'If an *Inordinate Desire* be *Lust*: / *Pygmalion*, loving what none can enjoy, / More *lustful* was, than the hot youth of *Troy*'.[72] Several seventeenth-century allusions to the story depict Pygmalion's love specifically as foolish or hopeless. John Taylor's 'A Whore' (1630) suggests that a lover would rather live alone than love a stone: '*Pigmalion*,

---

[69] Richard Johnson, 'A Lover's Song in Praise of his Mistresse', *A Crowne-Garland of Goulden Roses* (London, 1612), no page numbers.

[70] John Davies, *Microcosmos* (Oxford, 1603), p. 168.

[71] Robert Gomersall, *The Levites Revenge* (London, 1628), p. 23.

[72] Abraham Cowley, *The Collected Works*, ed. by Thomas O. Calhoun, Laurence Heyworth and J. Robert King, 2 vols (London and Toronto, 1993), II, 37.

with an Image made of Stone, / Did love and lodge: (I'le rather lye alone)'.[73] Henry King's 'Paradox. That Fruition Destroyes Love' (1664) describes '*Pigmaleon's* dotage on the carved stone' as a delusion.[74] Matthew Stevenson's narrator would rather have gone through the pointless exercise of loving a stone than have to court an ugly woman: 'But to make serious love to such an one, / Pigmaleon-like, I'd sooner court a Stone'.[75] On the other hand, William Basse characterized Pygmalion with a modesty which is usually reserved for his statue: '*Pygmalion* at her cheekes and chin would trip, / And at hir browes would blush and look awry'.[76] Others too refer to the story in a positive way: John Davies asks 'What Images would not seem rude, and raw / Before Pigmalion?'.[77]

The use of the Pygmalion story in the lover's complaint continues throughout this century. Edmund Waller's 'On the Discovery of a Ladies Painting' (1645) puts forward the usual statement that Pygmalion's situation has some bearing on the predicament of a narrator-lover.[78] Sir Aston Cokayne's 'Now after Tedious Weeks of Being Mute' (1658) is another example:

> Had I your Picture reasonably wrought,
> No lady like it should command my thought;
> *Pigmalion-like* I would adore't, until
> You did prove kind, or me my griefes did kill.[79]

Furthermore, we see the continuation of other sixteenth-century features. The association of the theme with cosmetics (as seen in Edward Guilpin's *Skialethia* [1598]) is continued by John Heath in 'To Mistris E. S.' (1619):

> Our latter Artists, who make up a face
> Of seeming beautie, for to blinde such eyes
> As with Pigmalion them doe Idolize'.[80]

These lines were copied by Samuel Pick in his poem 'To his deare Mistris, H. P.' (1639).[81] Robert Gomersall associates Pygmalion's statue with painted women:

---

[73] John Taylor, *All The Workes* (London, 1630), p. 108. These lines, and a substantial quantity of the rest of this poem, were plagiarized by Walter Scot (1614?–1694) for his poetic history: *A True History of Several Honourable Families of the Right Honourable Name of Scot* (Edinburgh, 1688), p. 4.
[74] Henry King, *Poems, Elegies, Paradoxes, and Sonnets* (London, 1664), p. 76.
[75] Matthew Stevenson, *Poems* (London, 1673), p. 121.
[76] William Basse, *The Poetical Works*, ed. by R. Warwick Bond (London, 1893), p. 61.
[77] John Davies, *Wittes Pilgrimage* (London, 1605), no page numbers.
[78] Edmund Waller, *Poems* (London, 1645), pp. 60–61.
[79] Aston Cokayne, *Small Poems Of Divers Sorts* (London, 1658), p. 47.
[80] John Heath, *The House of Correction* (London, 1619), no page numbers.
[81] Samuel Pick, *Festum Voluptatis* (London, 1639), p. 5.

'a painted Woman will cause love' (p. 23), and the narrator of John Donne's 'A Paradox of a Painted Face' states that he knows that the beauty of his beloved is 'artificiall, borrowed [...] yet for this / I idoll thee, and begge a luschyous kisse'.[82] The poem ends with the exhortation: 'Jove grant me then a repairable face, / Which whil'st that colours are, can want noe grace; / Pigmalion's painted statue I wold loue, / Soe it were warme or soft, or could but move' (I, p. 232).

The Eighteenth Century

The eighteenth century saw a further increase in short references to Pygmalion, though there is only one British poem dealing solely with the subject of Pygmalion. This decline in major references may be attributable to a decline in the popularity of Ovid. Douglas Bush writes:

> One symptom of altered taste, to be inferred from silence as well as from express statements, is the loss of prestige that Ovid underwent. [...] Ovid had held a high place in the tradition of European poetry, during long periods he had outshone the greater ancients. [...] The response of the early Augustans was less ardent, but it was exceedingly voluminous; every gentleman of letters translated parts of the *Metamorphoses* or the *Heroides* or the *Ars Amatoria*. But the appeal of Ovid quickly declined.[83]

The association of the Pygmalion story with the lover's complaint continues in the short references. This kind of allusion is seen at its best in Soame Jenyns's 'The Choice':

> Had I, Pygmalion like, the pow'r
> To make the nymph I wou'd adore;
> The model shou'd be thus design'd,
> Like this her form, like this her mind.[84]

The poem goes on to outline the various qualities the speaker decides that his

---

[82] John Donne, *The Complete Poems*, ed. by Alexander B. Grosart, 2 vols (London, 1872), I, 229.
[83] Douglas Bush, *Mythology and The Romantic Tradition in English Poetry* (New York, 1963), p. 32.
[84] Soame Jenyns, *The Works*, 4 vols (London, 1790), I, 147–150 (p.147). The poem belongs to the mid-eighteenth century (Miles, p. 379).

beloved should possess.[85] Furthermore, the transformation of the statue achieved greater prominence in these references. Words like melted, softened, warmed and glowed were frequently used to describe the metamorphosis of the statue. For example, Henry Travers describes Venus bidding the statue's 'vital Pow'rs exert their Strife, / And warm each varied Atom into Life'.[86] Though such vocabulary is occasionally used to describe the metamorphosis in other eras, the words gain a new significance in the eighteenth century as they are often accompanied by references to fires and flames. For example, Soame Jenyns writes of the statue in 'The Art of Dancing' (1728): 'But breasts of Flint must melt with fierce desire, / When art and motion wake the sleeping fire' (I, 4). Joseph Mitchell, in 1731, observes that 'Life *Pygmalion's* Iv'ry fir'd'.[87] Richard Savage also mentions Pygmalion and Prometheus within a few lines.

> If Life *Pygmalion's* iv'ry fir'd,
> Sure some enamour'd God this draught inspir'd!
> Or if you rashly caught Promethean Flame,
> Shade the sweet theft, and mar the beauteous frame! (Savage, II, 148).

Henry Travers's statue 'imbib'd the Flame' in 1731, and James Woodhouse has his 'statuary's soul inflame' in 1764.[88] Pygmalion is even confused with Prometheus in 'Ode To Poetic Fancy' by Anna Seward: 'While Zeuxis' pencil, Orpheus' lyre, / Pygmalion's heaven-descended fire, / The smiling pleasures bring'.[89] References like these herald the beginning of a close association between Pygmalion and Prometheus. These connections were later consolidated by the Romantics (for example, Mary Shelley's *Frankenstein* [1818]). The importance of the Prometheus story for Romantic writers has been well documented.[90]

Prometheus's fire is also associated with Pygmalion in George Ellis's rendering of Chaucer's Wife of Bath's tale in 'The Canterbury Tale' (1778):

> Here nature seem'd to mock Pygmalion's art,

---

[85] For further references of this type, see George Granville, 'To Myra. Loving at First Sight', *The Genuine Works in Verse and Prose*, 2 vols (London, 1732), I, 16–17 and Christopher Pitt, *Poems and Translations* (London, 1727), p. 168.

[86] Henry Travers, *Miscellaneous Poems and Translations* (London, 1731), p. 75.

[87] Joseph Mitchell, *Three Poetic Epistles to Mr. Hogarth, Mr. Dandridge, and Mr. Lambert* (London, 1731), p. 3. The lines quoted and others were later plagiarized by Richard Savage in 'To Mr. John Dyer', *The Works*, 2 vols (London, 1777), II, 147–149 (148).

[88] Travers, p. 75; James Woodhouse, *Poems on Sundry Occasions* (London, 1764), p. 96.

[89] Anna Seward, *The Poetical Works*, 3 vols (Edinburgh, 1810), II, 106.

[90] Burton R. Pollin, 'Philosophical and Literary sources of *Frankenstein*', *Comparative Literature*, 17 (1965), 97–108; Christopher Small, *Ariel Like a Harpy: Shelley, Mary and Frankenstein* (London, 1972).

All that proportion, all that form can give,
Venus once more had play'd Prometheus' part,
And bid the beauteous wonder love and live.[91]

Chaucer's tale did not contain a reference to the Pygmalion story, but Dryden, nevertheless includes a reference to it in his translation (*Fables* [1700]). The allusion forms part of the description of the metamorphosis of the old woman, whom the knight is compelled to marry, into a beautiful young woman:

He look'd, and saw a Creature heavn'ly Fair,
In bloom of Youth, and of a charming Air.
With Joy he turn'd, and seiz'd her Iv'ry Arm;
And like *Pygmalion* found the statue warm (Dryden, p. 1717).

The trope is particularly appropriate here, as both stories, Pygmalion and the Wife of Bath's tale, are about the metamorphosis of a woman. George Ogle's collection of stories from *The Canterbury Tales* (1741) also uses Dryden's rendering of the tale, calling it 'The Desire of Woman: Or the Wife Of Bath's Tale', and therefore includes the Pygmalion reference.[92]

The paucity of renarrations of the myth in this period seems curious when we consider the popularity of the story in the rest of Europe, where Rousseau's *Pygmalion* was well-liked. Rousseau's play, a scène-lyrique with musical accompaniment, was written in 1762, first performed in 1770 and published in 1771. It caused a great surge in the popularity of the Pygmalion story in France, and its fame gradually spread to other parts of Europe. Rousseau's interest in the theme did not appear in isolation. J. L. Carr reveals that the Pygmalion story gained in popularity in eighteenth-century France because it linked the human and the divine:

> Artistic creation may be said to be the outcome of man's desire to influence inanimate nature. The statue legend, therefore, illustrates the point of contact between art and magic; into the statue, made in the image of Venus herself, some part of the goddess of love has been transfused.[93]

There are examples of its use in French poetry and drama prior to 1762, and the theme was used by artists such as François Boucher and Jean Restout in the 1740s and more extensively in the latter part of the eighteenth century, after Rousseau's

---

[91] George Ellis, *Poetical Tales. By Sir Gregory Gander* (Bath, 1778), p. 26.
[92] George Ogle, *The Canterbury Tales of Chaucer* (London, 1741), p. 103.
[93] J. L. Carr, 'Pygmalion and the Philosophes. The Animated Statue in Eighteenth Century France', *Journal of the Warburg and Courtauld Institutes*, 23 (1960), 239–255 (p. 244).

play. While Pygmalion had occasionally been the subject of operas prior to 1700, the story became an extremely popular theme for operas, cantatas, and opera-ballets in Europe during this period. Many of these were loosely based on Rousseau, or used Rousseau's play as a libretto.

A significant development on the French stage is the emergence of the comic Pygmalion. Examples include Jean-Antoine Romagnesi, *Pygmalion* (1741), Anonymous, *Pigmalion* (1741), Edme Sulpice Gaubier de Barrault, *Brioché* (1753), Louis Poinsinet de Sivry, *Pygmalion* (1760), Fontenelle, *Pigmalion* (1764), Michel de Cubières-Palmézeaux, *Galathée* (1777 or 1778). The Pygmalion story was not, however, included in the earlier comic *Ovide Bouffon* by Louis Richer.[94] There is also a comic tradition associated with the story in the French opera of the period. It is not until the nineteenth century, however, that the story becomes the subject of comic plays in Britain.

Rousseau's influence on British poetry was not felt until the turn of the century, despite an early anonymous translation. This translation, composed in rhyming couplets, conveys very little of the style of the original work, which is highly conversational; the translation contains countless brief diversions into classical mythology and history which do not appear in the original. William Mason's English verse translation of 1811 is more literal.[95] The *Metamorphoses* was translated (in parts and in its entirety) by Dryden (1700) and others during this period.[96] These translations often formed part of short collections of stories from the *Metamorphoses*. Most notable are John Hopkins's 'Pygmalion and his Iv'ry Statue' (1700) and Henry Baker's 'Pigmalion and the Statue' (1737).[97] Despite the abundance of translations of the *Metamorphoses* in Europe, 'the impression remains that the influence of Ovid in literature has decreased. [...] Other research shows, however, that interest in mythology survived' (Vinge, pp.253–256). The following chapter will explore the significance of the Pygmalion story for English Romantic writers, who look to Rousseau for inspiration.

Finally, the eighteenth century sees the first use of the name 'Galatea' for the statue; the name is probably taken from the story of Acis and Galatea in the *Metamorphoses*. Although Rousseau was not the first writer to give the statue this name, his *Pygmalion* is undoubtedly the origin of its wider use and it is through him that Pygmalion's statue comes to be so named in Britain.[98] From Rousseau

---

[94] Louis Richer, *L'Ovide Bouffon; ou Les Metamorphoses Burlesques* (Paris, 1650).

[95] William Mason, *The Works*, 4 vols (London, 1811), II, 365–377.

[96] Dryden's popular version was included in *Ovid's Metamorphoses*, ed. by Samuel Garth (London, 1717), pp. 343–346.

[97] John Hopkins, *Amasia*, 3 vols (London, 1700), III, 37–40; Henry Baker, *Medulla Poetarum Romanorum*, 2 vols (London, 1737), II, 223–227.

[98] Edward P. Harris claims, incorrectly, that André François Boureau-Deslandes was the first to call the statue 'Galathée'; Boureau-Deslandes's statue has no name. Edward P. Harris, 'The Liberation of Flesh from Stone: Pygmalion in Frank Wedekind's *Erdgeist*', *The Germanic Review*,

onwards, poets and writers on the Pygmalion story (including compilers of handbooks on mythology and translators of Ovid's story) often refer to the statue as 'Galatea'. For some, the name has become part of the story itself. Mary Innes's *Penguin Classics* translation of the *Metamorphoses* calls the statue Galatea in the title of the story and in the index to the translation, though the name does not appear in Ovid's version of the myth.[99]

---

52 (1977), 44–56 (p. 45).

[99] Ovid, *Metamorphoses*, trans. by Mary M. Innes (Harmondsworth, 1986), p. 231 and p. 361.

Chapter 2

'Don't look at J. J. Rousseau': Pygmalion and the Romantics

Though Ovid's tale greatly influenced the nineteenth century, it was Rousseau's one-act play, *Pygmalion* (1770), which inspired the British Romantics to tackle the theme.[1] Rousseau's representation of Ovid's sculptor as a narcissist, more interested in his own creativity than his statue as a separate entity, prompted a number of different responses. From the 1780s, Rousseau's play was extremely popular and widely performed and translated throughout Europe. In Britain, however, probably because of the writer's reputation, the work was only of interest to the few, namely those writers who were already sympathetic to his ideas.

On the whole, Rousseau's theories were treated with suspicion in late eighteenth and early nineteenth-century Britain. Edmund Burke's famous attack on the writer, and the widespread association of his ideas with those of the French Revolutionaries, encouraged unfavourable reactions to Rousseau's work by the first-generation Romantics and the periodical press.[2] Rousseau was condemned for his vanity, emotionalism and self-indulgence. Although ambivalent about Rousseauean sensibility, Mary Wollstonecraft denounced Rousseau's opinions on the restriction of women's education to the domestic sphere. Support for Rousseau came from Hazlitt, Byron and Percy Shelley: 'By reason of time, temperament, and political difference, Burke's influence lay much less heavily on Byron and Shelley than on Wordsworth and Coleridge' (Duffy, p. 53). Hazlitt and the later Romantics are interested in Rousseau's deliberation on the boundaries between art and life, his elevation of the artistic personality, and his homage to love. While Rousseau's influence can be seen more generally in work of these Romantics, their explicit reactions to *Pygmalion* show them directly engaging with his ideas.

There are very few translations of *Pygmalion* before 1800. Leigh Hunt wrote that he knew of none when he undertook the task himself in 1820: 'We are not aware that this piece of Rousseau's has hitherto appeared in English'.[3] Hunt had clearly missed William Mason's accomplished translation first published posthumously in 1811, and an anonymous American review and translation of

---

[1] First performed in Lyons in 1770.
[2] Edward Duffy, *Rousseau in England* (Berkeley, California, 1979), pp. 133–134 (pp. 31–32).
[3] J. H. Leigh Hunt, 'Rousseau's *Pygmalion*', *The Indicator*, 1 (1820), 241–246 (p. 241).

some extracts of the play in *The Port Folio*.[4] The American writer suggests that 'these extracts [from Rousseau's play] will be sufficient to give some ideas of a production, not familiar, I presume, to the English reader' (p. 326) and regards Rousseau's topic as a little old-fashioned:

> Who but one conscious of the magic power of eloquence, could flatter himself with being able to impart the smallest degree of interest, at the present day, to so antique a tale; so wild and extravagant a fiction, as that of a man falling in love with the image of his own creation (p. 324).

Notwithstanding the dearth of translations, a general indicator of popularity, the play and the myth are significant for this group of early nineteenth-century writers.

Rousseau's *Pygmalion* is a highly indulgent monodrama which follows the changing moods of the artist as he contemplates his statue. Pygmalion's emotions range from self-doubt, to an overwhelming belief in his own ability. The monologue begins abruptly in the midst of Pygmalion's laments for the lifelessness of his veiled sculpture. Blaming his own lack of imagination, he attempts to reinvigorate his mind by unveiling the statue. On seeing the statue, he is struck by its sanctity and prostrates himself, declaiming Galatea a goddess and praying to her. His adoration quickly turns towards himself as the originator of such beauty, and Pygmalion declares himself to be greater than the gods. Contemplating further work on the statue, he realizes that her only fault is that she is too perfect. Pygmalion impetuously offers to die in order that she might live, and volunteers to live as her. This appeal closely associates the artist's identity with that of the statue. Quickly, he realizes that he would be disadvantaged, as he could not be the man who loved her if he actually were the beloved statue. He asks instead that the gods look into his heart and grant his desires, and appeals specifically to Venus, as a universal nature goddess, to right the disorder caused by the denial of his wishes. Galatea is brought to life and, enacting Lacan's 'mirror stage', she touches her own body and realizes that she has a self, then touches another statue and recognizes that it is other. Galatea finally touches Pygmalion, who puts her hand to his heart. Indicating the closeness of their relationship, Galatea does not recognize it as other. In conclusion, Pygmalion declares that he will live for her.

Mary Wollstonecraft is the first British writer to accentuate the idea of the sculptor projecting an identity onto the statue. In her critique of Rousseauean sensibility, *The Wrongs of Woman: Or, Maria* (1798), the heroine of the novel, Maria, imagines the ideal man to be like Rousseau's St Preux, the hero of *La*

---

[4] William Mason, 'Pigmalion, A Lyrical Scene', *The Works*, 4 vols (London, 1811), II, 365–377.'Notes of a Desultory Reader', *The Port Folio*, 4, 3rd series (New York, 1814), pp. 323–326.

Nouvelle Héloïse. Maria, who has been wrongfully imprisoned by her husband, falls in love with the benevolent Henry Darnford, who has been incarcerated in the same prison. Recognizing how the world will view her love, Maria wrestles with her conscience:

> Having had to struggle incessantly with the vices of mankind, Maria's imagination found repose in pourtraying [sic] the possible virtues the world might contain. Pygmalion formed an ivory maid, and longed for an informing soul. She, on the contrary, combined all the qualities of a hero's mind, and fate presented a statue [i.e. Darnford] in which she might enshrine them.[5]

Here the heroine takes the role of the imaginative artist and ironically makes a Galatea of Darnford, the passive 'man of feeling'. Although Wollstonecraft read widely amongst the works of Rousseau, whether she read Rousseau's play is unknown, but her identification of the sculptor's role as essentially a projection of personality onto the statue aligns it with Rousseau's interpretation. It is also clear from this reference that she either directly or indirectly knew Ovid's version because of her description of the statue as having been made from ivory, Rousseau's Galatea being a marble statue.

Wollstonecraft's reference marks the beginning of a new interest in the tale by British writers. It is followed by Robert Southey's 'Sonnet 4: The Poet Expresses His Feelings Respecting A Portrait In Delia's Parlour' (1799), one of *The Amatory Poems of Abel Shufflebottom*.[6] Loosely based on Samuel Daniel's Delia sonnets, Southey's brief reference similarly reverses the genders. The poet wishes to be the painting of a portly gentleman displayed in Delia's parlour, so that he can gaze upon her freely and be gazed upon by her. This causes him to worry that the picture might indeed come to life like Pygmalion's statue, warmed to life by Delia's beauty. The jealousy subsides and the poet repeats his first wish, to be the man in the painting. Here coming to life and being loved are closely linked, as they are in Ovid. Southey is likely to have been influenced by the Renaissance conception of the story in this amusing poem on the lover's complaint.

The main Romantic responses to the tale belong to the 1820s. Leigh Hunt translated and reviewed Rousseau's *Pygmalion* in 1820, regarding it as 'exquisitely managed'.[7] The play inspired William Hazlitt (as did Rousseau's *Confessions* and his *La Nouvelle Héloïse*) to write his story of unrequited love,

---

[5] Mary Wollstonecraft, *Mary and The Wrongs of Woman*, ed. by Gary Kelly (Oxford, 1998), p. 99.

[6] Robert Southey, *The Poetical Works*, 10 vols (London, 1837–8), II (1837), 117–120 (p. 120).

[7] For convenience, when citing Rousseau's *Pygmalion* I shall use Hunt's English translation and cite the original in the notes.

Liber Amoris; or The New Pygmalion (1823).[8] Hazlitt also discusses the Pygmalion story in *Characteristics* (1823, IX, p. 212). Byron also alludes briefly to the Pygmalion story in *Don Juan* (1819–1824), saying of Dudù: 'She looked (this simile's quite new) just cut / From marble, like Pygmalion's statue waking, / The Mortal and the Marble still at strife, / And timidly expanding into life'.[9] Percy Shelley mentions Pygmalion in passing in the 'The Witch of Atlas' (1820).

> Then by strange art she kneaded fire and snow
> Together, tempering the repugnant mass
> With liquid love – all things grow
> Through which the harmony of love can pass
> And a fair Shape out of her hands did flow –
> A living Image, which did far surpass
> In beauty that Bright shape of vital stone
> Which drew the heart out of Pygmalion.[10]

Furthermore, Shelley, who had most likely read Rousseau's *Pygmalion* and Hunt's review, includes Rousseau as a character in his final and unfinished poem 'The Triumph of Life' (1822).

The most overt and extensive engagement with Rousseau's play comes from the less well known Romantic poet, playwright and devotee of Shelley, Thomas Lovell Beddoes. Beddoes, a Bristol-born poet and writer of gothic closet-drama, was the son of the eminent physician and friend to Coleridge, Southey and Wordsworth, Dr Thomas Beddoes. He remains on the fringes of British Romanticism, probably due to his unique interests and his self-imposed exile in Germany for much of his writing career. The poet is known for his literary (and medical) fascination with death: 'I search with avidity for every shadow of a proof or probability of an after-existence, both in the material and the immaterial nature of man' (20 April 1827).[11] Educated at Bath grammar school and at Charterhouse, where he distinguished himself as a prize-winning classicist, Beddoes went up to Pembroke College, Oxford in 1820, publishing his first collection of verse there, and taking his BA in 1825. He later qualified as a doctor in Germany.

'Pygmalion. The Cyprian Statuary' (1823–5) is part of a group of poems

---

[8] William Hazlitt, *The Complete Works*, ed. by P. P. Howe, 21 vols (London and Toronto, 1930–1934), IX (1932), 99–162.

[9] George Gordon Noel Byron, *Byron's Don Juan: A Variorum Edition*, ed. by Truman Guy Steffan and Willis W. Pratt, 4 vols (Austin, Texas, 1957), III, p. 27. There is a second brief reference in III, p. 208.

[10] Percy Bysshe Shelley, *The Complete Poetical Works*, ed. by Thomas Hutchinson (London, 1965), p. 379.

[11] *The Works of Thomas Lovell Beddoes* ed. by Henry Wolfgang Donner (Oxford, 1935), p. 630.

written while the poet was at Oxford and collected under the heading *Outidana: Or Effusions, Amorous, Pathetic, and Fantastical* (1821–1825). 'Pygmalion' is likely to be one of the 'fantastical' or 'amorous' poems. Beddoes's introverted sculptor rejects the beautiful women of his island in favour of his stone statue. Pygmalion's prayer asks for the image to be brought to life and is an appeal to Venus to save him from death. His thoughts tend towards mortality and the emptiness of his life causes him to feel 'lifeless'.[12] Disappointed by the statue's inanimate state, Pygmalion grows weak with yearning for her to come to life. Finally, he steps into Charon's boat, but is united with the statue either in death or on another plane of existence.

Beddoes openly acknowledges his debt to Rousseau in a letter to his friend (and later his biographer) Thomas Forbes Kelsall, with whom he discussed much of his work. His letter is quite specific about the influence of Rousseau; in it Beddoes concedes that the play is a better version of the story than his own poem:

> I wrote this Pyg stuff this morng. – what d'ye think of it? Don't look at J. J. Rousseau – his is much better, because prose. I have not hit at what I aimed at – the beautiful philosophy of the story – but have fallen as usual into diffuseness and uninteresting delay (25 April 1825).[13]

This Rousseauean act of confession, and self-justification through an association with the earlier text, invites us to make a comparison: the act of 'looking' at Rousseau elucidates Beddoes. The poet's choice of images and his exploration of 'self' and 'other' are indebted to Rousseau. There are, however, some important differences between the poets, differences which highlight the lack of uniformity (and variety of development) in Romantic thought, as well as Beddoes's own anxieties. Beddoes's 'Pygmalion', though indulgent, is restrained in comparison with Rousseau's.

Beddoes's interest in Rousseau's *Pygmalion* has largely gone unexplored in the critical literature on this poem. Sarah Annes Brown overlooks the Rousseau connection, assessing the poem from the general standpoint of 'Ovidianism'. Brown, acknowledging Beddoes's classical scholarship, is certain that Beddoes derives his poem from Ovid, though she is perhaps over-cautious in her theory of how he came to know of Ovid's work, conjecturing that the Pygmalion story 'would, presumably, have been sufficiently well known for Beddoes to have read it in a summary elsewhere [i.e. other than in Ovid] or derived it from a

---

[12] Thomas Lovell Beddoes, *Plays and Poems*, ed. by Henry Wolfgang Donner (London, 1950), pp. 98–104 (p. 102).
[13] Thomas Lovell Beddoes, *The Works*, ed. by Henry Wolfgang Donner (Oxford, 1935), p. 601.

conversation'.[14] Beddoes used two sources for his poem: Rousseau's *Pygmalion* and Ovid's version. The exclusion of Rousseau's *Pygmalion* and the reliance on Ovid as Beddoes's sole source leads Brown to several problematic assumptions about the poem's inception and interpretation. Brown suggests, for example, that Beddoes's interest in Renaissance writers may inform his colouring of the tale (Brown, p. 156). Although he is interested in Renaissance plays, 'Pygmalion' shows little interaction with its Renaissance predecessors and is more absorbed with coming to a late-Romantic understanding of the problem of Rousseau. The poem enacts a late-romantic engagement with the early romantic vision. While Brown points out that Beddoes's emphasis on the power of Pygmalion's creative mind distinguishes him from Ovid, she is at a loss to provide a reason for this deviation; the answer lies in Rousseau.

There are many points of comparison between Beddoes's and Rousseau's versions. Broadly, Beddoes incorporates Rousseau's suggestion that there is an important emotional connection between the artist and his statue. Both see the Pygmalion story as a metaphor for this close relationship. But whereas Rousseau's play leads to a successful union between the artist and his creation, Beddoes's poem concludes with an ambiguous ending, and possibly with the failure of the imagination to bring about such a close connection before death. If Pygmalion dies it is because Beddoes conceives the character of Pygmalion, and the nature of his love for the statue, differently.

For Rousseau, the story is exaggerated to exalt the artistic self into a creator who wavers between *amour-propre* (self-referential love) and *amour de soi* (love of another). Just as Shelley demands of the spirit of the west wind 'Be thou me', so the sculptor identifies with his subject, treating it as an extension of himself. This Romantic emphasis breaks down the distinction, central to neoclassicism, between subject and object. The statue is representative of the artist's internal ideal, and is therefore a part of him. Rousseau's Pygmalion demonstrates that he both loves the statue because he has made her, and loves himself for the same reason: 'I am intoxicated with self-love; I adore myself in that which I have made' (Hunt, p. 243).[15] Rousseau's Pygmalion celebrates self-referential art, a point of contention in many Romantic responses to Rousseau's literature, particularly in Beddoes and Leigh Hunt. Rousseau's interest in narcissism is confirmed by his *Narcisse*, in which he tells the story of Valère, a man so vain that he falls in love with his own portrait thinly disguised as a woman.[16]

Beddoes, on the other hand, advocates that one should avoid writing about

---

[14] Sarah Annes Brown, *The Metamorphosis of Ovid: From Chaucer to Ted Hughes* (London, 1999), p. 156.

[15] 'Je m'adore dans ce que j'ai fait' (Rousseau, p. 10).

[16] See Paul de Man, *Allegories of Reading. Figural Language in Rousseau, Nietzsche, Rilke, and Proust* (New Haven and London, 1979), p. 166.

oneself. As Rousseau's *Confessions* show, the genesis of *Pygmalion* had much to do with Rousseau's 'attempt to come to terms, as an artist, with the experience of his affair with Sophie d'Houdetot and his quarrel with the *philosophes*', and so the play has some currency as a semi-autobiographical work.[17] John Hummel points out that: 'even when it is not overtly autobiographical, Rousseau's work is never very far removed from autobiographical concerns, and we cannot ignore them' (p. 273). The play itself is about an artist putting himself into his art and enjoying the result. Even the statue confuses herself with her creator: 'Ah it is I again', she sighs when she touches Pygmalion (Hunt, p. 246).[18] Galathée implies here that Pygmalion is an extension of her, that his heart belongs to her, and possibly that by being touched she can feel herself again, by being able to sense the surface of her fingers. This interest in the self is commented on by Leigh Hunt in his review. Hunt suggests that 'Pygmalion's self predominates over the idea of his mistress, because the author's self pressed upon him while he wrote' (Hunt, p. 241). Hunt associates Rousseau's approach with vanity. Hunt further expresses his suspicion of egotistical writing in his essay 'I and We': 'There is an egotism of the letter, and maybe an egotism of the spirit, in writing of the first person singular'.[19] Beddoes also expresses his difficulties with autobiographical art:

> I will not venture on a psychological self-portraiture, fearing, and I believe with sufficient reason, to be betrayed into affectation, dissimulation, or some other alluring shape of lying. I believe that all autobiographical sketches are the result of mere vanity – not excepting those of St. Augustin [sic] and Rousseau – falsehood in the mask and mantle of truth. [...] How sleek, smooth-tongued, paradisiacal a deluder art thou, sweet self-conceit! (Beddoes [1935], p. 664).

This attitude is reflected in Beddoes's portrayal of the character of Pygmalion. Although Hunt and Beddoes thought highly of Rousseau's *Pygmalion*, they take issue with the egocentricity implied by Rousseau's account of the creative process. Hunt wishes that Rousseau had modified his portrayal of Pygmalion as an artist who falls in love with his statue *because* it is his own work, objecting to the narcissistic implications of the work. He argues that Pygmalion should sculpt a woman with whom he could fall in love because she represents a human being and not just his own genius. Hunt sees a necessity for art to be connected to the natural world, and not to be excessively internalized. For Beddoes, the author shines on

---

[17] John H. Hummel, 'Rousseau's *Pygmalion* and the *Confessions*', *Neophilologus*, 56 (1972), 273–284 (p. 273).
[18] 'Ah, encore moi' (Rousseau, p. 16).
[19] Leigh Hunt, *Literary Criticism*, ed. by L. H. Houtchens and C. W, Houtchens (New York, 1956), pp. 208–214 (p. 208).

his work with 'light creative'; and although his Pygmalion is a solitary figure, the statue is not a Rousseauean mirror which reflects the artist.

Rousseau and Beddoes emphasize the solitude and isolation of Pygmalion in order to elevate a the artist's importance or singularity. Rousseau's Pygmalion is self-analytical; for him, the statue acts as a touchstone enabling him to focus on his self-exploration. The genre gives scope for this exploration of the artistic ego. Until the statue speaks at the end of the piece, Pygmalion is the only character in a one-act play. Beddoes's Pygmalion, on the other hand, is introverted. The interposition of the narrator, and the figurative descriptions of Pygmalion's loneliness emphasize his solitude. 'Lonely Pygmalion' is 'self inhabited', 'his mind had space /And none went near'; he is the 'centre / Of an inspired round', and 'the middle spark / Of a great moon setting aside the dark and cloudy people' (Beddoes, p. 99). A similar image of the solitary figure parting the multitude, which is described as cloud-like, can be found in Shelley's critique of Rousseau, 'The Triumph of Life' (1824):

> The crowd gave way, and I arose aghast,
> Or seemed to rise, so mighty was the trance,
> And saw, like clouds upon the thunder-blast,
> The million with fierce song and maniac dance (Shelley, p. 510).

Beddoes's Pygmalion, a solitary who communicates only with Venus, emphasizes his uniqueness: 'let me not die, like all, / For I am but like one' (p. 102). Through his solitariness, Beddoes's Pygmalion achieves the self-awareness which enables him to create: 'His soul was bright and lonely as the sun / like which he could create' (Beddoes, p. 99), and accordingly Beddoes sees solitude as a positive state. Unlike his Romantic forbear, Victor Frankenstein, Beddoes's solipsistic genius is not corrupted by his alienation from society. Beddoes's poem remains morally neutral, as the absence of the Propoetides implies. Victor's Frankenstein's absence from society is shown by Mary Shelley to be a Godwinian evil, as Victor is separated from its moral influence. Whereas Shelley's text is heavily influenced by Godwin's late-enlightenment views on the evils of solitary confinement, Beddoes, exhibits the later Romantic (and Rousseauean) fascination for introspective creativity.[20]

---

[20] William Godwin, *Things As They Are; Or The Adventures of Caleb Williams*, ed. Maurice Hindle (London, 1988). Godwin is, however, inconsistent on this point, arguing in *Political Justice* that solitude is an evil, on the grounds that man is a social animal, and in his novel *Caleb Williams* the opposite. Caleb, when imprisoned, is reliant on his imagination to keep him sane: 'I became myself a poet; and, while I described the sentiments cherished by the view of natural objects, recorded the characters and passions of men, and partook with a burning zeal in the generosity of their determinations, I eluded the squalid solitude of my dungeon, and wandered in idea through all the varieties of human society' (p. 198). There is a tension between

It is possible to see the community of interest between Rousseau's suggestions, in *Pygmalion*, that the artist's work is his re-creation of himself and is not an object that can be properly distinguished from the artist, and Hazlitt's account of the breakdown of a real distinction between subject and object in his concept of 'gusto'. 'Gusto' is an aesthetic which synthesizes the subject and the object, preserving the individuality or essence of both entities, and at the same time using the nature of one to reveal the nature of the other; the artist's imagination, then, is responsible for combining the internal image and the external world. External objects are moulded by

> thoughts and feelings, into an infinite variety of shapes and combinations of power. This language is not the less true to nature, because it is false in point of fact; but so much more true and natural, if it conveys the impression which the object under the influence of passion makes on the mind (V, 4).

Hazlitt's aesthetic is based on the principle that the artist is not distinct from nature. He stresses the complexity and variety of nature and the intimacy between the perceiver and the perceived.

Approval of Rousseau's view of the Pygmalion story (that the statue is the creation of another self) is given by Hazlitt in *Characteristics* (1823):

> It is impossible to love entirely, without being loved again. Otherwise, the fable of Pygmalion would have no meaning. Let any one be ever so much enamoured of a woman who does not requite his passion, and let him consider what he feels when he finds her scorn or indifference turning to mutual regard, the thrill, the glow of rapture, the melting of two hearts into one, *the creation of another self in her* – and he will own that he was before only half in love! (IX, 212, my italics).

For Hazlitt, the statue as an internal or platonic ideal is an appealing concept. There are strong overtones of *Liber Amoris or the New Pygmalion* (1823) in this passage. This autobiographical work follows Rousseau in emphasizing the unresponsiveness of his beloved Sarah: 'Her words were few and simple; but you can have no idea of the exquisite, unstudied, irresistible graces with which she accompanies them, unless you can suppose a Greek statue to smile, move and speak' (IX, 143). Her statue-like role is to look beautiful, to inspire, and, it is hoped, to return love. Hazlitt refers again to the Pygmalion story in 'Notes of a Journey Through France and Italy' (1826) when he writes of the Venus of Medici seen in a public gallery: 'In a word, the Venus is a very beautiful toy, but not the

---

Godwin's social ideals and his views on the imagination.

goddess of Love or even of Beauty. It is not the statue Pygmalion fell in love with; nor did any man ever wish or fancy his mistress to be like it' (X, p. 167).

The corollary of treating the artist as an heroic narcissist is the neglect of the statue. The focus on Pygmalion's self excludes the statue's self to the extent that she is recast as almost indistinct from his personality. Like Rousseau's submissive Sophie in *Émile*, who is destined to seek only vicarious fulfilment through her husband and children, and Wollstonecraft's Darnford, whose personality is created by Maria, Galathée is an equally passive ideal. Just as Galathée has little choice and even less to say, so Hazlitt's Sarah has, in the eyes of her pursuer, been remade to fit the ideal of a marble woman. Sarah's rejection of her suitor is initially seen as modesty, but eventually the writer reassesses his view when she compromises herself with another man. Sarah has a choice of whether to love her obsessive wooer; but her identity is constructed entirely by the writer and she is guarded jealously: 'I should almost like you to wear a veil, and to be muffled up from head to foot' (p. 9). Beddoes's statue-woman, is very similar. As Hiram Johnson writes, 'the women of his poems both early and late are pale, unreal creatures lacking in all substance'.[21]

Beddoes, like Rousseau, uses the story to argue for an identity of subject and object, though he does not believe that Rousseau's self-referentiality is the way to achieve this identity. Furthermore, Beddoes is in agreement with Leigh Hunt that there is too much 'self' in Rousseau's text. Nevertheless, both Rousseau and Beddoes aim at the same point: the linking of the transformation of the statue with the removal of the boundary between art and life. While they view the transformation of the statue in similar terms, Rousseau merely employs the rhetoric of self-annihilation (for example: 'My heart, consumed by her charms, longs to quit my own body to give warmth to her's' [Hunt, p. 244]; 'Ah! let Pygmalion die, to live in Galatea. [...] It shall suffice me to live in her' [Hunt, pp. 244–245]).[22] It is likely that Beddoes's Pygmalion literally destroys himself. Both writers imagine a transfer of life from the artist to the statue: 'Is there not gone / My life into her which I pasture on, / Dead where she is not?' (Beddoes, p. 103). The death of the artist is to be a sublime or epiphanic moment. For Rousseau this is part of the dialectic – Pygmalion's process of reasoning through his dejection to the sublime union. His Pygmalion only toys with the idea of overcoming the distinction between himself and the statue by giving up his life to her:

> I imagine in my delirium that I could spring from myself, that I could give her my life, that I could animate her with my soul. Ah, let

---

[21] Hiram Kellogg Johnson, 'Thomas Lovell Beddoes', *The Psychiatric Quarterly* (New York, 1943), p. 4.

[22] 'Mon coeur embrasé par ses charmes, voudroit quitter mon corps pour aller échauffer le sien' (Rousseau, p. 12). 'Il me suffira de vivre en elle' (Rousseau, p. 14).

Pygmalion die, to live in Galatea! – What do I say, O heaven? If I were she, I should no longer see her; I should not be he that loves her! – No, let my Galatea live; but let me not become Galatea. Oh! let me always be another, always to wish to be herself, [to see her], to love her, to be beloved (Hunt, p. 244).[23]

Gesturing towards self-annihilation, Pygmalion quickly moves on to another theme. Rousseau's rhetoric returns to the issue of the artist putting himself into his work to achieve the 'sublime' connection of subject and object. Beddoes's Pygmalion, on the other hand, creates animate art (and a connection of subject and object) only through the death of Pygmalion.

Beddoes's story is, however, not clear cut. The poet leaves us with an ambiguous ending: Pygmalion and the statue-woman are united on a plane which is not in the world of normal experience. By line 214 it is clear that Pygmalion is dying:

> from the shore
> His foot is stretching into Charon's barge.
> Upon the pavement ghastly is he lying
> Cold with the last and stoniest embrace,
> Elysium's light illuminates all his face,
> His eyes have a wild starry grace
> Of heaven into whose depth of depths he's dying
> A sound, with which the air doth shake
> Extinguishing the window of moonlight.
> A pang of music dropping round delight,
> As if sweet music's honiest heart did break.
> It stung by as if something was unfurled
> That held great bliss within its inmost curled.
> Roof after roof the palace rends asunder,
> And then – a sight of joy and placid wonder! –
> He lies beside a fountain on the knee
> Of the sweet woman-statue, quietly
> Weeping the tears of felicity (Beddoes, p. 104).

The first eight lines of the final stanza express sudden actions, the last four are prolonged actions. The transformation is over after the first eight and a new situation emerges in the final four lines: Pygmalion and the 'woman-statue' are

---

[23] 'Je crois dans mon délire pouvoir m'élancer hors de moi. Je crois pouvoir lui donner ma vie & l'animer de mon ame. Ah! que Pygmalion meure pour vivre dans Galathée – que dis-je, ô ciel! si j'étois elle, je ne la verrois pas, je ne serois pas celiu que l'aime! non, que ma Galathée vive, & que je ne sois pas elle. Ah! que je sois toujours un autre, pour vouloir toujours être elle, pour la voir, pour l'aimer, pour en être aimé' (Rousseau, p.13).

together and happy, though where they are is uncertain. The references to Charon and Elysium suggest that Pygmalion dies, yet the ending is happy. According to Harold Bloom,

> The postulate of Beddoes' poetry is a world in which every metaphor resolves itself as another figure of death. For Beddoes the separation between subject and object is bridged not by any imaginative act, as in Blake, Wordsworth, and Shelley, but by dying. [...] Beddoes abandoned hope in the earth's renewal. In him the apocalyptic impulse of Romanticism degenerated into the most ironic of its identifications, and death and the imagination became one.[24]

The images in the last stanza of Beddoes's poem are certainly apocalyptic. The light is extinguished, there is a flash of light and 'roof after roof the palace rends asunder' (p. 104). Nevertheless, the sculptor and the statue share the same world. This final description of death contrasts with Beddoes's earlier more negative description in the prayer to Venus:

> The grave [...] is a fearful coop
> Dark, cold, and horrible – a blinded loop
> In Pluto's madhouse' green and wormy wall.
> O save me from't (Beddoes, p. 102).

If Pygmalion dies at the end of the poem, and I think this is likely, it would not be out of step with Beddoes's other work which explores the fragility of life, and love affairs which frequently end in death. The closet-drama, *The Bride's Tragedy*, and the poem 'The Phantom Wooer' (which depicts an invitation to die as an erotic request) are two prime examples. Hiram Kellogg Johnson argues that in Beddoes's work a perfect union between lovers can be only found in death: 'This idea adumbrated in his earliest works, reappears repeatedly. Time and again we find lovers bidding their mistresses to that [...] "private place, the grave"' (Johnson, p. 13). Brown concurs that 'The ending is too oblique to allow of a certain interpretation, but the sculptor is apparently weeping happily at the end of the poem' (p. 166). She offers an alternative reading, suggesting that Pygmalion may undergo an 'interiorised and unmagical transformation' in the same way that the metamorphosis at the end of *The Winter's Tale* is an illusion. Gail Marshall on the other hand, suggests that 'romantic satisfaction is guaranteed' in this poem (p. 21).

Notwithstanding the ambiguities, the clash of life and death as opposites leads, in Beddoes's 'Pygmalion', to an epiphanic conclusion. Extensive use is made of contrasts and juxtaposed opposites throughout both interpretations of the

---

[24] Harold Bloom, *The Visionary Company* (London, 1961), pp. 433-434.

Pygmalion story. Beddoes goes further than Rousseau, in using antinomy. These oppositional tropes are a stylistic pointer to the climax of the narrative: the transformation of art to life (or at the very least a commonality of experience). Antinomy and juxtaposition are not part of Ovid's version. It is therefore very likely that Beddoes was influenced by Rousseau here. In particular, Beddoes opts for Rousseau's choice of linked images of hot and cold, art and nature, man and goddess, and life and death. These contrasts all point towards a similar end: warmth, nature, man and life are all connected; as are cold, art, goddess and death. The difference between the world of the statue, with its added associations of rigidity, sterility, and lack of love and the world of the artist, associated with creativity, warmth, movement, and love, is emphasized. Paul de Man suggests that Rousseau uses a 'system of antinomies that confront each other at the beginning of the play' (p. 178). The images of hot and cold are contrasts and do not necessarily imply a contradiction as de Man implies. For example, Rousseau's Pygmalion says:

> All my fire is extinguished, my imagination is frozen; the marble comes cold from my hands. [...] What arrows of fire seem to issue from this object to burn my senses, and to carry away with my soul unto their source! Alas she remains immoveable and cold, while my heart, consumed by her charms, longs to quit my own body to give warmth to hers. [...] Celestial Venus [...] all thy flames are concentrated in my heart, and the coldness of death remains upon this marble (Hunt, pp. 242–245). [25]

Here, the qualities of hot and cold have been attributed to two separate entities, the images are used as contrasts and there is no contradiction implied. Beddoes, unlike Rousseau, uses both contrast and antinomy, several of his descriptions implying a contradiction. For example, the statue is referred to as a 'stone bud' (Beddoes, p. 101). Pygmalion calls her 'my sweet rock – my only wife' (Beddoes, p. 102), suggesting that she is both animate and inanimate at once. The marble slab from which the statue is carved is described in terms of both warmth and coldness: 'the cold stone' is 'less porous than a lip which kisses melt / And diamond hard' (p. 100). The density and the smoothness of the marble, a cold surface, compares with the warmth of a kissed lip. Hot and cold contrasts in the poem are extended to include the sun and moon, light and dark. These contrasts are a thematic link with Beddoes's philosophy of 'self' and 'other'. Beddoes's use of contradiction in

---

[25] 'Tout mon feu s'est éteint, mon imagination s'est glacée, le marbre sort froid de mes mains. [...] Quels traits de feu semblent sortir de cet objet pour embraser mes sens, et retourner avec mon ame à leur source! Hélas! il reste immobile et froid, tandis que mon coeur embrasé par ses charmes, voudroit quitter mon corps pour aller échauffer le sien. [...] Tous tes feux sont concentrés dans mon coeur, & le froid de la mort reste sur ce marbre' (Rousseau, pp. 7–13).

addition to contrast, looks forward to the less-definitely optimistic result of his version of the narrative.

Beddoes follows Rousseau's revision of the tale in many respects. There are notable elements found in Ovid which are omitted by both writers. For instance, there is no scene in which Pygmalion gives presents to the statue; Pygmalion neither visits the temple to pray for a woman like his statue nor thanks Venus after the event. In addition to omitting the parts of Ovid's version which Rousseau has ignored, Beddoes inserts actions which are found in Rousseau but not in Ovid. For example, both emphasize the loneliness and isolation of Pygmalion, discuss his exchanging places with the statue, and each narrative ends dramatically after the transformation scene. Naturally, Beddoes makes some alteration to the detail of Rousseau's version. Rousseau sets his story in Tyre, possibly as a short-hand way of referring to the fallen women whom Pygmalion rejects in Ovid's tale, or as J. L. Carr suggests, Rousseau had confused Pygmalion, the king of Cyprus, with Pygmalion, the prince of Tyre, who was the brother of Dido (p. 240). Carr notes that Fontenelle's version of the story (1764) made the same mistake, even though eighteenth-century dictionaries distinguished the two Pygmalions. Beddoes, on the other hand, sets his story in Cyprus, probably for classical authenticity. When Rousseau's *Pygmalion* was anonymously translated into English verse in 1779, the versifier likewise notices that Rousseau had set his play in the wrong place but decided to stick to Rousseau's original:

> in Conformity to the Original, represented *Pygmalion* the Sculptor as King of Tyre: Tho' it seems to be settled on unquestionable Authority, that he was a very different Personage, and lived at Cyprus, four hundred Years before the Tyrian Monarch of that Name.[26]

Mason's prose translation also keeps Rousseau's situation of the play in Tyre. Beddoes is likely to have taken his information from Ovid. Leigh Hunt did not know of any English translation of Rousseau's play, and so it is doubtful that this earlier translation was widely available, and indeed 'was intended only for the Closet', and not for the stage (p. 2). Beddoes's poem shares several features with Ovid which are omitted by Rousseau. Beddoes, unlike Rousseau, leaves the statue unnamed. The first British use of the name 'Galatea' in an original work was not until W. S. Gilbert's *Pygmalion and Galatea* (1871). Furthermore, Beddoes imitates Ovid in his description of the blush which occurs as the statue comes to life and he describes the sculpting of the statue, whereas Rousseau does not.

As one would expect, there are many differences between Beddoes's early nineteenth-century descriptive narrative and Rousseau's eighteenth-century conversational style which, to use Leigh Hunt's words, is 'declamatory and full

---

[26] Anonymous, *Pygmalion, A Poem* (London, 1779), p. 2.

of ejaculation' – a style which, Hunt notes, does not appeal to English tastes (Hunt, p. 241). The most obvious difference is in the choice of genre. Beddoes renders the conversational and dramatic qualities of the play into narrative poetry, and manifestly distances himself from Rousseau's deliberate intellectualizing of the theme. Beddoes, according to his letter felt that his own poem was inferior and diffuse, and he was ultimately unhappy with it. In a letter (4 December 1825) he asks Kelsall to consider printing 'Death's Jest-Book' with 'Pygmalion' (p. 610), but by 15 May 1837 he is less keen: 'Pygmalion is, if I recollect aright, considerable trash' (p. 662).

The change from a dialectical style to a diffuse Keatsian narrative reflects an important shift in emphasis within the story on the part of Beddoes. The sensuousness and precision of the descriptions contribute to a stifling atmosphere which is matched, in some respects, by the oppressive interiority of Rousseau's play. Beddoes shares Rousseau's conviction that the story could be used to explore the fusion of subject and object, and both authors see the transformation of the statue as an epiphanic moment when boundaries and distinctions are overcome. Beddoes nevertheless holds Rousseauean autobiographical art in less esteem, and therefore cannot follow the extremes of his predecessor. Beddoes's attitude to autobiography explains the major alterations to the story; his interest in death, a theme which enters much of his work, prompts him to explore the fusion of subject and object in the moment of expiration – the indeterminacy between contrary states is such that readers have found it hard to decide whether the characters live or die at the end of the poem. Beddoes accuses himself of having been distracted from his purpose in writing 'Pygmalion', and his digressions are mainly descriptive asides. This spirit of digression, however, the poem shares with Rousseau's vacillating monologue, which follows the moods and thoughts of his artistic hero.

Chapter 3

Adam's Dream:
Post-Romantic Renarrations

> The Imagination may be compared to Adam's dream – he woke and found it truth.[1]

According to E. B. Burgum, anyone 'who seeks to define Romanticism is entering a hazardous occupation which has claimed many victims'.[2] The definer of 'post-Romanticism' has an equally difficult task. 'Post-Romanticism' commonly describes two types of reaction to Romanticism: that of those who continued to expound the theories of Romanticism, but were not part of the first or second phases of Romanticism, and those who developed Romanticism. The first type is best seen in the juvenilia of poets who later developed Romanticism, for example, the early poems of Tennyson and Robert Browning. Post-Romanticism, as a development of Romanticism, dispenses with the political aspects of the movement and is more concerned with the mind and the emotions. This interest, derived largely from Wordsworth and Rousseau, evolves into a preference for exploring unconventional or unusual mental states: 'The great subject' writes Donald Thomas, was to be the grotesque, as a rival to the sublime'.[3]

> Of the facets of Victorian poetry that owed most to Romantic innovation, the confessional or autobiographical mode of writing appeared almost universally. [...] Poetry as mood or state of mind was important. [...] By no means all mental states portrayed in post-Romantic poetry were of madness, uncertainty, delusion, or alienation. Yet these seem to be characteristic of the new style as its critics pointed out in the case of Tennyson's *Maud*, Browning's dramatic monologues, or even the interior debates of Clough's poetry (Thomas, p. 8).

Walter Pater's description of Leonardo da Vinci's *Gioconda* is an example of the post-Romantic response to art. Thomas argues that Pater is interested in 'the bizarre, rather the than the beautiful, the grotesque rather than the sublime' (p. 6). Pater's emphasis on dream as an inspiration for the artist cannot be ignored however:

---

[1] John Keats, *Letters*, ed. by Robert Gittings (Oxford, 1987), p. 37.
[2] Cited in Lilian Furst, *Romanticism: The Critical Idiom* (London, 1969), p. 1.
[3] Donald Thomas, *The Post-Romantics* (London, 1990), p. 5.

> From childhood we see this image defining itself on the fabric of his [Leonardo's] dreams; and but for express historical testimony, we might fancy that this was but his ideal lady embodied and beheld at last. What was the relationship of a living Florentine to this creature of his thought? By what strange affinities had the dream and the person grown thus apart, and yet so closely together? Present from the first incorporeally in Leonardo's brain, dimly traced in the designs of Verrocchio, she is found present at last in *Il Gioconda*'s house. [...] Again, was it in four years and by renewed labour never really completed, or in four months and as by a stroke of magic, that the image was projected? It is a beauty wrought out from within upon the flesh, the deposit, little cell by cell, *of strange thoughts and fantastic reveries and exquisite passions*. Set it for a moment beside one of those white Greek goddesses or beautiful women of antiquity, and how would they be troubled by this beauty, into which the soul with all its maladies had passed![4]

Pater's *Gioconda* expresses the bizarre, but it also demonstrates a fascination for the dream-image which the painting embodies. Furthermore, Pater recognizes the importance of dream for the post-Romantic poet Dante Gabriel Rossetti: 'Dreamland [...] is to him [...] no mere fancy or figure of speech', dreamland is 'a real country, a veritable expansion of, or addition to, our waking life' (Pater, pp. 92–94). Dreams are an inspiration to post-Romantics, just as they are to Romantic art. They embody idealism and lend a freedom and significance to imaginative thought.

The Post-Romantic Dream

The influence of Romantic ideas is felt generally throughout the nineteenth century, and renarrations of the Pygmalion story by writers interested in Romantic models of creativity form a group. Post-Romantic writers characterize Pygmalion as a man inspired by a specific creative vision. The statue is an embodiment of the woman he sees in his dream. This situation follows Keats's description of the imagination: 'The imagination may be compared to Adam's dream – he awoke and found it truth. [...] Imagination and its empyreal reflection is the same as human Life and its spiritual repetition' (Gittings, p. 37). Adam is given a vision of the birth of Eve and awakes to find her standing before him. It is the ease of the translation from idea to art which makes this a representative model for Romantic creativity. The birth of the statue is a kind of phantom pregnancy, during which the male creative act becomes internalized in the mind and produces a life-like

---

[4] Walter Pater, *Selected Works*, ed. by Richard Aldington (London, 1948), p. 266.

mental image of a woman. The idea of Adam's dream can be traced back to the Chester mystery plays:

> The second play of the Chester cycle (mystery plays) contains the relatively novel idea of Adam's dream, which grew out of the simple statement that God put Adam to sleep when he took the rib to make woman. In this dream, which Adam later relates to Cain and Abel, the great Flood, the Incarnation, and the Last Judgement are prophesied.[5]

Keats, however, takes the idea from Milton's *Paradise Lost*. The dream-vision, as Nietzsche points out, also has classical origins:

> As Lucretius envisages it, it was in a dream that the magnificent figures of the gods first appeared before the souls of men; in dream the great image-maker saw the delightfully proportioned bodies of superhuman beings; and the Hellenic poet, if asked about the secrets of poetic procreation, would likewise have reminded us of dream.[6]

The sculpture of dream-inspired visions forms part of Nietzsche's late nineteenth-century account of Apolline Greek art. For Nietzsche, dreams denote the fundamental creativity in human nature, linking mankind with the divine. 'The semblance of dream', he argues, 'is the precondition of all the arts of image-making'(p. 15). Nietzsche's Apolline dream sculptor is of primary importance to his conception of Romantic art, and he speculates that the dreams of the Greeks may have 'had that logical causality of line and outline, colour and grouping, and a sequence of scenes resembling their best bas-reliefs' (p. 19).

What role does the artist's self have in this kind of creativity? Nietzsche denies the lyrical its status as art; the artist's over-association with his subject leads to the breakdown of order. This stance is a response to a decadent culture. Apolline art eschews subjective lyricism, which is representative of chaotic Dionysianism, in favour of cool objectivity and 'disinterested contemplation' (p. 29). Nietzsche presents conflicting views of the dream-sculptor's artistic act. The sculptor preserves his individuality and at the same time loses himself in 'the pure contemplation of images' (p. 30). In this way, Nietzsche perpetuates the difficulties of Romantic aesthetics. This ambivalence towards self-abandonment and self-preservation is seen in the Romantic responses to the Pygmalion story. The consequence of centring the Pygmalion story on a dream raises again the issue

---

[5] David Lyle Jeffrey, *A Dictionary of Biblical Tradition in English Literature* (Michigan, 1992), p. 19.
[6] Friedrich Nietzsche, *The Birth of Tragedy*, ed. by Raymond Guess and Ronald Speirs, trans. by Ronald Speirs (Cambridge, 1999), p. 15.

of the nature of the artist's role: he is either inspired by a dream or creates in a dream. The latter, Adam's dream, illustrates the directness of the link between the inspired state and the creative action. The link is so direct that the poet is rendered passive. The former illustrates a process of extreme visionary inspiration which involves the writer more closely: he is inspired and then he writes. These are different models, but they share the important link between creativity and dream. Post-Romantics often reveal their acceptance of Apolline passivity through their deployment of Romantic passive-creative models (such as 'Adam's dream'), yet their responses to the dream are not always passive, dream is sometimes treated as an inspirational rather than a creative act.

Keats's Adam's dream recalls Milton's *Paradise Lost*; there is no mention of it in Genesis. Adam describes a vision given to him by God in which he sees one of his ribs taken from his body in order to produce Eve. When he awakes, he finds that his dream has come true and Eve has indeed been created. Adam says that he

> sought repair
> Of sleep, which instantly fell on me, called
> By nature as in aid, and closed mine eyes.
> Mine eyes he closed, but open left the cell
> Of fancy my internal sight, by which
> Abstract as in a trance methought I saw,
> Though sleeping, where I lay, and saw the shape
> Still glorious before whom awake I stood,
> Who stooping opened my left side, and took
> From thence a rib, with cordial spirits warm,
> And life-blood streaming fresh; wide was the wound,
> But suddenly with flesh filled up and healed:
> The rib he formed and fashioned with his hands;
> Under his forming hands a creature grew,
> Manlike, but different sex, so lovely faire. [...]
> She disappeared, and left me dark, I waked
> To find her.[7]

The 'Adam's dream' model is a form of 'unconscious invention': the Romantic aesthetic which freed the poet from the action of creating poetry by inspiring automatic writing.[8] In *Paradise Lost* Adam is unconscious, and yet passively involved in the act of creation. For Keats, and others, the poet experiences this as an increased facility of creativity, a Shelleyan 'unpremeditated art'. Blake, writing of his poem *Milton*, acknowledges this process:

---

[7] John Milton, *The Poems*, ed. by John Carey and Alastair Fowler (London, 1968), pp. 838–840.

[8] A term used by M. H. Abrams in *The Mirror and the Lamp*, pp. 214–217.

> I have written this Poem from immediate Dictation, twelve or sometimes twenty or thirty lines at a time, without Premeditation & even against my Will; the Time it has taken in writing was thus render'd Non Existent, & an immense Poem Exists which seems to be the Labour of a long Life, all produc'd without Labour or Study.[9]

The visionary experience often involved closing off some or all of the senses in order to affect an escape into the visionary realm. The description of the vision is accompanied by inner sense figures – a vocabulary used to emphasize the ability of the mind to sense in the way that the ordinary senses do. Coleridge and Wordsworth make much use of this type of imaginative experience and its accompanying language of inner sense, and Mary Shelley's *Frankenstein* demonstrates this Romantic interest in dream and its accompanying discourse.[10]

Frankenstein is particularly relevant here because of its thematic links with the Pygmalion story. In her introduction of 1831, Shelley describes the way in which she conceived the story before going to sleep. Her creative imagination works 'unbidden', like Adam's dream, and a visionary world is described, the inner sense taking on the attributes of the outer:

> When I placed my head on my pillow, I did not sleep, nor could I be said to think. My imagination, unbidden, possessed and guided me, gifting the successive images that arose in my mind with a vividness far beyond the usual bounds of a reverie. *I saw with shut eyes, but acute mental vision,* – I saw the pale student of unhallowed arts kneeling beside the thing he had put together. I saw the hideous phantasm of a man stretched out, and then, on the working of some powerful engine, show signs of life, and stir with an uneasy, half vital motion. Frightful must it be; for supremely frightful would be the effect of any human endeavour to mock the stupendous mechanism of the Creator of the world.[11]

The narrative, we are told, appeared in the author's mind while she was experiencing a waking-dream (p. 10). Whether this was the case in the actual conception of the story is not an issue here; we are merely concerned with the interest which the Romantics showed in unconscious invention and dream-vision. Mary Shelley's ideas on this 'waking dream' are very much a mixture of the two figures. The use of 'unconscious invention' suggests that this passage may have some links with the Adam's dream model found in Milton and Keats. Shelley is both inspired by a dream and relieved of the burden of creativity. The

---

[9] William Blake, *The Complete Works*, ed. by Geoffrey Keynes (London, 1966), p. 823.
[10] See Judson S. Lyon, 'Romantic Psychology and the Inner Senses: Coleridge' *Publications of the Modern Language Association,* 81 (1966), 246–260.
[11] Mary Shelley, *Frankenstein*, ed. by M. K. Joseph (Oxford, 1971), p. 9, my italics.

Frankenstein story is extracted from the author like an Eve from her originator. She calls it her 'offspring' and her 'hideous progeny' (p. 10). These ideas have been inspired by Milton's work, which Shelley cites throughout her novel. Mary had read *Paradise Lost* in 1815, and Percy Shelley read it aloud to her in November 1816.

Dreams pervade Romantic prose and poetry, and several theories emerge from their writings. Hazlitt, for example, whose views on dream are mainly expressed in his critiques of phrenologists Johann Gaspar Spurzheim and Franz Joseph Gall, rejects the idea that we can rationalize or sense in dreams (Hazlitt, XII, 138). He calls Spurzheim 'the Baron Munchausen of marvellous metaphysics' and a 'German quack doctor' for suggesting that people were capable of having clearer thought whilst dreaming than when awake. In short, Spurzheim suggests that dreams are a creative state and Hazlitt opposes this by arguing that ideas in dreams are merely random. Hazlitt's concept of dream must entail some kind of mental coherence, however, if we are to accept his apparently contradictory statements about the necessity of dreaming the truth: 'we are not hypocrites in our sleep' (XII, 23). Furthermore, he considers love 'an involuntary passion' and therefore one which, when true, should be dreamt about. Dreams are, he writes, a test of how much you love: 'I think myself into love and dream myself out of it' (XII, 23). His inconsistency is testimony to his insistence upon the critical freedom to hold conflicting views. Coleridge, in contrast to Hazlitt, argues that we are not able to reflect on the truth or falsehood of an idea when dreaming, because we cannot exercise the will. Coleridge's experience of dreams owes something to his own opium reveries. The most famous Romantic dream is, of course, that which produced 'Kubla Khan' (1816). The preface to the poem describes a dream-vision (a vision which the post-Romantic dreamer-poet aspired to have) as an instance when the imagination was at its most productive and free:

> The Author continued for about three hours in a *profound sleep, at least of the external senses*, during which time he has the most vivid confidence, that he could not have composed less than from two to three hundred lines; if that indeed can be called composition in which all the images rose up before him as *things*, with a parallel production of the correspondent expressions, *without any sensation of consciousness of effort*. On awaking he appeared to himself to have a distinct recollection of the whole, and taking his pen, ink, and paper, instantly and eagerly wrote down the lines that are here preserved [my italics].[12]

The preface refers to states which are akin to 'unconscious invention' and the

---

[12] Samuel Taylor Coleridge, *The Complete Poetical Works*, ed. by Ernest Hartley Coleridge (Oxford, 1912), p. 296.

dream-vision and a closing down of the external senses to concentrate on the inner. Coleridge's intoxication makes this a Dionysian dream, and this is evidenced in the violent and prophetic subject matter, where destructive forces are sublimated onto Kubla and the landscape.

Dreams imply a transcendence of the ordinary, an invitation to elevate inner life. The transcendent discourse that arises, emphasizing new internal senses also has a mystical dimension. The soul is given a capacity to feel deeply. The sentient soul is clearly not the same kind of soul that Christianity understands, it is an organ which can experience pain and hunger and, as an extension of the mind, can think and feel. Arthur O'Shaugnessey's poem 'Death' (1870) provides an example of late Romantic usage:

> I close my eyes and see the inward things:
> The strange averted spectre of my soul
> Is sitting undivulged, angelic, whole,
> Beside the dim internal flood that brings
> Mysterious thoughts of dreams or murmurings
> From the immense unknown.[13]

The sentient soul is a visionary organ which explores internal and unseen dream-worlds. It is described using language which mixes the religious and material. The soul is a second (and often inner) self with heightened awareness; it is a transcendent consciousness seemingly responding to physical sensations and forms part of the post-Romantic response to the elevation of the inner life.

Arthur Hallam (1811–1833)

In the year before his death, Arthur Henry Hallam, the great friend of Alfred Lord Tennyson and the inspiration for *In Memoriam*, wrote the dramatic monologue 'Lines Spoken in the Character of Pygmalion' as charade for an evening's entertainment. Hallam is the first to bring an inspirational dream into the Pygmalion story. In a letter to Emily Tennyson (20 November 1832), he describes a performance of this monologue in which he had acted the part of Pygmalion and his friend Charlotte Sotheby had played the statue. Hallam expresses a wish to act out the scene with Emily Tennyson, whom he admired, implying that he would like to place her on a pedestal – a wish reminiscent of Hazlitt's desire to be a Pygmalion to the statuesque Sarah in *Liber Amoris*.

---

[13] Cited in Lothar Hönnighausen in *The Symbolist Tradition in English Literature: A Study of Pre-Raphaelitism and 'Fin de Siècle'*, European Studies in English Literature (Cambridge, 1988), p. 208.

> My most decided success was in the character of Pygmalion. Charlotte Sotheby was my Statue: she looked it to perfection: when the curtain drew up, & shewed her standing motionless on the pedestal, draped in white, & a white veil concealing all her head except the beautiful features not unlike in truth the work of Grecian art – when I, dressed as a sculptor, chisel in hand, poured forth a speech (in verse) of my own composition in praise of my supposed statue, ending with a prayer to Venus that she might live, & at the word slowly and gracefully the form began to move, to bend forward, to descend, to meet my embrace – the room rang with acclamations, & I – I thought of several things, but of none so much, as of the pleasure I should have in describing this to you, & perhaps on some occasion acting it with you.[14]

Hallam's poem opens at the moment when Pygmalion has finished sculpting. It describes the statue as having been inspired by a dream: 'Lo! now it stands before me, / Even as long years ago I dreamed of it' (Hallam, p. 111). The work on the statue, however, has not been easy in this case: he has 'toiled / days, nights, months, years' to finish it (p. 111). It is, nonetheless, the 'creature' of Pygmalion's soul' (p. 111). Pygmalion admires the statue and then prays that she be brought to life. Venus, who performs the miracle, is described as the 'Queen of my dreams', and when Pygmalion sees the statue-woman coming to life he thinks that he is again dreaming (p. 112).

The poem inspired awe and delight in its first parlour audience, and it is clearly intended as a parlour spectacle or charade. A similar scene occurs in George Eliot's *Daniel Deronda* (1876), in which the heroine, Gwendolen Harleth, acts out the statue scene from *The Winter's Tale* as a parlour game designed to impress her admirers.[15] A slightly different type of charade game is performed in *Jane Eyre* (1847).[16] The early nineteenth century charade was 'A kind of Riddle, in which each syllable of the word to be guessed, and sometimes the word itself also, is enigmatically described, or (more recently) dramatically represented (acted charade)' (*OED*). The form of Hallam's charade is distinctly unusual in that its ludic element is not alluded to, and is indeed prevented by the poem's title.

The history of the charade dates back to the eighteenth century. Its origins are illuminated by a French writer, Rondeaulet, who, in 1776, published a treatise on the subject. It was translated into English in 1777 by a writer who called himself Tobias Rigmerole. He writes:

> The Introduction of the CHARADE, that happy Effort of human Genius,

---

[14] Arthur Henry Hallam, *Writings*, ed. by T. H. Vail Motter (New York, London, 1943), p. 111.
[15] George Eliot, *Daniel Deronda*, ed. by Barbara Hardy (London, 1986), pp. 89–91.
[16] Charlotte Brontë, *Jane Eyre*, ed. by Margaret Smith (Oxford, 1986), pp. 184–186.

has distinguished the Year MDCCLXXVI in a Manner that must be the Envy of all preceding ones. The pleasing Talk I have imposed upon myself is that of explaining and illustrating this elegant Novelty; and I hope the Method in which I shall treat my Subject, will render it clear to all Capacities, and will recommend it to the Wonder and Imitation of future Ages. [...] And notwithstanding the Person who first gave it Birth, may at present chuse to keep his Name an inscrutable Secret, yet there is no doubt but he will soon own it with a rapture.[17]

Early charades were generally written in verse, the shortest being two lines, and the longest approximately twelve lines, and the object of the game was to guess the word which was being described. The description of the answer-word, and the nature of the word itself, had to adhere to certain rules. The solution was generally a word of two syllables or more; each syllable or part of the word formed a complete word in itself. For example, 'foot' and 'step' made 'footstep'. The description was often divided into sections, each section containing a clue to a syllable of the word. The phrasing of the clue is pretty standard and usually takes the format of the speaker asking his audience which word is being represented. This happens in the following fashion: 'My first is [...] / My second is [...] / My third is [...]'. Sometimes, a clue to the whole word was given at the end: 'My whole is [...]'.[18] The solutions to the charades could be any polysyllabic word which had parts that could make smaller words.

Hallam's poem does not take the usual format for an early nineteenth-century charade as exemplified by the puzzle-books of the era. Rather, his poem takes the form of an 'enigma'. The enigma is a charade-like puzzle which involves giving a clue to a whole word without breaking it into smaller words; it takes the form of a poem spoken by the person or thing which is solution word. The *OED* cites examples of this word being used as early as 1539. As one would expect in the case of a puzzle game, the solution word, 'Pygmalion', is not mentioned in the poem, but the discourse of the poem does not imply a guessing game. Rather, the puzzle-poem is elevated into a monologue in which Pygmalion's role as the speaker of an enigma (and therefore as self-definer) is closely allied to his traditional concern with describing the beauty of his statue. In the enigma, the statue is important insofar as she helps to define Pygmalion, yet there is a tension between the enigmatic and the poetic genres. Pygmalion's speech falls into two kinds: it is a prayer directed towards Venus as the goddess who will transform the statue, and it is also the soliloquy of a Rousseauean Pygmalion musing on his talents. The speech does not seem to be directed at an audience which must guess the name of the speaker. The audience, the usual addressee in the enigma, is

---

[17] Tobias Rigmerole (pseud.), *A Treatise on the Charade* (London, 1777), p. 2.
[18] See James Glassford, *Sphinx Incruenta* (Edinburgh, 1835).

passed over in order to suggest something more akin to a mini-narrative or tableau than a definition. The speaker in an enigma is not someone who is in the process of making their story, but someone who can recognize what they are famous for and describe themselves in a detached and oblique manner. Pygmalion talks of his dream-inspired statue as if he does not know that she will become human and the circumlocutory discourse which should delay the solution has been completely abandoned. Hallam's Pygmalion wants us to know who he is immediately. Furthermore, the poem's subject matter is unusual because it is classical. Classical names were extremely uncommon as solution words. Lewis Carroll is the exception. He wrote a charade (on 23 January 1879) on the subject of Galatea after he had seen Marion Terry in a performance of W. S. Gilbert's *Pygmalion and Galatea*. The solution word to this charade was 'Galatea', and Carroll split the word into 'Gala' and 'tea' in order to make his charade.[19]

Dream is important to this poem as a device for closure. Pygmalion says of the statue's metamorphosis in the final lines:

> I dare not look again – my brain swims round –
> I dream – I dream – even now methought she moved.
> If 'tis a dream, how will I curse the dawn
> That wakes me from it! There – that bend again –
> It is no dream – Oh speak to me and bless me (Hallam, p. 112).

Dream art is associated with fantasy and wish fulfilment; it is such an ideal form of art that during the metamorphosis reality is mistaken for dream. When Pygmalion concludes that the statue is alive, the poem, the performance, and the fictional reality end. Hallam's Pygmalion preserves his individuality through his gesture towards self-definition and at the same time loses himself in 'the pure contemplation of images' through performing the act that defines him. Hallam's poem is conceivably a charade in the sense that it was intended to be a love-game acted out by himself and Emily Tennyson, but was in fact acted out with another friend.

'The New Frankenstein'

'The New Frankenstein' (1837), an anonymous short story, picks up on the hints of the Pygmalion story which are found in Mary Shelley's original novel, and explores Romantic aesthetics further.[20] The exact nature of the influence of the Pygmalion story on Mary Shelley's *Frankenstein* has been disputed. Several

---

[19] Lewis Carroll, *The Magic of Lewis Carroll*, ed. by John Fisher (Harmondsworth, 1975), pp. 128–130.

[20] Anonymous, 'The New Frankenstein', *Frasers Magazine*, 17 (1838), 21–30.

critics have noted that Mary Shelley knew of the Pygmalion story before she wrote *Frankenstein*, and although she does not mention the story, the overtones of the Pygmalion situation are evident. Burton R. Pollin's exploration into the sources for the influence of the Pygmalion story on Mary Shelley's *Frankenstein* suggests that a French play by Madame de Genlis (1746–1830) and Ovid's *Metamorphoses* are Shelley's primary sources for the Pygmalion theme. Mary Shelley's journal suggests that she had read Madame de Genlis's play. The play, *Pygmalion et Galatée; ou La Statue animée depuis vingt-quatre heures*, contains a prefatory note which indicates that it was to be played after the 'scène lyrique' on the same theme by Rousseau. Madame de Genlis

> Filled her dozen and a half short scenes with criticism of the composition of society, delivered through a conversation between the pure, ingenuous Galatea and an old servant. They discuss the cruelties and injustices of the world. Galatea is shocked at slavery, tyranny, the extremes of poverty and wealth, hunting, and deception. [...] The play *Pygmalion* helped to suggest the device of awakening and the actual injustices of society with which both naive intellects become acquainted (Pollin, p. 101).

Madame de Genlis, like Rousseau, takes the name Galatea for her statue. (The writer of 'The New Frankenstein' does not.)

Several critics have explored the Pygmalion myth's connection with Shelley's novel. David Ketterer suggests that the female monster, which Victor Frankenstein aborts, may have been inspired by the Pygmalion story on the grounds that 'there is no evidence of Prometheus playing a part in the animation of a female figure'.[21] Christopher Small suggests that the Pygmalion story does not influence the novel's central action, proposing that

> there is a difference to be seen here between the act of Prometheus and that of Pygmalion, whose overwhelming desire for the woman he has made as a work of art brings her to life (or causes Aphrodite to do so in pity for him).[22]

According to Small and Ketterer, the Pygmalion story could not have influenced the creation of the male monster. We can, however, only speculate on the nature and extent of the influence of the Pygmalion story on *Frankenstein*.

'The New Frankenstein', dismissed by Chris Baldick as 'rather inept', is

---

[21] David Ketterer, *Frankenstein's Creation: The Book, The Monster, and Human Reality*, English Literary Studies, 16 (Victoria, Canada, 1979), p. 20.

[22] Christopher Small, *Ariel Like a Harpy: Shelley, Mary and Frankenstein* (London, 1972) p. 50.

significant here because of its handling of the Pygmalion story, its use of dream, and its acknowledgement of the popularity of Spurzheim and Gall.[23] It recounts a tale told to the narrator by an unnamed German Frankenstein-like scientist who claims he has attempted to give a mind to a galvanized monster. A German translation of *Frankenstein*, read as non-fiction, inspires the scientist: 'The part [...] that most interested me was the creation; the scene that rivetted me most, the creation scene' (p. 23). When reading the novel one night, the scientist's tutor, Starnstein (a name echoing that of Frankenstein), mysteriously appears and deposits the galvanized monster in the scientist's room. It is quickly discovered that the monster has no mind and so the scientist resolves to give him one: '"I shall create a mind for you, and such a mind as man, till now, never possessed!"' (p. 23). His research into phrenology, craniology and animal magnetism enables him to discover a transportable brain-gas, which he calls 'cerebral afflatus' (p. 24). The story takes a humorous turn when the scientist travels around Europe extracting brain gas from such Romantic dignitaries as Goethe (whose gaseous imagination fills the largest bottle), Percy Shelley and Coleridge.

> The great poet's [Shelley's] animal magnetic sensibility is well known, and it had been, if possible, increased by a late visit to the Prato Fiorito, where he had fainted with the excess of sweetness of the jonquils that carpet that enamelled mead. He was, at that moment, full of the conception of his *Ode to Intellectual Beauty* (p. 25).

The scientist then applies his bottled Romantic imagination to the monster's brain. Though the idea of Romantic imagination being transported in gaseous form is comical, it acts as a metaphor for Romantic influence on art. While the scientist waits to see the outcome he brings to mind a painting of Pygmalion and his statue seen in a Paris exhibition:

> The artist had chosen the moment when the intensity of the sculptor's passion, which is impassable to Love, warmed the marble statue into life. As the Italians said to one of their school, the French painter had made use of *carne macerato* instead of colour. We might almost see the roseate light of life and youth, as through an alabaster vase, gradually illuminating the perfect form of the nympholept's creation; and the creator himself contemplating, with delight and wonder, the object of his adoration (p. 26).

The transformation of Pygmalion's statue is an echo of the metamorphosis of the monster into a sentient Romantic genius. The German calls this process

---

[23] Chris Baldick, *In Frankenstein's Shadow. Myth, Monstrosity, and Nineteenth-Century Writing* (Oxford, 1987), p. 141.

'Phrengenesis' or mind-creation.

The scientist expects the monster's first impulse to be worship, but 'far from this, what was my vexation and disappointment to mark the look of unutterable scorn and hate with which he regarded me' (p. 27). At length, the monster acquires the ability to speak, but he cannot be understood. The Romantic gas causes his 'merciless Imagination' to fly 'with the speed of thought from subject to subject, from topic to topic' in a perpetual 'flux and reflux' (p. 27). The episode is an exposition on the post-Romantic text:

> It was a labyrinth inextricable – an ill-linked chain of sentences the most involved, parentheses within parentheses – a complication of images and figures the most *outré*. In short, imagine to yourself the mysticism of Kant, the transcendental philosophy of Coleridge, the metaphysics of Shelley and Goethe, the poetry of Lycophron, mingled and massed together in one jargon, compounded of Greek, Latin, Italian, French, Spanish, German and English, not to mention tongues known and unknown (p. 27).

The scientist repents his act, his conduct weighing upon him 'like remorse upon the guilty' (p. 27) and he concludes that 'the Theosophs were right in separating the mind from the soul, in considering them diametrically opposite relations – as different principles, as the physic and the phrenic. And I became satisfied that my paradox had no soul' (p. 27). At the end of the tale, the scientist travels to Egypt in search of a soul from Osiris. He finds the sarcophagus of the Theban 'Adamite king'. The mummy is wrapped up except for the face, and has open eyes. His intrusion causes the whole necropolis to shake, and a multitude of chanting fiends appears. All the tombs open, the dead rise, a red spiral flame materializes and turns into Starnstein: 'It was, yet it was not, my old tutor' (p. 30). After reaching this pitch of suspense, the story concludes abruptly with the words 'Then I awoke, and found it was a dream' (p. 30).

This tribute poem gestures towards the frame narrative structure of *Frankenstein*. Whilst the dream-frame is a plot-device, the text touches on the relevance of dream for the Romantic. The scientist talks of dividing

> the life of man into two sets of sensation, but not of equal value in my eyes – a waking sleep, and a sleeping sleep; for it seemed to me that no one could dispute the superior advantages of the latter in perceiving the only world that is worth perceiving – the imaginary one (p. 21).

As in the 1831 introduction to *Frankenstein*, dreams are valued for their creativity. The whole story, it seems, is attributed to 'waking sleep'. The narrative exhibits a cluster of ideas on the nature of Romantic influence (the monster standing for a work of art); it explores the nature of the post-Romantic when the Romantic influence is poured into the brain of the monster. The monster then *becomes* the post-Romantic text: his brain is a confusion of influences, his thoughts, a 'labyrinth inextricable' (p. 27). The German scientist is both mind-creating and mentally creative during the dream-state. He spins an autobiographical tale only to alter its significance with the final deflating sentence: it is no longer about the scientist, but is his dream.

James Payn (1830–1898)

One of the most striking interpretations of the Pygmalion story as a variation on the Romantic theme of 'Adam's dream' appears in a collection of poems by James Payn in 1853. Payn is largely remembered as a novelist, he wrote around a hundred of them, the most popular being the *Lost Sir Massingberd* (1864). Though little remembered today, Payn was a well known figure in the literary world of the nineteenth century. From 1859 to 1874, he edited *Chambers Edinburgh Journal* and was a regular contributor to *Household Words* (the periodical started by Charles Dickens in 1850). From 1882 to 1896, he edited *The Cornhill Magazine* which serialized novels. Payn's 'Pygmalion' is an early poem, published when he was twenty-three years old, and had just left Cambridge.[24] Payn, like Robert Buchanan after him, in later life became scornful of the use of classical subjects for poetry, arguing that the position of classical authors in British education was unjustified:

> For what is very curious, the advocates of the classical authors – those I mean whom antiquity has more or less hallowed – instead of pitying those unhappy wights who confess their want of appreciation of them, fly at them with bludgeons, and dance upon their prostrate bodies with clogs.[25]

Perhaps the 'unhappy wight' was Payn himself, who is recorded as having been a poor classical scholar at Eton.

Payn's 'Pygmalion' is a highly descriptive narrative poem containing several long monologues spoken by the sculptor himself. It opens with an address to the warm sea which woos the 'virgin Isle' of Cyprus, and, setting the scene for the lonely Pygmalion, the narrator describes the sea's distress at never being able to rest near its beloved. The young Pygmalion appears in the midst of a festival in honour of Aphrodite, and proclaims that he is sated with life. He asks that women seek other lovers, but is no hater of women. The women of the island have, in the past, distracted him and in giving them attention he has neglected his career as a

---

[24] James Payn, *Poems* (Cambridge, 1853), pp. 4–14.
[25] James Payn, *Some Private Views* (London, 1881), p. 43.

sculptor. Once hailed as the 'New Prometheus' (the sub-title of Mary Shelley's *Frankenstein*), he is now praised with less enthusiasm. In order to remedy this, Pygmalion builds himself a home in 'the hollow of a vine clad hill' (p. 9). Payn's Pygmalion rejects the Dionysian 'clasps and kisses' to retreat into an internal creative world. Falling asleep during his orisons to Aphrodite, a beautiful woman appears:

> Too bright for life, too warm for sculptor's hands,
> A Goddess or a Dream, before him stands
> Perfected Maidenhood; from foot to face
> As fair and flawless as the lily's grace;
> The lips are parted, but she will not speak,
> Nor draw the breath; the roses on her cheek
> Nor fade nor glow; the white arm, pointing still
> Whereto the servants of his disused skill
> Lie taskless, will not fail from its command
> Till all that fair similitude be plann'd (pp. 10–11).

Once Pygmalion has completed the dream-inspired statue, he entreats Aphrodite to bring it to life. The poem ends with the narrator joining in with Pygmalion's request.

The narrator compares Pygmalion's dream, in analogical fashion, with the vivid dreams of others. Pygmalion's joy is like that of a young man who dreams that a 'thronèd maid' whom he cannot have 'wakes to find / That fair, won wife within those arms entwined' (p. 10); Pygmalion is like the homesick school-child who has 'visions' of his home and wakes to see his mother tending him; he is compared to the 'pent-up dweller in the breezeless town', who, like Coleridge's 'gentle-hearted Charles' (who in 'This Lime-Tree Bower My Prison', 'pined / And hunger'd after Nature, many a year, / In the great City pent'), dreams of meadows and mountains every night.[26] The city dweller wakes to find himself listening to a brook, birds, waving trees, and distant herds of wild animals. The happiness of these people is as great as Pygmalion's. The comparisons with the love-lorn man, the school-child, and the town-dweller are all drawn while Pygmalion is sleeping. Pygmalion's joy at completing the statue ('carved by Venus' grace') is compared to the reaction of the poet who has experienced 'unconscious invention':

> As Poet with his poem, to last line
> Complete in harmonies and thoughts divine,
> Self-certain of th'inexplicable power
> That shook from out his soul the silver shower,

---

[26] Samuel Taylor Coleridge, *Poems and Prose* ed. by Kathleen Raine (Harmondsworth, 1986), p. 35.

> So joys Pygmalion at the marble base
> Of his rare Statue, carved by Venus' grace (p. 11).

Pygmalion has, like Adam, performed 'unconscious invention' with similar supernatural help. As in Hallam's poem, Payn links the soul to his creativity: Payn's Pygmalion has a 'thirsty sculptor soul' which looks for an ideal (p. 9). The soul is also something which feels: Pygmalion's 'soul grows weary' and he experiences 'soul-sorrow' (p. 7 and p. 13). He also sees his previous sculptures as 'the born children of my soul' (p. 7). Pygmalion's suppliant request with 'claspèd hands' echoes the clasping of the Dionysian women he has rejected (p. 13).

William Cox Bennett (1820–1895)

Continuing the association of the Pygmalion story with dream, William Cox Bennett's 'Pygmalion' (1857) concentrates on exploring the vision Pygmalion has of the statue before he sculpts it. Bennett was the son of a Greenwich watchmaker who carried on his father's business and is more famous as a song-writer than as a poet.[27] Bennett's 'Pygmalion' displays his endorsement of Romanticism: the rainbow, æolian harp, and even a brief excursion into Coleridge's philosophy of the 'One Life' leave us in no doubt that he is a post-Romantic. Bennett is even interested in the Prometheus story, a theme popularized by the Romantic poets.

The introductory poem to Bennett's *Poems* (1862) acknowledges his appreciation of the visionary nature of poetic inspiration: 'Forms beyond my vision fleeting, / Shadowy phantoms, O how fair!'.[28] Pygmalion's monologue describes his 'white vision' of a woman which floods its 'glory' through his soul. The soul takes an active part in the visionary experience. Pygmalion, while he strives to make the vision in his mind clearer, describes 'how even to agony my soul was wrought, / To tears and frenzy' (*Poems*, p. 105); his soul hungers for the image and it listens to the statue: 'Silent, and yet how tuneful with sweet speech, / Utterance divine, that from the listening soul / Drew echoes, though the dull ear heard it not!' (*Poems*, p. 106). He craves the image, but it is too ethereal to be defined and is represented in mystical terms. The vision shapes his thoughts, but is not easily understood or retained in the mind. Pygmalion struggles with its intangibility trying to make it more focused. The movement of the image from impermanence to permanence happens in an instant: 'in one golden moment' a 'veil' is drawn from the dream-image enabling Pygmalion to see her more clearly in his mind's eye (p. 105). Pygmalion worships her and sets about replicating her

---

[27] *The Chambers' Cyclopædia of English Literature*, ed. by David Patrick, 3 vols (London, 1938), III, 548.

[28] William Cox Bennett, *Poems* (London, 1862), p. 1. The poem first appears in *Queen Eleanor's Vengeance and Other Poems* (London, 1857).

image in marble, a task that takes some effort: 'I took / Marble, and wrought, and wrought' (p. 106).The resulting statue is so perfect that Pygmalion imagines that it speaks. Pygmalion, inspired by a mystic spirit, offers prayers to the gods asking that the statue be brought to life in return for his devotion to them. He argues that the gods do not understand human suffering because they only experience heavenly bliss and that Pygmalion's craving for the statue is the fault of the gods. In desperation, Pygmalion appeals to them on the grounds that they too have experienced love. In remembrance of their own hours of passion, he hopes that they will act for him and enable him to know love. His address to Venus recalls her passion for Adonis and Pygmalion offers to sculpt her as a nude, so that all of Cyprus might worship her. Pygmalion's prayers are heard and the statue comes to life. A soul 'dreams' from her dewy eyes, and she is a 'new Pandora'.

Conceiving the inspiration for the statue as a vision provides Pygmalion with a clear motivation. The prominent use of the artist's solitude emphasizes this heightened introspection. Having omitted Pygmalion's disappointment with the women of his island, Bennett gives the sculptor a recurring dream to inspire him to sculpt the statue. The other-worldliness of the vision contrasts with the tangibility of the transformed statue. The statue is alive even to the 'tendrils of her hair' (p. 106) – hair which marks her out to have changed from the Apolline dream to the passionate Dionysian: her lips are as red as Hyacinthus's blood, and her long tresses are 'nets of gold, / Fit as lorn Ariadne's streaming hair/ To catch flush'd Dionusus [sic]' (p. 109). Under a mystical influence Pygmalion understands the statue's Dionysian nature before she is brought to life, and his soul hears her tuneful music likening it to 'the passionate sobs and swells' of the harp. His comparison of her with Pandora, who unleashes the evils of the world also draws on the etymology of her name. She is 'all-gifted', as the transformed statue's beauty implies. Bennett's 'Pygmalion' is both Apolline and Dionysian. Pygmalion's dream inspires him to become a god-like image maker, an act which defines his separateness from his subject. Pygmalion's reaction to her transformation indicates his willingness to abandon himself to passivity and Dionysian pleasure. He exists, at the end of the poem, only to see, hear and love the statue; the statue becomes Pygmalion's existence and he loses himself:

> I had hearing but to drink her words;
> Mine eyes had vision but to feed on her.
> Hope – memory – thought – existence – from my brain
> She smote the world – earth – heaven – and all but her,
> And joy and grief – life and death – and all but her (p. 109).

Pygmalion's staccato speech encapsulates the breakdown of his mental coherence as the infringement of grammatical boundaries implies Dionysian excess. A similar differentiation between Apolline grace and self-defeating pleasure-seeking is seen in Bennett's 'The Judgement of Midas', where Apollo warns Midas to ignore worldly 'pleasures and delights of the sense' (p. 167) and Pan advises the opposite. Enticed by Pan's seductive speech, Midas embraces worldly pleasure and is made to regret his folly.

George MacDonald (1824–1905)

George MacDonald, a Scottish-born writer and lecturer who made his living in England, is best remembered for his fantasy stories and fairy tales such as *The Princess and The Goblin* (1872). *Phantastes* (1858) is a rare treatment of the Pygmalion story in novel form. Categorized as 'a fairy tale for adults', it was written 'over a period of two months' after the recent deaths of his father and two brothers.[29] C. S. Lewis, who was greatly influenced by MacDonald's work, describes the novel as the great work of 'mythopoeic art' which had baptized his imagination.[30] Auden also points to MacDonald's interest in myth and dreams:

> For the writing of what may comprehensively be called Dream Literature [...] the primary requirement is the gift of mythopoeic imagination. [...] George MacDonald is pre-eminently a mythopoeic writer. [...] His greatest gift is what one might call his dream realism, his exact and profound knowledge of dream causality, dream logic, dream change, dream morality: when one reads him, the illusion of participating in a real dream is perfect.[31]

There is no doubt that MacDonald was fascinated by dream. His poetry series, 'A Book of Dreams' (1857), describes a variety of dream experiences.[32] One poem describes a dreaming soul:

> Our souls, in daylight hours, awake
> With visions sometimes teem,
> Which to the slumbering brain would take
> The form of wondrous dream (p. 82).

Another suggests the possibility of the dreamer controlling his dreams: 'Now I will mould a dream, awake, / Which I, asleep, would dream' (p. 107). MacDonald's poetry also demonstrates his fascination with sculpture. In the first

---

[29] George MacDonald, *Phantastes*, ed. by Derek Brewer (Woodbridge, 1982), p. x. and p. viii.
[30] George MacDonald, *Phantastes and Lilith*, ed. by C. S. Lewis (London, 1962), p. 10.
[31] George MacDonald, *The Visionary Novels: Lilith, Phantastes*, ed. by Anne Freemantle, with an introduction by W. H. Auden (New York, 1954), pp. v–vii.
[32] George MacDonald, *Poems* (London, 1857).

of 'Eighteen Sonnets, About Jesus', he supposes what would have happened if Christ had been a sculptor (p. 287); and another poem, 'The Unseen Model', takes as its subject the sculpting of a statue of Psyche. Like the post-Romantic Pygmalion stories, here the sculptor is inspired to sculpt by a vision: 'In my brain last night the vision arose, / To-morrow shall see its birth!'.[33] In the 'flickering lamplight', the man sculpts what he thinks is a statue of Psyche (the soul), but when day comes, the sculptor realizes that he has been sculpting the statue of a girl he had once loved and forgotten, and who has since died (II, 102). Sculpting in the dark shadows has caused him to sculpt from his dim memories. The sculptor is doomed to love the inanimate statue, and from then on, whenever he carves a statue of woman it takes the same form.

Phantastes is influenced by German and English Romanticism; the Romantic epigraphs to each chapter to proclaim this bias. The novel is modelled on the German Romantic *Märchen* (or artistic fairy tales for adults). As Michael Mendelson suggests, the novel

> marks the first appearance in MacDonald's work of the *Kunstmärchen*, or artistic fairy tale developed by writers such as Tiecke, Novalis, La Motte-Fouqué (the author of *Undine*), and E. T. A. Hoffmann. [...] The Romantic authors of the *Kunstmärchen* were fascinated by the mysteries of experience, the dark places of the mind, and the world beyond the finite; as such, they found in the inherent enchantment of the fairy tale a perfect vehicle for exploring our confrontation with the unknown.[34]

As George P. Landow points out, MacDonald follows the German *Märchen* in employing 'a dream or a dream-like structure'.[35] This structure reveals that 'to him the world of the spirit must be seen in terms of human psychology, the human inner world (Landow, p. 127). Roderick McGillis suggests that Percy Shelley's *Epipsychidion* has much in common with *Phantastes* 'not only in incident, but also in mood'.[36] MacDonald embraces 'not only the self and phenomenal reality, but also a transcendent reality that enlarged human spiritual possibilities'.[37]

---

[33] George MacDonald, *The Poetical Works*, 2 vols (London, 1893), II, 101.

[34] Michael Mendelson, 'The Fairy Tales of George MacDonald and the Evolution of a Genre', in *For the Childlike*, pp. 31–49 (p. 32).

[35] George P. Landow, 'And the World Became Strange: Realms of Literary Fantasy', in *The Aesthetics of Fantasy Literature and Art* ed. by Roger Schlobin (Notre Dame, 1982), p. 127.

[36] Roderick McGillis, 'The Community of the Centre. Structure and Theme in *Phantastes*', in *For the Childlike*, pp. 51–65 (p. 53).

[37] Frank. P. Riga, 'From Time to Eternity: MacDonald's Doorway Between' in *Essays on C. S. Lewis and George MacDonald*, ed. by Cynthia Marshall, Studies in British Literature, 11 (Lewiston, Queenstown, Lampeter, 1991), pp. 83–100 (p. 84).

The Pygmalion episodes in *Phantastes* are complex because they occur in the context of a dream and because they constitute not so much a series of episodes as a thread which runs throughout the novel and through the dream of its hero, Anodos. In his exploration of his dream-land, Anodos, as in many *Kunstmärchen*, journeys in search of knowledge, only to find himself back home when he has reached his destination. The narrative is complex and heavily laden with dream allegory. The novel employs the imaginative dream vision model in which the ordinary senses are closed off and a visionary world is evoked. All of the sensations Anodos experiences in the inner world of his dream landscape are inner senses. The way in which Anodos enters and leaves the world points to this language being used. He enters by falling asleep and dreaming that he has woken to find the external objects of his room transformed. His washbasin has become a stream, the flowers on his carpet he now perceives as real, the foliage carved on his dressing table is likewise real. When Anodos leaves the dream world, he describes the return of his ordinary senses: 'A pang and a terrible shudder went through me; a writhing as of death convulsed me; and I became once again conscious of a more limited, even a bodily and earthly life' (p. 164). The Adam's dream model is suggested when Anodos, while dreaming, finds a marble statue of a woman.

Like Nietzsche's Greeks who dream in bas-relief, Anodos finds a 'time worn bas-relief' in a cave in his dream-world (p. 29). The bas-relief scene represents

> Pygmalion, as he awaited the quickening of his statue. The sculptor sat more rigid than the figure to which his eyes were turned. That seemed about to step from its pedestal and embrace the man, who waited rather than expected (p. 29).

Anodos suggests that in such a cave as this, Pygmalion could have 'set up his block of marble and moulded into a visible body the thought already clothed with form in the unseen hall of the sculptor's brain' (p. 29). Exploring the cave further, Anodos finds another Pygmalion thread: a block of marble 'white enough and delicate enough for any statue, even if destined to become an ideal woman in the arms of a sculptor' (p. 29). The marble, when its moss covering is removed, is revealed to be an alabaster statue of a beautiful, reposing woman with her hair 'fallen partly over her face' (p. 30). The protagonist recognizes her as his Platonic soul-mate. Her face is 'perfectly lovely; more near the face that had been born with me in my soul, than anything I had seen before in nature or art' (p. 30). She is 'vainly sleeping / In the very death of dreams' (pp. 30–31). Anodos is obsessively concerned with her statue-like state, likening her to an 'alabaster tomb' (p. 30), a 'pale coffin' (p. 31), an 'antenatal tomb' (p. 31), a 'stony shroud' (p. 32), a 'pearly shroud of alabaster' (p. 36), and a 'marble prison' (p. 37). The combination of poetry and song, and not prayer, animates the statue. Music, the

Dionysian art, is also heard during the transformation of Beddoes's statue.

The Pygmalion subject moves from the confines of the artistic realm of the bas-relief to a free-standing world in which the statue and Anodos share the same background. Sleeping Beauty, the half marble prince of an enchanted city, Ariel, and Niobe are remembered in connection with this scene. Niobe is also mentioned by Beddoes, whose 'Pygmalion' MacDonald cites for a chapter epigraph:

> And she was smooth and full, as if one gush
> Of life had washed her, or as if a sleep
> Lay on her eyelid, easier to sweep
> Than bee from daisy (p. 27).

Like Beddoes, MacDonald makes death an important element of the story. Rolland Hein suggests that the marble woman

> appears to symbolize the spirit of the Ideal, or the Perfect, and, as such, is in MacDonald's thought a surrogate for the divine Presence. [...] These deep longings toward the Ideal which men feel have often been prime motivations for artists and much of what MacDonald is saying in *Phantastes* intrigues those who are interested in a Romantic theory of art.[38]

Hein argues, furthermore, that the novel in general addresses 'the problem of man's search for satisfactions for his personal desires and longings. The Christian concern arises because the natural process of seeking satisfactions for human desires is self-centred, and self-centredness is spiritually destructive' (Hein, p. 55). Much of the rest of the novel is indeed taken up with Anodos chasing the ideal woman, until he finally relinquishes his obsession and humbly comes to terms with the fact that she loves another man.

Phantastes examines the interchangeability of art and life and transformations from illusion to reality. There are several episodes in the novel which illustrate this. Anodos mistakes the dangerous Maid of the Alder for his fleeing newly-transformed woman. The Maid reveals her true nature and transforms herself into an ugly hollow shell: 'It had for a face and front those of my enchantress, but now of a pale greenish hue in the light of the morning, and with dead lustrous eyes' (*Phantastes*, p. 39). When in the Fairy Palace, Anodos reads the story of Cosmo von Wehrstahl, a student at the university of Prague, who falls in love with a beautiful princess who appears to him only in a mirror. The princess tells Cosmo that he must break the mirror in order to free her, but that she cannot be certain

---

[38] Rolland Hein, *The Harmony Within. The Spiritual Vision of George MacDonald* (Michigan, 1982), p. 61.

that they will be together if this is done. Cosmo is torn between his love for the imprisoned ideal and his fear of losing her. The real princess, meanwhile, is very ill in another part of the city. To emphasize the connection between the Pygmalion story and this story of the transformation from mirror image to life, the ill princess is seen as 'more like marble than any other woman. The loveliness of death seemed frozen upon her face, for her lips were rigid, and her eyelids closed' (p. 90). Cosmo eventually breaks the mirror and the princess regains her liberty; however, Cosmo is wounded and dies in the arms of his princess. The story illustrates MacDonald's central theme of coming to terms with idealism and accepting the harshness of reality.

The chapter following the story of Cosmo opens with a quotation from *The Winter's Tale*, another text in which a statue comes to life. The Pygmalion episode which follows this involves several stages in which Anodos's statue passes from art to life and back again. Once again, dream is important. One of the most striking of these occurs while Anodos is in the Fairy Palace. He experiences a vision in which 'a succession of images of bewildering beauty' passes before his 'inward eye' (p. 93). This vision reminds him that 'only in the marble cave, before I found the sleeping statue, had I ever had a similar experience' (p. 93). In the palace, Anodos finds a corridor which contains 'various statues, of what seemed both ancient and modern sculpture' (p. 95). He dreams that he sees them moving: 'All the statues were in motion, statues no longer, but men and women – all shapes of beauty that ever sprang from the brain of sculptor, mingled in the convolutions of a complicated dance' (p. 95). Standing apart from these statues, motionless, the 'marble beauty' appears again (p. 95). Taking the dream to be a prediction of what will happen, Anodos, when he awakes, searches amongst the statues for his marble woman. Pausing in front of a vacant pedestal, he tries to conjure her form onto it with a song. The woman appears gradually:

> As I sang the first four lines, the loveliest feet became clear upon the black pedestal; and ever as I sang, it was as if a veil were being lifted up from before the form, but an invisible veil, so that the statue appeared to grow before me, not so much by evolution, as by infinitesimal degrees of added height (p. 99).

The form appears as a woman and not as a statue; though Anodos finds it difficult to tell whether she looked 'more of a statue or more of a woman; she seemed removed from that region of phantasy where all is intensely vivid, but nothing clearly defined' (p. 103). When the song is finished, the woman changes back into a statue. When Anodos lifts her from the pedestal, comically ignoring a sign saying 'Touch Not!' (p. 94), the statue comes to life again and runs away. He has tried again to possess the ideal, and failed. The pursuit continues through a door and into another landscape, and down a hole. Underground, a group of goblins inform him that the woman belongs to another man. Ultimately, Anodos gives up his prize: if the other man was 'a better man, let him have her' (p. 107), he says. He meets the victor and concedes that he 'could have thrown' his 'arms around him because she loved him' (p. 152). His experience, then, has ultimately led to some kind of maturity.

The Pygmalion theme in this novel sparks off a series of transformations between contrary states in a concatenation of dream narratives. Just as the novel builds up a network of levels, with its dreams within dreams, so these further transformation scenes build upon the initial conception of the Pygmalion story. The result is less of a collage, which implies the stories are unconnected, and more of a *découpage*, in which each layer, each transformation story, enhances the significance and meaning of the whole, building from the 'tiny woman form, as perfect in shape as if she had been a small Greek statuette roused to life and motion' who rouses the protagonist to explore his dream-world (p. 2), to Anodos's delusion that the ideal woman is there for the taking, to the final realism of the hero's loss. The text demonstrates the creativity of visions, and emphasizes the reality of the dream-world. Life is experienced as a platonic 'world of shadows' (p. 165) and, by contrast, the dream world is introduced by a narrator who is convinced of its reality: 'I awoke one morning with the usual perplexity of mind which accompanies the return of consciousness' (p. 1). The effect of Anodos's experiences on the novel's narrator is to create an extreme optimism and belief in human good.

William Hurrell Mallock (1849–1923)

William Hurrell Mallock's 'Pygmalion to his Statue, become his Wife' (1869) recounts the story in the form of a monologue spoken by Pygmalion to the transformed statue.[39] Mallock, the author of *The New Republic* (1877), is largely remembered as a social satirist whose later work contains thinly disguised portraits of his contemporaries. 'Pygmalion to his Statue', written when the author was twenty, and shows an enthusiasm for post-Romantic themes. Mallock's early work is devoted to the Apolline-Dionysian view of Greece. 'A Boy's Dream', tells of a boy who prefers to dream of ancient Greece rather than live in his own time.

> Yes, let me here forget my life, my home,
> In a rapt dream o'er these hypastral seas,
> Charmed by the luminous fall of silver foam.
> [...] Oh, dreamy, foamy moonlight! dreamy shore!
> Oh, dreamy ecstasy! (pp. 11–12).

---

[39] William Hurrell Mallock, *Poems* (London, 1880).

Chapter 6

The Twentieth Century: Towards a Conclusion

The Galatea Story

The Pygmalion story prior to the 1880s predominantly represents Galatea in two ways: she is either accepting and appreciative of her lot as a wife, demurely fulfilling Pygmalion's ideal, or she is a disappointment to Pygmalion, who views her with disgust. Prior to the eighteenth century, Galatea is consistently portrayed as inferior to Pygmalion, inconstant, dependent, immodest, criminal, and an easy prey to temptation. Rousseau's *Pygmalion* helped to disseminate a less negative view of Galatea, although his sculptor reduces the statue to a projection of himself. In forging his own fantasy around the statue-like Sara, Hazlitt's Pygmalion similarly forgoes interaction with another in favour a narcissistic replica. Concurrent with this is Hazlitt's desire to treat the woman as a goddess, and thus make her something untouchable and incapable of responding.

From the 1820s until the end of the nineteenth century we find a number of recurrent themes which express standard male views of women's bodies. Galatea is like a flower or a child and is immobilized by her heavy hair. For James Payn she is 'as fair and flawless as the lily's grace' (p. 11). Joseph John Murphy's statue-woman has 'a flower's soft bending grace'.[1] Writers emphasize the whiteness of the statue and of the woman she becomes. Beddoes writes: 'all her marble symmetry was white / As brow and bosom should be' (*Plays and Poems*, p. 101). This, of course, reflects her statue state, but it is also an reflection of the purity and beauty required (by men) in womankind. Galatea's voice and actions are often child-like: Beddoes's Pygmalion calls her 'my delicious child' (p. 102), Buchanan's statue-woman has 'prattled infants' speech',[2] and George Eric Lancaster's Pygmalion asks his statue to lift up her arms to him 'like a child'.[3] Joseph John Murphy talks of her possessing 'the purity of childhood' (p. 66), as does Andrew Lang's Pygmalion, who wants 'a woman with a child-like heart / "And passionately pure"' (p. 301). Galatea is without rights and exists only as a dependant. Ronald Ross's Galatea occupies the uneasy position of being both child and woman.

> What are you still but a child?

---

[1] Joseph John Murphy, *Sonnets* (London, 1890), p. 66.
[2] Robert Buchanan, *Undertones* (London, 1863), p. 178.
[3] George Eric Lancaster, *Pygmalion in Cyprus* (London, 1880), p. 5.

late in life and dates from about 1860 onwards. He writes that 'the supernatural and the Future Life [...] have occupied my whole soul to the exclusion of almost every subject which the Gorillas of this world most delight in, whether scientific, political, or literary'.[43] Charles Tennyson characterizes his brother's poetry as containing 'long tracts of Swedenborgian philosophy, for the introduction of which the poet seems to have used the classical stories as a rather perfunctory excuse'.[44] This has subsequently become the general view of Frederick's Tennyson's poetry. *The Cambridge History of English Literature* helps to perpetuate this assessment, suggesting that Tennyson

> was deeply interested in metaphysical problems. He retells old myths with the purpose of making them messengers of his own thought on immortality and the unseen world. But his message is a little indistinct. Occasionally, as in *Psyche*, he loses himself in a Swedenborgian quagmire. [...] Nature and love and death and immortality are the foci round which his thought, as that of his greater brother, moved, and on each he has written occasional haunting lines.[45]

'Cyprus, Pygmalion' forms part of a series of stories devoted to various Greek islands. Pygmalion's story is naturally associated with Cyprus, as it is in Ovid's version, though the goddess takes the name Urania (the surname of Venus). Pygmalion yearns for a quiet spot away from his people, where he can worship beauty undisturbed. The 'loose laughing daughters of the isle' are incomparable to the 'one Form, invisible to sight, / visible to the Soul' (p. 39). Pygmalion sees the 'Ideal' vision form day and night, and eventually it grows 'more real than all things outward' and he begins to see 'more with an inner sight than with mine eyes' (p. 39). The post-Romantic perception of the vision, using inner-senses to perceive enables Pygmalion to nurture an internal Swedenborgian spiritual world. Pygmalion thinks that the 'spirit-picture' has been caused by some unconscious influence; it is in his 'soul' and it is 'a dream' (p. 40). Pygmalion, still praying, questions what has happened: Has a god made a heaven inside him and given him such a clear image of beauty which makes him lose all thought of human beauty? The devotion to the spirit implies a neglect of Urania, for which Pygmalion is penitent. The goddess's consolation is to be that Pygmalion is impregnable to human influences and is only affected by internal things. He worships at 'that inner Shrine / Where She [the image] is glorified' and will not sleep until he has

---

[43] *Letters to Frederick Tennyson*, ed. by Hugh J. Schonfield (London, 1930), p. 132.
[44] Frederick Tennyson, *The Shorter Poems*, ed. by Charles Tennyson (London, 1913), p. xxx.
[45] *The Cambridge History of English Literature*, ed. by A. W. Ward and A. R. Waller, 15 vols (Cambridge, 1916), XIII, 47–48.

prayed for a dream of her. This dream will enable him to impress the image more deeply on his 'inner sense' and inspire him to transfer the image to 'dead marble' and make external what is internal (pp. 42-43).

Pygmalion's sculpture is an 'incarnation of the dream' which makes 'the metaphysical an ultimate in nature' (p. 44). The sculpture produces a dramatic change in Pygmalion's attitude to the image. No longer internalized, the statue's separateness from him inspires his need to bring it to life. Could not desire, patient toil, and strong will make her live, he asks? A 'delirium of phantasy' comes over him and he imagines that the statue has come to life (p. 45). Discovering, that it is still stone, Pygmalion falls into a swoon and lies 'lost to all knowledge of the world without / And the world within' (p. 45) during which his 'inner eyes were open'd, and I saw / Round me, as in a dream, heroic men' who were as tall as gods (p. 46). The heroes describe the nature of mankind, pantheism and platonism. A discussion of what would happen if the statue were brought to life ensues: the hero suggests that she would come into the world soulless and uneducated, and being captive, she would crave her liberty.

The voices depart and Pygmalion, still dreaming, wanders through a wood, where he sees a woman who has the same face as the marble statue. His passion causes him to wake up, crying, in his chamber. During this vision, night has fallen. A dazzling golden radiance lights up his chamber and Pygmalion hopes that this light might give the statue life. He makes sure that he is not dreaming: 'I smote my brow, that I might know for sure / That I was not adream' (p. 53). It is Urania, who now answers Pygmalion's prayer because his 'heart was fix'd upon a godlike dream, / A pure white image of a purer thought' (p. 54). The goddess explains that the dream of the beautiful woman was sent to him, and that it is the face of a real woman he had once glimpsed in the past. This echoes MacDonald's *Phantastes*. Although time has passed since and he has forgotten her, the marble statue is a replica of the woman. The woman has, in the meantime, dreamed of Pygmalion. Pygmalion is sceptical, saying that the woman could be anywhere or already married. He pleads for his statue to be brought to life. Urania agrees and the statue comes to life. She steps off the pedestal and throws off her veil. The goddess invites Pygmalion to 'take her', adding that the statue's heart is a mirror which will reflect all of his love (p. 59). Pygmalion learns the difference between beauty born of 'Phantasy' which is an 'imperfect, unsubstantial, insecure' ghost of Love, and natural beauty (pp. 60-61).

Pygmalion's active internal nature draws on Swedenborgian theories on the internal nature of mankind. Pygmalion thinks that the gods have 'made a heaven / Within me' because his vision of the woman is so perfect (p. 40). Swedenborg similarly proposes that 'A man whose moral life is spiritual has heaven within himself. [...] Man's nature is such that he must have the Divine within him as a creative source'.⁴⁶ Pygmalion's concentration on the internal image within his soul enables him to privilege his inner sight over his external senses. Pygmalion is advised, by one of the heroic men, not to assume that 'what is outward is Reality, / The Inward but a Shadow' and that 'the Form ⟨ Is the true Man, and not his Minister' (p. 48). Pygmalion is so devoted to his internal life that he ceases to function normally and is given over to a mystic life. Pygmalion disregards the Socratic theorization of the heroic voices and embraces his experience of love. His relationship with the transformed statue is close: 'As were my thoughts, ev'n such were hers' (p. 62). The lovers parrot each other, losing their individuality (Rousseau-like), in their passionate mirroring '"My own," she cried, I answer'd her, "My own!"' (p. 63). Tennyson completes the story with this Dionysian scene of self-abandonment and unity.

Echoing Romantic dream figures, the post-Romantics use dream as an inspiration for creativity and as a creative act in itself. The story, which previously had no dream element in it, metamorphoses into one in which dream plays a principal part, the dream vision becoming central to the motivation of the artist and the way in which he creates. Accompanied by inner sense figures, which emphasize the internalized nature of the vision, post-Romantic dreams continue the pursuit of the ideal. Preoccupation with internal ideals leads to some dependence on a Romantic passive-creative aesthetic as Pygmalion's art is facilitated by internal aid. Sculpture, the Nietzschean act of self-definition, centred on realizing the perfect dream in art, does not result in a purely disinterested response. Pygmalion is driven by a pleasure-seeking Dionysian will to transgress boundaries, to bring life to art and to lose himself in his passion for Galatea or reject her outright. These post-Romantics remain largely unconcerned with the moral questions which arise from the story. The statue operates as an ideal woman whose role is to expedite the fulfilment of Pygmalion's goals. Principally this involves a period of self-examination followed by the sculptor's rejection of the Apolline ideal and his subsumption into a united existence with his Galatea. The progression from idealism to love, though sometimes difficult, is most often successful. For certain writers in the mid-Victorian period, however, circumstances dictate that the moral issues arising from this development of Pygmalion's character have to be addressed.

---

⁴⁶ Emanuel Swedenborg, *Essential Readings*, ed. and trans. by Michael Stanley, (Northamptonshire, 1988), pp. 56–59.

Chapter 4

The Pre-Raphaelite Pygmalion and Mid-Victorian Hellenism

The Pygmalion story in the mid Victorian period acts as a vehicle for debate on the morality of Greek art in which questions are raised about the nature of Hellenic spirituality and, in particular, about the way in which the Hellenic female body should be rendered. The story is particularly relevant in this context because it describes a male sculptor creating his ideal (naked) woman in a frank and erotic manner. In her ivory form the statue is so realistic that Pygmalion cannot tell the difference between art and life:

> The face is that of a real maiden, whom you would think living. [...] So does his art conceal his art. Pygmalion looks in admiration and is inflamed with love for this semblance of a form. Often he lifts his hands to the work to try whether it be flesh or ivory; nor does he yet confess it to be ivory. He kisses it and thinks his kisses are returned (Ovid, II, 83).

Ovid describes the danger that Victorian critics feared: the ability of art to inspire lust. Mid-Victorian renarrations of the story form part of this discussion of the moral safety of Hellenism. Writers and critics are interested in whether Pygmalion's transformed statue had a soul or whether it was merely a body. If the statue attained only the status of body on her transformation, then Pygmalion's love for her must be condemned as carnal lust (and, by extension, the Greek nude must be seen as excluding the spiritual). The willingness to diverge from Ovid in nineteenth-century named versions of the Pygmalion myth legitimately motivates us to question why these writers made certain choices about their narratives. The difficulties that the post-Romantics have found with the conflicts in the story, suggested by the morality of idealism and the carnality of love, are crystallized here where the Greek becomes both a symbol of purity and of desire.

In the mid nineteenth century, the Pygmalion myth, as part of Greek iconography, becomes a token in the war of words between the Pre-Raphaelites and their detractors. It not only echoes one of the main debates of the 'Fleshly Controversy' (on the representation of the body in art) but it is also taken up and retold by the principal disputants of the Fleshly Controversy: the war in words initiated by the critic Robert Buchanan. The portrayal of the physical nature of the statue is censured by the anti-Pre-Raphaelite Robert Buchanan, and is a criticism which is at the heart of the Fleshly Controversy. Buchanan appraises the relative importance of the spiritual and sensual (or fleshly) qualities of contemporary art and literature in a bitter attack aimed at destroying the reputations of D. G. Rossetti and A. C. Swinburne.[1] He argues that their work lacks the moral content needed to prevent it from being perceived as erotic (or fleshly) literature. Moreover, he accuses them of supporting the idea that 'poetic expression is greater than poetic thought and by inference that the body is greater than the soul' ('The Fleshly School of Poetry', 335). Focusing on Rossetti, Buchanan criticizes his emphasis on physicality and his supposed disregard for the spiritual element of poetry. Buchanan was reacting to Rossetti's occasional poetic (con)fusion of the body and the soul: for example, 'Thy soul I know not from thy body, nor / Thee from myself, neither our love from God'.[2] Swinburne was criticized by the *London Review* for a similar offence committed in *Poems and Ballads*: 'He seems to have some idea of a heaven; but he tells us in plain language... that it is a poor matter compared with a courtesan's caresses'.[3] These separate categories are replaced, in Rossetti's work, by a kind of physical spirituality in which the soul is appreciated through the body.

This is akin to Pater's roughly contemporary concept of the spiritual nature of Greek art. Pater argues that during its moral and artistic zenith (5th century BC) Greek sculpture was capable of depicting the human soul: 'The work of the Greek Sculptor, together with its more real anatomy [than the Egyptian], becomes full [...] of the human soul. [...] The true Hellenic influence brought a revelation of the soul and body of man'.[4] Pater understands Greek sculpture to be a complex combination of the material and the spiritual: the body is sensualized and spiritualized. He admires the close connection between Greek sculpture and Greek religion:

> It was the privilege of Greek religion to be able to transform itself into an artistic ideal. [...] [The Venus of Melos] is in no sense a symbol, a suggestion, of anything beyond its own victorious fairness. The mind begins and ends with the finite image, yet loses no part of the spiritual motive. That motive is not lightly and loosely attached to the sensuous form, as its meaning to an allegory, but saturates and is identical with it.[5]

---

[1] Robert Buchanan, 'The Fleshly School of Poetry: Mr D. G. Rossetti', *The Contemporary Review*, 18 (1871), 334–350. This was published under the pseudonym 'Thomas Maitland'. Buchanan published an expanded version of this article under his own name: *The Fleshly School of Poetry and Other Phenomena of the Day* (London, 1872). See John A. Cassidy in 'Robert Buchanan and the Fleshly Controversy', *PMLA*, 67 (1952), 65–93.

[2] Dante Gabriel Rossetti, *The Poetical Works*, ed. by William Michael Rossetti (London, 1898), p. 179.

[3] A. C. Swinburne, *The Critical Heritage*, ed. by Clyde K. Hyder (London, 1970), p.36.

[4] Walter Pater, *Greek Studies: A Series of Essays*, New Library Edition (London, 1910), VII, 239 and 256.

[5] Walter Pater, *The Renaissance: Studies in Art and Poetry*, (London, 1910), I, 204 and 206.

William Michael Rossetti, whose defence of *Poems and Ballads* angered Buchanan, suggests that the beautiful body and the soul were at one in Greek art, particularly in Greek sculpture: 'everything Greek has become to us a compound of beauty and of thought, a vestige and an evidence of human soul infused as into Parian marble, marble-like in its purity of appeal to us'(Hyder, p. 65).

Dante Gabriel Rossetti defended his position in 'The Stealthy School of Criticism' arguing that he had not ignored spirituality, but had openly discussed it.[6] Buchanan, expanding his earlier article into a longer pamphlet, and continuing the attack, concedes that Rossetti has some concept of the spiritual in art, albeit not an acceptable one.

> No one can rejoice more than I do to hear that Mr. Rossetti attaches a certain importance to the soul as distinguished from the body, only I should like very much to know what he means by the soul; for I fear, from the sonnet he quotes, that he regards the feeling for a young woman's person, face, heart, and mind, as in itself quite a spiritual sentiment. In the poem entitled 'Love-Lily' he expressly observes that Love cannot tell Lily's 'body from her soul' – they are so inextricably blended. It is precisely this confusion of the two which, filling Mr. Rossetti as it eternally does with what he calls 'notorious longing', becomes so intolerable to readers with a less mystic sense of animal function (*The Fleshly School of Poetry*, p. 69).

Buchanan argues, nevertheless, that Rossetti and the Fleshly School place 'the body' in the limelight, 'as if the simple and natural delights of the body had not been occupying our poetry ever since the days of the *Confessio Amantis*' (*The Fleshly School of Poetry*, p. 84). Buchanan proposes that the proper locus for poetic effort should be not the bodily but the spiritual: 'Perhaps, after all, since so many centuries of Sexuality have done so little for poetry, it might be advantageous to give Spirituality a trial, and to see if *her* efforts to create a literature are equally unsuccessful' (*The Fleshly School of Poetry*, p. 85).

The Fleshly Controversy was essentially about the suitability of certain subjects (including Greek subjects) for art and literature. Though Buchanan does not single out the Greek subject in *The Fleshly School of Poetry*, Hellenism is certainly an aspect of the texts he denounces here, and is a trait which he had picked out as objectionable four years earlier. Furthermore, Buchanan states openly in later works that the Greek subject has no relevance to contemporary life and was used in such a way as to encourage too much emphasis on the physical at the expense of the spiritual and moral. Other opponents of Swinburne, however, were happy

---

[6] D. G. Rossetti, 'The Stealthy School of Criticism', *The Athenaeum*, 16 December (1871), 792–794.

to support what was, by this time, a heavy investment in Greek culture. In defence of his work Swinburne sanctions his version of the Greek theme, relishing its homoerotic beauty and physical nature:

> I knew that belief in the body was the secret of sculpture, and that a past age of ascetics could no more attempt or attain it than the present age of hypocrites; I knew that modern moralities and recent religions were, if possible, more averse and alien to *this purely physical and pagan art* than to the others; but how far averse I did not know. There is nothing lovelier, as there is nothing more famous, in later Hellenic art, than the statue of Hermaphroditus (my italics).[7]

Swinburne's attackers favoured their own version of Hellenic morality, whilst Swinburne's Hellenic dream was condemned as immoral. Swinburne's poem on the statue of Hermaphroditus in *Poems and Ballads* (1866) celebrates the otherness of this beauty as a unique example of the platonic perfect whole. Hermaphroditus is the summation of the conflict between the sexes, a Dionysian whole. 'The double blossom of two fruitless flowers', s/he embodies a statuesque sterility that often accompanies Swinburne's lovers.

The propriety of descriptions of the female body was challenged by writers on both art and literature. Just as art critics were discussing issues such as the extent of flesh that could be shown without drapery, and the appropriate colours for avoiding eroticism, so literary critics like Buchanan contested sensual and candidly written descriptions of the female body in situations which could be perceived as indelicate. Robert Buchanan declares

> I have [...] never come across persons of the other sex who conduct themselves in the manner described [in the work of the Fleshly School]. Females who bite and scratch, scream, bubble, munch, sweat, writhe, twist, wriggle, foam, and in a general way slaver over their lovers, must surely possess some extraordinary qualities to counteract their otherwise most offensive mode of conducting themselves (*The Fleshly School of Poetry*, p. 44).

Nudity and Hellenism were often united in the art and literature of the period. For some, Hellenism justified nudity; for others, however, the link between these two subjects was a cause for concern. Critics of contemporary sculpture were worried about the Greek influence. Richard Westmacott comments in 1863:

> Our public exhibitions constantly abound [...] with the most unnecessary

---

[7] A. C. Swinburne, *The Complete Works*, ed. by Sir Edmund Gosse and Thomas James Wise, The Bonchurch Edition, 20 vols (London, 1925–1927), VI (1925), 366.

display of the entirely naked female figure, under conventional names
of Venus, Nymphs, and similar appellations. [...] [These are] possibly
a means of corruption [...] blunting those feelings of delicacy which are
the surest safeguard to the moral character of a nation.[8]

The Greek body could signify repose, serenity and purity; but it could also be conceived as salacious and debauched. The Controversy addresses these issues directly.

The Fleshly Controversy began properly with the publication of Swinburne's *Poems and Ballads* in 1866. There is, however, much evidence of a fleshly debate going on a few years before Robert Buchanan's first article (Cassidy, p. 65). During this period William Bell Scott, poet, artist, lecturer and Pre-Raphaelite sympathizer, and Robert Buchanan, the instigator of the Fleshly Controversy both composed versions of the story, raising new questions about the nature of the statue.[9] Scott, whilst head of the Government School of Art and design in Newcastle, published a series of lectures on aesthetics.[10] Outlining his views on the spiritual element in Greek art, he uses the Pygmalion story as a demonstration of his argument that there is a danger in making the physical more important than the spiritual. For him the Greek ideal in art lacks a spiritual element. It places too much emphasis on bodily beauty, ignoring moral beauty: 'the ideal of the Greeks' he says, 'is not spiritual but material' (*Half-Hour Lectures*, pp. 312–313). Scott's ideal theory is based around the necessity of producing the soul (or spiritual) in art: 'the soul is superior to the body' (*Half-Hour Lectures*, p. 307). He argues that what is immaterial or intangible (e.g. the intellect, hope, possibilities, the soul) is of greater value than the material or tangible (e.g. the body). This picture of an intellectualized ideal contrasts with the body-centred Greek ideal, which, according to Scott, 'was the natural man approaching the gods by the perfection of the body' rather than the soul (*Half-Hour Lectures*, p. 309). Advising his contemporaries against following the example of the Greeks and worshipping the body in art, Scott writes:

> If by a paganish love of the body, or a peculiar cultivation, we
> apprehend and feel fully the beauty of the antique, we are in danger of
> sharing the *infatuation of Pygmalion*, or of losing reason; of being lost
> in the admiration, amounting to worship, expressed by Winckelmann of
> the Apollo [my italics] (*Half-Hour Lectures*, p.309).

As a result of his idolatrous love of the body, Pygmalion becomes an emblem of

---

[8] Richard Westmacott, *A Lecture on Sculpture* (Cambridge, 1863), p. 23.
[9] Robert Buchanan, *Undertones* (London, 1863).
[10] William Bell Scott, *Half-Hour Lectures on Art* (London, 1861), pp. 299–321.

Hellenic excess and moral turpitude. Winckelmann writes of the Apollo in his *History of Ancient Art* (1764): 'For my image seems to receive life and motion like the beautiful creation of Pygmalion. How is it possible to paint and describe it'.[11] To avoid Pygmalion's mistake, Scott advises, we must not forget that we know 'moral goodness and intellectual greatness to be often inhabitants of mean and even ugly bodies' (p. 309). Scott's reference to Pygmalion, though brief, places the story within the framework of the spiritual-physical debate.

Robert Buchanan's contribution was a poem called 'Pygmalion the sculptor' in *Undertones* (1863). Written shortly before his attack on the Pre-Raphaelites, this slim volume of classical verse shows Buchanan approaching the story from a moral perspective. Though it is an early piece, 'Pygmalion' clearly exhibits the doctrine Buchanan later espoused in *The Fleshly School of Poetry* and he alters the myth considerably. Buchanan acknowledges his extensive modifications in the preface: 'Faults may be found with certain liberties taken with old theories, certain tentative interpretations of ambiguous myths'. The Pygmalion story is reconstructed as an exemplary tale warning (like Scott's reference) against over-indulgence in the physical form of Greek beauty. Here the chaste Pygmalion is engaged to be married to a woman who dies on the morning of their wedding day, before they marry. He hears her voice instructing him to sculpt a marble statue of her to ease his grief. Falling in love with the statue, Pygmalion prays for it to be brought to life. When she has been transformed, Pygmalion mistakes her for Psyche; but on discovering that she cannot speak, he realizes that she has no soul. (Psyche is here substituted for Ovid's Venus, highlighting the shift of interest from love to spirituality.) A plague breaks out in the city, the cause of which Pygmalion attributes to his transgression. He abandons the statue and becomes an Ancient-Mariner-like itinerant story-teller.

Buchanan's Pygmalion becomes an aberrant worshipper of the sculpted soulless beauty. He affirms: '"To the glorious windows of the eyes / No soul clomb up to look at the stars"' (p. 177). Pygmalion's love is an obsessive adoration of a morally dubious woman. She is sensuously pictured as a nude beauty gingerly hiding behind her long yellow hair:

> [...] gleaming ringlets tingled to the knees
> Veiling her nakedness like golden rain,
> And cluster'd round about her where she stood
> As yellow leaves around a lily's bud (p. 173).

Terrified of her creator she cowers vulnerably like an animal, soulless and without speech. After subduing her, Pygmalion ties a chord around her waist – the symbol

---

[11] Johann Joachim Winckelmann, *Writings on Art*, ed. by David Irwin (London, 1972), p. 140.

of her captivity. For Buchanan, this Greek icon is spiritually dead. Though conceived chastely, she comes to represent the sensuality of Pygmalion, and is therefore abandoned when he repents. The statue-woman does not live up to Pygmalion's expectations in this scenario, and he rejects her. Scott and Buchanan both characterize Pygmalion as a wanton idolater. For Scott, the love of beauty is set out as art-worship, possibly with homosexual overtones. Buchanan's Pygmalion both desires and is repulsed by his statue. He constructs her as an ideal, but she becomes a physical contradiction of the intangible and moral idea.

William Morris, like Buchanan, sees a difference between the love given to the statue (as ideal) and the love given to the woman she becomes, but the second kind of love is described in much more positive terms. 'Pygmalion and the Image' forms part of the first volume of *The Earthly Paradise* published in 1868. Morris, like Scott and Buchanan, interprets Pygmalion's love for the statue as a desire for the body or empty shell. Pygmalion says that he has 'nothing in his heart but vain desire, / the ever-burning unconsuming fire', he is 'a madman, kneeling to a thing of stone'.[12] Immediately prior to the transformation of the statue, however, Pygmalion begins to calm his obsession with its aesthetic and physical beauty, and comes to prefer reality: '"Ah, life, sweet life! the only godlike thing"'. He regrets having been too interested in the work of art:

> Yet did he loath to see the image fair
> White and unchanged of face, unmoved of limb,
> And to his heart came dreamy thoughts and dim
> That into some strange region he might come,
> Nor ever reach again his loveless home (IV, 201).

By the time he arrives home, he finds that his obsessive love has gone:

> on his heart there streamed
> Cold light of day – he found himself alone,
> Reft of desire, all love and madness gone (IV, 202).

Pygmalion falls in love anew with the living woman he finds there. Importantly, this statue-woman has a soul: '"My new-made soul I give to thee today"' (IV, 203). In this case, an interest in the purely physical is portrayed as an obsession; an interest in the physical and the spiritual together (i.e. the statue-woman with a soul) is lauded as love. Morris solves the physical-spiritual dilemma by transforming the nature of Pygmalion's love. This alteration is the result of a rationalization of his situation in the 'cold light of day'; he is thus allowed to appreciate both the spiritual and physical qualities of the statue-woman.

---

[12] William Morris, *The Collected Works*, 24 vols (London, 1910–1915), IV (1910), 194.

'Pygmalion and the Image' is the companion piece of Edward Burne-Jones's paintings.[13] Burne-Jones also took up the theme on several occasions. Between 1864 and 1868 he made 12 drawings for William Morris's poem 'Pygmalion and the Image'; these were never published in conjunction with the poem. Furthermore, he completed a series of sketches on the subject in 1867, a small set of paintings in 1870, and four larger paintings in 1879 (entitled: 'The Heart Desires', 'The Hand Refrains', 'The Godhead Fires', 'The Soul Attains' [plate 1]). The final title indicates that a spiritual nature has been given to the statue in this version. The subject was also treated in water-colours by John William Waterhouse in 1873 and by William Bell Scott in the form of an etching.[14]

In the same year that 'Pygmalion and the Image' was published, Swinburne made a very different contribution. Swinburne's 1868 review of George Frederic Watts's painting 'The Wife of Pygmalion: A Translation from the Greek' plays on Watts's attempt to portray the statue's animation: 'the soft severity of perfect beauty might serve alike for woman or statue, flesh or marble' (XV, 197) (plate 7). Watts had controversially combined the statuesque qualities of the Greek nude with the polychrome colours of the flesh: 'colour and movement were associated with passion and the lower sensual emotions'.[15] Many of Watts's paintings combine the classical with Venetian polychromic ideals. 'The Wife of Pygmalion' depicts 'a Greek bust as if it were a living woman and in a Venetian format and style'.[16] As Swinburne observes, sculpture and painting go hand in hand in the painting: 'without any forced alliance of form and colour, a picture may share the gracious grandeur of a statue, a statue may catch something of the subtle bloom of beauty proper to a picture' (XV, 197).[17] The relationship between the contrary states of art and life, body and soul, fascinate Swinburne:

---

[13] Jane Davidson Reid's *The Oxford Guide to Classical Mythology in the Arts 1300–1990s*, 2 vols (New York, 1993) notes that Burne-Jones's gouache picture entitled 'The altar of Hymen' (1874) depicts Pygmalion and the statue embracing with Hymen looking on (II, 960). The picture was based on one of his illustrations for Morris's poem.

[14] William Bell Scott, *Poems Ballads, Studies From Nature, Sonnets, etc.*, (London, 1875), p. 191. Jane Davidson Reid notes that Waterhouse's painting has been lost (*The Oxford Guide to Classical Mythology*, II, 960). The watercolour was exhibited and then sold for 50 guineas. Anthony Hobson, *The Art and Life of J. W. Waterhouse R. A. 1849–1917* (London, 1980), p. 179.

[15] Alison Smith, *The Victorian Nude: Sexuality, Morality and Art* (Manchester, 1996), pp. 121–122.

[16] Hilary Morgan, *Burne-Jones, The Pre-Raphaelites and their Century*, 2 vols (London, 1989), I, 116.

[17] *The Oxford Guide to Classical Mythology in the Arts* notes that Burne-Jones's gouache 'The Altar of Hymen' (1874) depicts Pygmalion and the statue embracing with Hymen looking on. It was based on one of his illustrations for Morris's poem.

Plate 1: Edward Burne-Jones, *Pygmalion and the Image – IV, The Soul Attains* (1878)

Plate 2: George Frederic Watts, *The Wife of Pygmalion: A Translation from the Greek* (1868)

So it seems that a Greek painter must have painted women, when Greece had mortal pictures fit to match her imperishable statues. Her shapeliness and state, her sweet majesty and amorous chastity, recall the supreme Venus of Melos (XV, 197).

In Swinburne's eyes, Watts's painting depicts the moment of transformation, where the subject is neither woman nor statue.

Morris's rendering of the story had a direct effect on William Bell Scott, who had previously associated Pygmalion's love for the statue with the obsessive worship of the body in art. His critical work *The British School of Sculpture* (1872) praises Morris's interpretation, calling it 'tender and human'.[18] The sculptor, he says, could 'elevate' the human body to 'perfection' in a god-like fashion: 'We seem to feel, with a sort of mysterious surprise, that the third step will follow, and the image become the thing itself' (*British School*, p. 3). Scott explains that

> one poet after another has essayed the history [of Pygmalion], till Morris has succeeded in clothing it in fitting verse. How beautiful is this description of the finished but as yet unvitalised marble!' (*British School of Sculpture*, p. 3).

Morris's version had shown Scott that Winckelmannian 'worship and adoration of the work of our own hands' was not a transgression: 'we find something like it in the enthusiasm of the critic, in whom learning and the love of art unite with an imaginative temperament'. Scott even cites Winckelmann with approval: 'The statue of the Apollo seems to be animated with the beauty that sprung of old from the hands of Pygmalion' (*British School*, pp. 4–5). Inspired by this, Scott tackles the Pygmalion subject again in *Poems* (1875), producing a sonnet ('Pygmalion') with an accompanying etching (plate 3) depicting the moment of the statue's transformation (*Poems*, p 193). Pygmalion's loyalty to Venus justifies the granting of his prayer for the statue's transformation.

---

[18] William Bell Scott, *The British School of Sculpture*, (London, 1872), p. 3. William Michael Rossetti suggests that Scott was not the publisher's first choice when they commissioned this book: '[Dante] Gabriel [Rossetti] tells me that he lately received a request from Virtues the publishers to write a book on English Sculptors: not having any inclination for such a job, he has referred the publishers to Scott'. *The Diary of William Michael Rossetti 1870–1873*, ed. by Odette Bornand (Oxford, 1977), p. 120.

Plate 3: William Bell Scott, 'Pygmalion' (1875)

> 'Mistress of gods and men! I have been thine
> From boy to man, and many a myrtle rod
> Have I made grow upon thy sacred sod,
> Nor ever have I pass'd thy white shafts nine
> Without some votive offering for the shrine,
> Carv'd beryl or chas'd bloodstone; – aid me now,
> And I will fashion for thy brow
> Heart-breaking priceless things: oh, make her mine.'
>
> Venus inclin'd her ear, and through the Stone
> Forthwith slid warmth like spring through sapling-stems,
> And lo, the eyelid stirr'd, beneath had grown
> The tremulous light of life, and all the hems
> Of her zon'd peplos shook. Upon his breast
> She sank, by two dread gifts at once oppress'd (*Poems*, p. 193).

The sonnet is a highly descriptive glorification of the classical subject: Venus's symbolic myrtle, the 'votive offering', the 'zon'd peplos' create the effect of the classical idyll, and the protagonist's love and devotion to Venus is celebrated. The metamorphosis, like the birth of the new growing-season, is positive. The tone changes, however, with the introduction of two unnamed 'dread gifts' which affect the statue on her transformation. These gifts could be seen as life (including physical and spiritual elements) and love. The statue's role, on her animation, is to love Pygmalion; this can be seen as a kind of oppression or even as awe-inspiring. There is, however, no overt statement of rejection from her. In the light of the attention Scott draws to the question of the spiritual nature of the statue in 1861, and his change of heart in 1872 on account of Morris's version, these gifts could be read as the beautiful body and the human soul: the gifts are dreadful because of the difficulty and seriousness involved in reconciling the two. Whichever way we read these 'two dread gifts', it is evident that Scott's conversion, by Morris, to the spiritualized classicism of the Pygmalion story was complete.

The Pre-Raphaelite sculptor-poet Thomas Woolner pays homage to Pygmalion in his twelve-book poem *Pygmalion* in 1881.[19] Although part of the Pre-Raphaelite group, Woolner is noted for his difference from other Pre-Raphaelite poets. Richard Jenkyns comments that 'Woolner, the only sculptor among the seven founders of the Pre-Raphaelite Brotherhood' shows 'no trace of Medieval influence. Instead he plainly descends from the neoclassical school'.[20] Woolner acknowledges that he saw the Pygmalion story quite differently from his

---

[19] Thomas Woolner, *Pygmalion* (London, 1881).
[20] Richard Jenkyns, *Dignity and Decadence: Victorian Art and the Classical Inheritance* (London, 1991), p. 104.

contemporaries. In a letter to W. E. Gladstone (20 December, 1881) he complains that the subject of Pygmalion has 'not been understood as an artist understands it'; furthermore, his letters suggest that he has 'never yet met with an individual who understood the story'.[21] As the artist-poets William Morris and William Bell Scott, and the artist Edward Burne-Jones, had already interpreted the story, this might constitute a criticism of their work. Woolner's poetic style, described by Coventry Patmore as 'sculpturesque', owes much to neoclassicism.[22] Pygmalion is, for example, 'bound up by those rules of Art / The Wise had found inexorably fixed' (p. 24). Woolner links his own sculpture with poetry, seeing poetry as a fitting substitute for sculpture when he could not get a commission.

> As I can get no chance of doing poetic sculpture it is pleasant that my poetry is so much liked; for one must get the poetry out somehow, or else feel very much disgusted with the world in general (Cox [II], p. 3).

He was particularly pleased with the favourable responses *Pygmalion* received from classical scholars and literary men: 'The very great scholars such as the Master of Trinity, Munro (editor of Lucretius), Aldis Wright, Cardinal Newman, and Mr Gladstone have sent me the most charming letters' (Cox [II], p. 3).

The poem explores the relationship between the artist, his model and the work of art. Furthermore, the poet is concerned with the issue of public opinion in the art world, suggesting that rumours can destroy a good reputation. Pygmalion's reputation is regained in the poem. Woolner's main concern is to retell the myth in a more credible form than had hitherto been seen; he views it as a problem for which he has the solution: 'I shall be anxious to know what you think, and if you think I have solved what seems to be an almost impossible problem, how a statue in marble came in legends to be turned into a live woman!'.[23] This is confirmed by the introduction, in which the narrator says that he or she will

> [...] venture into days remote and old,
> Till I the mystery unfold
> How passion deep, and Aphrodite's aid,
> Resolved to life that wondrous Maid,
> Pygmalion wrought in marble (p. 2).

---

[21] Amy Woolner, *Thomas Woolner. R. A. His Life in Letters* (London, 1917), p. 311. John F. Cox, 'Thomas Woolner's Letters to Mr and Mrs Henry Adams (II)', *Journal of the Pre-Raphaelite and Aesthetic Studies*, 2 (1981), 1–21 (p. 1).

[22] Benedict Read, 'Was There Pre-Raphaelite Sculpture?' in *The Pre-Raphaelite Papers*, ed. by Leslie Parris (London, 1984), pp. 97–110 (p. 98).

[23] John F. Cox, 'Some Letters of Thomas Woolner to Mr and Mrs Henry Adams (I)', *The Journal of Pre-Raphaelite Studies*, 1 (1981), 1–27 (p. 22).

Woolner's solution to the improbability of the statue's metamorphosis is to omit the transformation scene and replace it with a scene in which the sculptor realizes that he is in love with Ianthe, the model for the statue. Benedict Reade and Joanna Barnes suggest a further motive for the change:

> In the matter of the statue coming to life and being married to the sculptor, Woolner evades the issue that could have embarrassed a man who felt so strongly in favour of the Deceased Wife's Sister Act, which Holman Hunt ventured to disregard, that Woolner never spoke to his brother-in-law again.[24]

The Decadent poet Richard le Gallienne notes that in revising the story, Woolner is altering the symbolism of the myth and ignoring its archetypal function. Woolner treats the myth as a text, or as le Gallienne terms it, 'historically':

> Strange to say that the poem which one would naturally expect most really gives us least. The radical artistic flaw of Mr. Woolner's 'Pygmalion' seems to me in treating the story historically instead of as a symbolic myth. Galatea therein appears but as the model of Pygmalion, and Mr. Woolner seeks to explain the old story away by attributing its origin to a playful remark of Pygmalion's, who, bringing Galatea down from his work-room one day after the statue had been finished and admired, said to his mother, 'Behold the statue has found breath, and I am going to take it to wife'. A bystander hearing this took it for a miracle, and the story was speedily running through the town. Hence the legend, says Mr. Woolner. Maybe, but all its significance as a symbol is absolutely lost in so domestic an interpretation.[25]

For Richard le Gallienne the Pygmalion myth as archetype should be synonymous with the Pygmalion myth as text. To change the text is to lose the archetypal nature of the story and its symbolism. The Pre-Raphaelites, however, were concerned with restoring the Pygmalion story as a significant symbol for contemporary literary and aesthetic concerns, and this involved developing the narrative.

The mid-Victorian Pygmalion myth raises an issue which is central both to the Fleshly Controversy and to discussions on Hellenism: the representation of the spiritual in art. In the case of the latter debate the emphasis is on whether the Greek subject can progress beyond the body and include the soul, and whether, in any case, the Greek subject is morally acceptable. With regard to the former, the

---

[24] *Pre-Raphaelite Sculpture. Nature and Imagination in British Sculpture 1848–1914*, ed. by Benedict Reade and Joanna Barnes (London, 1991), p. 10.

[25] *The Poets of the Century*, ed. by Alfred Miles, 10 vols (London, 1879), V, 265–266.

emphasis is on whether the style and subjects chosen by the 'fleshly school' were sensual and paid insufficient attention to morality. The Pygmalion story unites these two debates. Its appeal was such that it even becomes significant for opposing camps. This is unsurprising as both the statue-woman and Pygmalion's attitude to her are polyvalent, and this ambiguity is located at the nexus between fleshly and spiritual. The dual status of the statue as artwork and as living person, as mere body and as ensouled body, connects Victorian classicism with the central concerns of Pre-Raphaelitism.

Chapter 5

Nineteenth-Century Pygmalion Plays: The Context of Shaw's *Pygmalion*

George Bernard Shaw's *Pygmalion* (1912) is the most famous renarration of the myth written in English, and it is unsurprising that critics have often compared the play with Ovid's version. The privileging of Ovid's text, however, has resulted in a lack of in-depth discussion of the connections between Shaw's play and other Pygmalion texts. When placed in the context of Ovid, Shaw's play has been almost universally interpreted as an unusual departure from the "original". Maurice Valency, for example, rejects the Pygmalion context outright on the basis of Shaw's deviation from Ovid: 'The Myth upon which *Pygmalion* is based has, of course, nothing to do with the legend of Pygmalion and Galatea'.[1] H. W. Massingham's contemporary review likewise distances Shaw's Pygmalion from Ovid's, calling the play 'a needless and painful defamation of the legend. The artist of the Greek fable is tenderly disguised as a lover; at his best, Pygmalion-Higgins is merely a diligent watcher of a test tube'.[2] These assertions are to some extent accurate, but they have led to the conclusion that, since Shaw's play is not like Ovid's 'Pygmalion' it is not like any 'Pygmalion', and that therefore the myth is irrelevant. To dismiss the Pygmalion context on this basis is misguided. Shaw's development of the myth comes out of two traditions: the thorough re-working of the Pygmalion myth by Victorian playwrights, especially W. S. Gilbert, and the nineteenth-century fascination for the Cinderella story.

Ovid as a Context for Shaw's *Pygmalion*

Ovid is clearly a problematic context for Shaw. The links between the two are at once both obvious and tenuous: obvious, because they both share the theme of the transformation of a person; tenuous, because Shaw's play does not contain, except metaphorically, any of the key episodes of Ovid's tale. Shaw has no statue, no sculptor, no island, no supernatural vivification, and no marriage between the two protagonists. It is similar only in a broad sense: there is a transformation, a woman is moulded by a man, and is given jewels and finery. The contextualization of the

---

[1] Maurice Valency, *The Cart and the Trumpet: The Plays of George Bernard Shaw* (New York, 1973), p. 319.
[2] *Nation*, 18 April 1914, p. 93, cited in T. F. Evans, *George Bernard Shaw: The Critical Heritage* (London, 1997), p. 228.

play through Ovid has been, with the exception of Timothy Vesonder's article, abandoned by critics.[3]

Vesonder attempts to justify an affinity between Ovid and Shaw on the grounds that Shaw intends Ovid's story to function as an ironic context. His reasons for this affiliation present a number of problems. In the first place, Vesonder argues that Shaw subverts the expectations of the audience by disallowing the marriage of Eliza and Higgins: 'Remembering at least subconsciously that the Pygmalion myth and the Cinderella folk tale end in the marriage of the principal characters, audiences expect Shaw to end his play similarly' (p. 40). This, he says, produced a negative reaction in Shaw's audience: the myths were incomplete. Vesonder then argues that Shaw intended this unsettling effect on the audience. Despite identifying this as intentional Shavian irony, Vesonder argues for a revision of this understanding of the play as ironic. He asserts that Shaw was right to end his play this way on the grounds that marriage is not the defining feature of the myth. In his opinion, these tales are defined by the transformation scene and this is, consequently, the 'controlling mythic idea' of the play:

> The core of the Pygmalion myth and of the Cinderella folk tale is the transformation, not the marriage: while Shaw does not use his sources as a prescription for his plot, he does preserve the fundamental pattern common to both stories. In this sense, he does not invert the myths so much as he retells them (p. 44).

On Vesonder's reading, the audience was right in supposing that Ovid was a context, but misunderstood Ovid by believing (wrongly) that the lack of a marriage element rendered Shaw's story incomplete. Vesonder ignores the problem that results from his argument: that there can be no Shavian irony if Shaw's Pygmalion story is after all (in Ovidian terms) complete. The only way in which both these accounts could be held at the same time is if we agree with the unlikely scenario that Shaw subverted the expectations of the audience, knowing that they would not understand Ovid as a context and supposedly misread it (a case of Shavian double-bluff perhaps?). Vesonder uses the audience's response to determine how the Pygmalion myth should be understood as a context. The negative reaction of the audience is contingent upon its recognizing the play as an unsuccessful version of Ovid's Pygmalion. When Vesonder suggests that Shaw's is a successful (or complete) version of Ovid, he creates a situation in which there are two conflicting contextual relationships: Ovid's text becomes a precedent. Reading the context in two ways is in itself not problematic; it only becomes so

---

[3] Timothy Vesonder, 'Eliza's Choice: Transformation Myth and the Ending of Pygmalion', in *Fabian Feminist: Bernard Shaw and Women*, ed. by Rodelle Weintraub (London, 1977), pp. 39–45.

when Vesonder argues that Shaw intended both (i.e. that his context should be misread to produce irony and that it should be read 'correctly' as non-ironic).

Vesonder's analysis raises the problem of the precise definition of the central features of the Pygmalion story. If Ovid and Shaw are to remain linked, then transformation has to be the story's defining feature. Transformation is the only major element that they share. Yet Shaw's transformation of Eliza is only as a metaphorical version of Ovid's vivification, and is not Shaw's sole theme. Shaw's portrayal of 'Galatea' is more complex than Ovid's, whose characterization of the transformed statue is simplistic. She is unchanging, she never speaks, she is born to love and finding her love immediately requited marries the sculptor. For the main part of the narrative, Galatea remains in an untransformed state. We know very little about her, except that she reacts passively and silently to her metamorphosis, blushes as she receives the kisses of her beloved, and bears him a child nine months later. We can infer from her timidity and blushes, and from Pygmalion's character, that Galatea is likely to be modest; Pygmalion sculpts her in response to his hatred for the fallen women of his island, and so she is a foil to the prostitutes of the story's opening. Nevertheless, her character remains sketchy. The link between Ovid and Shaw can only be made in very general terms, and the contextual connection is strained. Vesonder's account of the similarities between the two versions is noticeably painted with broad strokes. If we are to use Ovid to contextualize Shaw, the nature of the relationship between the two main characters, for instance, has to be sidelined. We cannot explore a connection between Ovid and the education theme, or even the complexities of Shaw's characterization of Eliza, as these have no precedent in Ovid's work. Viewed in this way, Shaw's play contains more to distinguish it from Ovid than to connect it.

On the other hand, when we compare *Pygmalion* with nineteenth-century plays on the same subject, we see that the protagonists' ambiguous relationship, Eliza's educational transformation, and even her characterization, have precedents. Furthermore, when viewed in the light of late nineteenth-century poetry on the subject of Pygmalion, and nineteenth-century plays on the Cinderella theme, we can see a strong precedent for the metamorphosis of the tale into one which expresses anxieties about class. The nineteenth-century context is more relevant than Ovid. Viewed solely in the Ovidian context, Shaw seemingly makes a gigantic leap in characterizing his Galatea as a complex, developing character and in situating her in an ambiguous social position. Furthermore, in keeping his protagonists apart, converting the supernatural transformation of the statue into a metaphoric account of Eliza's education, and making Higgins her teacher, Shaw appears to add new elements to the tale. Seen in the context of the nineteenth century, however, these elements are not innovations. *Pygmalion* is, rather, part of a series of renarrations which addresses and develops all of these key areas.

Shaw's Eliza is a much more complex character than Galatea. She is an innocent and vulnerable teenager who gradually metamorphoses into an independent and self-assured young woman. Her simplicity is characterized by childlike screaming when frightened or confused, and by her self-description: 'I'm a respectable girl', she protests.[4] Yet encoded within these protestations is a virgin-whore paradigm, a suggestion that Eliza has the potential for the opposite of respectability. This paradigm is defined, not by her character, but by the social framework in which she has been placed. As a single working-class woman she is under suspicion of being a prostitute. For example, in Act I, Eliza refers to Freddy Eynsford Hill by his Christian name, though she has never met him. Freddy's mother questions Eliza closely about her relationship to her son:

> THE MOTHER Now tell me how you know that young gentleman's name.
>
> THE FLOWER GIRL I didnt [sic] (p. 207).

Mrs Eynsford Hill is suspicious of Eliza's innocent reply, implying that the girl has accidentally revealed a secret connection between herself and Freddy.

> THE MOTHER I heard you call him by it. Don't [sic] try to deceive me.
>
> THE FLOWER GIRL (*protesting*) Who's trying to deceive you? I called him Freddy or Charlie same as you might yourself if you was talking to a stranger and wished to be pleasant (p. 207).

Eliza, defined by her social position, comes under suspicion on more than one occasion. We see her father sell her to Higgins for five pounds, claiming that this action has been forced on him by his poverty. Although both Eliza and Higgins disregard the transaction, ostensibly Eliza is placed in a situation in which she is bought by Higgins. By contrast, Eliza's character, we are assured, is so innocent that she instinctively recoils from the prospect of a marriage for financial security. In response to Higgins's suggestion that his 'mother could find some chap or other who would do very well' for her as a husband, Eliza says 'We were above that at the corner of Tottenham Court Road [...] I sold flowers. I didn't sell myself' (p. 265). The position that Eliza occupies conflicts with the depiction of her personality. Shaw presents a girl whose innocence protects her from a tainted world, but one whose social situation nevertheless prevents us from seeing her exclusively in this way. We cannot avoid the dual perspective that this conflict generates.

---

[4] George Bernard Shaw, *The Works*, Constable Edition, 33 vols (London, 1930–1938), XIV (1930), 208.

Shaw's appendix to the play draws a parallel between Eliza's transformation through education and the ability of the actress to cross social barriers in life and in the theatre. Just as Eliza plays a duchess, an actress could play a queen:

> Such transfigurations have been achieved by hundreds of resolutely ambitious young women since Nell Gwynne set them the example by playing queens and fascinating kings in the theatre in which she began by selling oranges (pp. 289–290).

At the embassy ball, Eliza is compared to the actress Lily Langtry: 'They tell me there has been nothing like her in London since people stood on their chairs to look at Mrs Langtry'.[5] In likening Eliza to an actress, Shaw highlights several characteristics: her independence as a working woman, her social mobility, her beauty, her ambiguous respectability, and her deception of the public. Like an actress, her role is to deceive her audience as to the reality of her origins. Just as Eliza's characterization as a single working woman makes claims on her innocent status, so does her role as actress. Her development from a simple working-class girl, who does not understand the duality of some of the things that she says, into an actress, whose role is to conceal her identity and replace it with another, on one level involves a loss of innocence: the actress is conscious of her artifice. Eliza must consciously maintain the illusion of her new state if she is to avoid the suspicion of artifice (and lack of innocence) of which she has already been accused by Mrs Eynsford Hill in Act 1. The double-natured Eliza, incorporating the public middle-class self and the private working-class self, has to hide her cockney origins completely in order to achieve her innocent status as a transformed woman. Eliza's audience has to be convinced that her lady-like elegance is not an illusion if they are to keep from seeing her as a self-conscious deceiver.

Shaw's most daring moment is to allow Eliza to contravene the social mores of the society into which she has been promoted, placing her in a situation in which her artifice could be detected. At Mrs Higgins's tea party we are shown the tension between the character that Eliza plays and her true nature, and she is in danger of being exposed as a fraud. Shaw himself was convinced that if Eliza showed any sense that she was playing for laughs in this contentious scene (in which she utters the immortal 'not bloody likely' [p. 253]), the play would be ruined: 'Unless it is said with perfect unconsciousness and sincerity, [it] will wreck the play on the first night'.[6] Eliza must be seen to be an innocent. Later at

---

[5] George Bernard Shaw, *The Bodley Head Bernard Shaw. Collected Plays*, ed. by Dan H. Laurence, 7 vols (London, 1970–1974), IV (1972), 742.

[6] This is taken from a letter to George C. Tyler (who was staging the play in New York) written on October 12th 1914. Alan Dent, *Mrs Patrick Campbell* (London, 1961), p. 263.

the Embassy ball, the true public test of her acting, Eliza relies on her innocence and thus avoids being seen for what she really is – a deceiver. This important scene, though a later addition, was, Shaw says, at 'the root of the play at its inception. But when I got to work I left it to the imagination of the audience, as the theatre could not afford the expense, and it made the play too long. [...] So when the play was screened, I added the omitted scene'.[7] Yet even this display of Eliza's naivety is not left unquestioned. As she explains to a language expert who addresses her in Hungarian that she cannot speak French, her ignorance is ironically taken for artifice: it is assumed that she is concealing aristocratic origins. The tension between Eliza's innocence and her artifice must be seen as a departure from Ovid's uncomplicated portrait of Galatea. Viewed in the context of the nineteenth-century plays, however, Shaw's characterization is not unexpected. W. S. Gilbert also depicts Galatea as a dual-natured character whose innocence could be misconstrued, and is dependent upon the extent to which she is seen to be conscious of the full meaning of her words.

Shaw's Nineteenth-Century Context: The Pygmalion Myth

Gilbert's *Pygmalion and Galatea* (first produced at the Haymarket Theatre, 1871), a highly successful 'mythological comedy', ran at several London theatres until the beginning of the twentieth century, and travelled extensively abroad.[8] Written before his partnership with Arthur Sullivan, it was Gilbert's first major success, marking a significant stage in his development as a playwright. G. E. Terry expresses his surprise at how successful it was: 'The house is full today cant [sic] understand it! must be a craze same as when Mrs Langtry appeared' (p. 30).[9] Generically, the play is unconventional. George Rowell regards it as a curious combination of 'arch Victorian humour with an undertone of genuine passion and despair'.[10] Gilbert's play was widely felt to be doing something new with the classical subject. The difference between it and other mythological comedies of the time was noticed by a reviewer in *The Times* who briefly compares it with Gilbert's other plays:

---

[7] George Bernard Shaw, 'How to Write a Play; An Interview with Hayden Church', *Glasgow Evening Times*, 7 February 1939, cited in *The Cart and the Trumpet*, p. 315.

[8] W. S. Gilbert, *Pygmalion and Galatea: An Entirely Original Mythological Comedy in Three Acts* (London, 1872). Jane Stedman notes that 'by the 1890s it had been played everywhere from Calcutta to St. Petersburg', *W. S. Gilbert: A Classic Victorian and His Theatre* (Oxford, 1996), p. 94.

[9] Russell Jackson, 'The Lyceum in Irving's Absence: G. E. Terry's Letters to Bram Stoker', *Nineteenth Century Theatre Research*, 6 (1978), 25-33, p. 30.

[10] George Rowell, *The Victorian Theatre 1792-1914: A Survey* (Cambridge, 1978), p. 94.

> [He] started with extravaganzas, differing from his many competitors by his temperance in the employment of buffoonery. Soon burlesque in his hands lost nearly all its attributes, and we had in the *Princess* a piece not assignable to any recognized class. [...] In his newest work [*Pygmalion and Galatea*] he assumes a classical tone, considers the antique unities, plunges into the depth of Greek mythology, and aims at a result altogether unique on the modern English stage. In Paris, especially at the Odéon, the public is more or less habituated to mythological comedies, but even these are usually in one act, and occupy a subordinate position in the evening's programme. The very attempt to make the simple myth of the enamoured sculptor and the vivified statue fill three acts shows much audacity on the part of the author (*The Times*, 12 December 1871, p. 4).

While *Pygmalion and Galatea* was running, the Haymarket was managed by John Buckstone. It was a theatre known for its comedies. Buckstone had been a great comic actor, retiring from the stage to manage and to turn his hand to writing plays. In earlier years he had worked with James Robinson Planché at the Haymarket. Harley Granville-Barker points to a connection between Planché's work and Gilbert's first plays.[11] Not only had both worked with Buckstone, but, as Granville-Barker suggests, in terms of comic theatre Gilbert took up where Planché left off. Planché is credited with having been the inventor of the modern burlesque and was the first to use classical mythology as a subject for burlesque.[12] Like all later examples of the genre Planché's burlesques were heavily dependent on ridicule and puns:

> Such mock-classical burlesques earned their laughs simply – with the audience at the minor theatres there was probably no choice. The joke derived from the grandeur of the figure represented – Greek hero or Roman god – and the bathos of his lines and antics. No doubt the acting of such pieces was often as crude as the writing. [...] In these classical burlesques Planché, like his colleagues, relied mainly on putting irreverent sentiments into revered mouths. [...] His audience's taste insisted on punning as a principal source of laughter (Rowell, pp. 67–68).

Burlesque was an extremely popular form of theatre in the mid-nineteenth century, though 'in decline by the time Gilbert began to make his way' (Granville-Barker, p. 120). Broadly, it evolved into two distinct types: high and low. High burlesque

---

[11] Harley Granville-Barker, 'Exit Planché – Enter Gilbert', in *The Eighteen Sixties*, ed. by John Drinkwater (Cambridge, 1932).

[12] William Davenport Adams, *A Book of Burlesques* (London, 1891), p. 44.

involved a trifling subject being elevated through the style of presentation; the, more popular, low burlesque depended on the degradation of a lofty theme.[13] It acted as an outlet for anti-establishment irreverence in a time when legal restrictions dictated that political issues were excluded from the stage (see Rowell, p. 66). An important aspect of the burlesque was its use of song; it was, effectively, an early form of musical. As well as comprising songs and drama, the typical burlesque formed part of a structured evening of entertainment. It 'was the affair of an hour, not more, split into five or six scenes for variety's sake' and 'played through without any interval' (Granville-Barker, p. 138).

The Pygmalion myth existed in burlesque form before Gilbert came to it in the early 1870s. *Pygmalion; or the Statue Fair* (Royal Strand Theatre, 20 April 1867) by William Brough is a Hudibrastic burlesque which mocks the theme rather than travesties a particular text.[14] Brough's classical burlesque was intended to be a visual spectacle and it played alongside other comedies: J. Kenny's *Sweethearts and Wives* ('a popular comedietta in two acts') and F. Hay's *The French Exhibition* ('a new and original farce'). *The Times*, judging the play according to the standard set up by the Strand, suggests that

> *Pygmalion* is most excellent; in almost every line we find a pun, and all the accompaniments of the modern extravaganza abound in it. The dresses of the king Astyages and his court are grotesquely classical; the Grecian key pattern appears in all sizes, and the head-dress of the princess is a masterpiece (20 April 1867, p. 8).

This play is significant in the development of the Pygmalion story in that it is the first time the vivification of the statue is portrayed as a punishment inflicted on Pygmalion by Venus because of the sculptor's dislike of women. This development is picked up later by certain classical dictionaries, and is incorrectly assumed to be part of the original story. Brough's burlesque also initiates a new focus on the development of the character of Galatea, who, despite being unnamed (she is called 'The Statue'), is newly conceived as an innocent in a complex world.

Central to his play is a two-stage animation of the statue. In the first instance the statue is brought to life without a mind. She describes herself as 'a block of stone endowed with human life' (p. 28). In spite of her deficiency, the statue has the power of speech and, in effect, lacks not a mind but knowledge, experience and the ability to love. Though we are told otherwise, it is clear that she has some sort of mental life after her first animation. Like Shaw, Brough highlights the social deficiencies of his statue. She has an appetite for food but not for love. In response to Pygmalion's adoration ('Say but that you've a heart for me will throb'

---

[13] John D. Jump, *Burlesque* (London, 1972).
[14] William Brough, *Pygmalion; Or, the Statue Fair* (London, 1867).

[p. 22]), she displays her ignorance of the lover's discourse: 'Though I've no heart, I feel I've a digestion'. Her innocence is an effective obstacle to love. When Psyche, with a kiss, gives her the ability to love, she is described as having a human mind breathed into her (p. 29). This signals a close connection between love and knowledge. As *The Times* puts it, Psyche 'endows the aforetime only hungry statue with a mind to think and a heart to love' (20 April 1867, p. 8).

Though it has its origins in the burlesque tradition, Gilbert's play was a new direction in classical comedy. Like Brough, Gilbert embellishes the Ovidian tale. He develops it into a vehicle for the central idea that duplicity and the 'lie courteous' are necessary for the smooth running of society. Galatea is an innocent girl who comes to life after Pygmalion has been married for some time. This puts her, like Eliza, in an ambiguous social position, since she has been brought to life with an ardent love for Pygmalion. There is good evidence to suggest that Gilbert knew that his play would be perceived to be daring. He writes in 1870:

> It has become a recognized principle in the unwritten law of criticism that no married man (in an original piece) may be in love with anybody but his wife, and in like manner no single lady may see any charm in a married man.[15]

This is precisely the situation of *Pygmalion and Galatea*. The difficulties of the play largely concern Gilbert's portrayal of the transformed Galatea both as an innocent (she does not understand the implications of protesting her love for Pygmalion) and as a passionate woman. Paradoxically, Galatea's innocent protestations of love are at the same time a portrayal of knowing female sexuality. Gilbert's humour relies on this conflict between the two perspectives. Galatea's overt avowals of love for Pygmalion jar with her characterization as an innocent. For instance, she cannot see the point of monogamy:

> GALATEA   It's a strange world:
> A woman loves her husband very much,
> And cannot brook that I should love him too;
> She fears he will be lonely till she comes,
> And will not let me cheer his loneliness
> (Gilbert, p. 17).

Like Eliza, Galatea is condemned for speaking her mind freely, and not curtailing her speech to suit those around her. When she gives voice to her vanity, Pygmalion says to her 'in thine innocence / Thou sayest things that never should be said' (p. 16). Although she does not herself understand the apparent

---

[15] W. S. Gilbert, 'A Hornpipe in Fetters', *The Era Almanack* (1870), p. 91.

inconsistencies that exist in society, others around her do, and judge her by them.

In order to allow her to appear newborn, Gilbert gives to Galatea just enough vocabulary with which to communicate while giving the impression of naivety and a lack of education. Her innocence and inexperience are seen in her selective vocabulary (rather than, as in the case of Eliza, accent and grammar), and in her knowledge. The selectivity of Galatea's innate knowledge was a point of contention with several contemporary critics, who were irritated by the inconsistencies. Gilbert, however, uses this feature of her character to his own advantage. In allowing Galatea's naive responses to become a vehicle for the revelation of truths, Gilbert creates an ironic situation in which the neophyte can teach. This mirrors the duality seen in the portrayal of her sexuality – the innocent can be passionately in love with a married man. On the one hand she is child-like, lacking an extensive vocabulary, and with an Edenic concept of love; on the other, she can be perceived as experienced, post-lapsarian, knowledgeable, (possibly) artificial, and exhibiting forbidden love.

Shaw was sensitive to the way in which the innocence of Eliza could so easily be shattered by playing her with any sense that she was aware of the offence that she might cause. The actresses playing Gilbert's Galatea likewise emphasized the innocence of their character in performance. By highlighting her statue-like otherworldliness and child-like purity, they could effectively negate any suggestion that Galatea showed any sort of sexual awareness. Eliza is also otherworldly. At the embassy ball 'she walks like a somnambulist in a desert' (*The Bodley Head*, IV, 741). On paper, Galatea exploits the tension between innocence and experience. She has lines which show her to be immodest and brazen, and yet, paradoxically, confirm her innocence. Her character, according to Gilbert, polarizes in order to preserve this tension: 'When Galatea is a statue, she cannot be too statue-like: when she comes to life, she cannot be too womanly'.[16] In performance, however, she was less controversial. By emphasizing Galatea's innocence, actresses defused the obvious problems which this potentially *risqué* play raises.

There seem to be good reasons for treating the performances themselves as further variants on the myth. Firstly, the open-ended, performative, aspects of any play allow its enactments to have a status that is to some extent independent of the text. Secondly, the vast amount of evidence that we have about the way in which Gilbert's play was performed makes it clear that these performances could plausibly count as genuine variants of the myth, tantamount themselves to renarrations. Thus, the productions provide further contexts for Shaw beyond the written text of Gilbert's play. The evidence that we have about Gilbert's play can

---

[16] Pierpont Morgan Library, New York, The Gilbert and Sullivan Collection, MS letter from W. S. Gilbert to Clement Scott, 10 December 1883.

be found in contemporary reviews and letters. As I hope to show, these further contexts are illuminating when compared with Shaw's treatment of the Pygmalion theme.

The first of the serene Galateas was Madge Robertson. Robertson was, on the whole, considered to be 'ethereal and naive' (*The Times*, 12 December 1871, p. 4).[17] *The Graphic* describes her as 'a very incarnation of innocence and beauty' (16 December 1871 [p. 590]). Whilst promoting this image of the role, *The Graphic*, nevertheless, refers to the 'delicate situation' of the leading characters. An explanation that 'much humour and satire is evolved, without the least violation of the poetical spirit of the situation' (p. 590) suggests an awareness that the audience might find the subject matter problematic. The paper reassures us that the scenes in which Galatea confesses her love for the married Pygmalion were 'delivered with an earnestness and an absence of all consciousness of impropriety' (p. 590). If Galatea was more like a work of art than a living woman, then the play could cause little offence; unlike, as *The Times* informs us, the plays of the French:

> The beauty of the situation is beyond question, the author, by his perfectly ideal treatment, avoiding all suspicion of immorality, where a less delicate and poetical writer would have given room for offence. Galatea is not the subject of a possible *liaison*, but merely the embodiment of an artist's devotion to art, and thus Pygmalion's dilemma has nothing in common with those social perplexities which we find in such variety on the stages of Paris (12 December 1871, p. 4).

Marion Terry's interpretation of the role (Haymarket, January 1877) elicited the most varied response (plate 4). Terry performed the role tamely and with 'remarkable purity and virginal charm'.[18] The actress went on to play Mrs Higgins for Shaw, who showed some disagreement with her interpretation of the role of Henry's mother. He writes in a letter to Mrs Patrick Campbell on 29 January 1920 that he is 'most anxious about Marion. She reads the part straight off with perfect

---

[17] Gail Marshall's suggestion that reviews of Robertson's performance 'are scarce' is incorrect (p. 61). Robertson received notices in *The Times* (12 December 1871), *The Graphic* (16 December 1871), *The Graphic* (27 January 1872), *The Athenaeum* (16 December 1871), *The Orchestra* (15 December 1871), and *The Illustrated London News* (16 December 1871). For a discussion of some of these see my 'The Mythographic Context of Shaw's *Pygmalion*', pp. 121–122. Further reviews can be found in the Theatre Museum Library Collection (Haymarket, 1871).

[18] This review comes from a collection of unidentified clippings held in the Theatre Museum Library (hereafter *TML*), Covent Garden, London. In many cases these reviews are not credited to journals, and their origin has proved elusive. As the library arranges its material according to the theatrical venue and date, this information is provided so that the reader can find the reviews easily. The quotation comes from *TML*, Haymarket Theatre, January 1877.

accent and point; but she has not the slightest intention of playing a matron'. In the role of Galatea, Terry was criticized by some for being passionless, and lauded by others for embodying the statuesque qualities needed in order to draw attention away from the play's indelicacies. *The Times* compares her passionless Galatea with the more animate portrayal of Cynisca (Pygmalion's wife) by Henrietta Hodson: 'The human Cynisca stands out in refreshing contrast to the "mythological" Galatea'. *The Athenaeum* confirms that it would be a 'mistake to regard Galatea as endowed with passion' (27 January 1877, p. 127). *The Figaro*, likewise, cannot imagine that the role was meant to be played with more expression:

> And yet it seems not unworthy of discussion whether Miss Marion Terry's less expressive reading of the part does not more accurately carry out the author's intention. Surely the contrast between the natural love of *Cynisca* and the supernatural love of *Galatea* is heightened when there is a something characteristic of a statue in the statue's emotion. Surely it will not be contended that the general affection felt by *Galatea* for him who has given her life is of the same order as the warm, passionate devotion of a woman for her husband. [...] Miss M. Terry, who consistently suggests in the gestures and tones of *Galatea* that she is, as it were in a dream – a spirit accidentally wandering to a world not her own (27 January 1877, p.127).

The Standard, though believing the statue to be not 'quite an earthly being', argues that Galatea is permitted to show emotion and fully realize her womanhood, but that she is only allowed to do so immediately before she changes back into stone.[19] This again avoids impropriety.

Retaining a passionless innocence whilst speaking passionate lines was not universally lauded however. There was one critic for whom Marion Terry's interpretation did not improve the play. Galatea, the reviewer claims, is not a part which should be played by an inexperienced actress. It requires more than mere 'simplicity and girlishness':

> Galatea is not a girl, but a perfected woman. She breathes at the supreme moment of her womanhood, and a soul is given to her shapely form. Unless Galatea is a woman, the comparison to Cynisca hopelessly breaks down, and, as it seems to us, the essence of the poem is diluted. [...] She [Marion Terry] constantly possesses on her face an air of supreme repose and movements and attitudes alike are singularly graceful. But this is only a third of what goes to make up the true Galatea. Where is the flow of her absorbing love for Pygmalion; where

---

[19] *TML, The Standard*, 22 January 1877 (Haymarket, 1877).

Plate 4: Marion Terry as Galatea (1877)

> the intensity of her new nature as she describes with fervour the joy of life or the sorrow occasioned by the sinking of the beautiful day? Alas we look for them in vain [...] We want the full richness of expression; we demand the bitter wail of despair. [...] The sorrow of Galatea must be intense and heartfelt, not merely prettily accentuated and tame. [...] We demand from Galatea, when she does breathe, some heart, some strength, some soul, and some expression.[20]

The reviewer of *The Figaro*, however, sees a major benefit from the characterization of Galatea as tame and statuesque: the neat contrast she provides with the passionate Cynisca. The unidentified review above argues the opposite: that playing Galatea in this manner changed the play beyond recognition.

The question of whether Galatea should be tamed or left to express her womanhood was still an issue in 1883. Miss Mary Anderson's Galatea at the Lyceum, like her predecessor's, concentrated on classical serenity at the expense of womanliness (plate 5):

> Actresses there have been who have given us more than this statuesque posing, who have transformed Galatea into a woman of flesh and blood, animated by womanly love for Pygmalion as the first on whom her eyes alight. Sentiment of this kind, whether intended by the author or not, would scarcely harmonize with the satirical spirit of the play, and the innocent prattle which Miss Anderson gives us in place of it meets sufficiently well the requirements of the case dramatically, leaving the spectator free to derive pleasure from his sense of the beautiful, here so strikingly appealed to, from the occasionally audacious turns of dialogue in relation to social questions, from the disconcerted airs of Pygmalion at the contemplation of his own handiwork, and from the real womanly jealousy of Cynisca (*The Times*, 10 December 1883, p. 7).

The intention was again to play down the daring aspects of the play, with a curtailment of the womanly nature of the transformed statue. The passion of the play, in this production, was emphasized, instead, by the character of Cynisca: 'womanly passion of the true ring happily found expression where it ought to find it, in the character of Cynisca' (*The Times*, 1883, p. 7). The result of playing down the womanly nature of Galatea is that she is upstaged by Cynisca: 'The curious spectacle was thus presented, for which the author is, perhaps, in some degree answerable, of a subordinate character [Cynisca] playing down and effacing the principal one' (*The Times*, 1883, p. 7). By this time, the role of Cynisca was seen as a reasonably challenging part for a young actress. The review of the 1888 production at the Lyceum notes that the play was 'being specifically revived for

---

[20] *TML*, unidentified newspaper clipping, Haymarket, January 1877.

the purpose of enabling this young actress [Miss Julia Neilson] to play the tolerably exacting part of Cynisca' (*The Times*, 22 March 1888, p. 5). Anderson was regarded as a 'disappointment' by *The Athenaeum*; her Galatea was 'inanimate' (15 December 1883, p. 786). Frederick Wedmore, of *The Academy*, compares her interpretation with the, in his opinion, more lively performance given by Madge Robertson (Mrs Kendal):

> The Galatea of Mrs Kendal approaches nearest to humanity as we know it, and it is from that that the Galatea of Miss Anderson is farthest removed. In Mrs Kendal's Galatea, the moment the transformation is effected from the Greek marble to the flesh and blood of all time, every attribute of the woman is pronounced, every feeling fully possessed – it is only the experience that is lacking. But in Miss Anderson's Galatea the transformation from the marble is made and yet not made; the feeling is very undeveloped, and something of the coldness of the statue still clings to the flesh (29 December 1883, p. 441).

The Athenaeum also compares Anderson's interpretation with what it saw as the more lively characterization by Madge Robertson:

> To those [...] who remember the womanliness and the pathos of Mrs Kendal, who endowed the animated statue with a full tide of life, the new rendering seems inanimate. [...] What is most nearly tragic in conception is lost, insomuch as the relapse into marble of a being who has never warmed into perfect life fails to present the idea of extreme cruelty (15 December 1883, p. 786).

Although these notices contradict many of the contemporary reviews of Madge Robertson's performance, they nevertheless illustrate the concern with the interpretation of Galatea's character.

Mary Anderson seems to have been the most serene of the Galateas and bore the most criticism for her interpretation. Despite the general taste for the statuesque, Anderson was criticized for being too cool. Even her make-up and costume were specifically designed to make her look and act like marble after her transformation:

> Miss Anderson and others who have appeared as the statue turned to life (Galatea) have managed to be at least white like marble, but never before has cloth been made to look so stony. Mr Millet gets all the praise, and that is not right, for every woman knows that it was far easier

Plate 5: Mary Anderson as Galatea (1883)

to design the costume which turns Mary into statuary than to realize it in cloth. An exquisite Greek tunic falls over her tall, slender figure in a perfection of graceful drapery and a kind of heaviness suggestive of marble. This curious effect is produced by weighing the fabric with metal at various points, by shirring and staying in just the right spots, and by fastening certain portions of the actress's body with concealed bands. Not only was she a statue when posed as marble on a pedestal, but when moving about the stage every attitude was perfectly statuesque. The costume seemed incapable of being thrown out of artistic and beautiful lines. Her face, neck and arms were whitened; her wig was quite like cut stone, and her feet were in stockings that fitted each separate toe. If she wore anything much underneath this drapery it was not enough to conceal any movement of her limbs. She looked very handsome, though a trifle too bony; and to my mind, the exposure of a portion of her side below the arm was just a little too daring, though the effect was palliated by the semblance of marble![21]

We have good reason to suppose that Gilbert, whose relationship with Anderson seems to have been, at times, strained, was not entirely happy with her performance. According to Anderson's autobiography, *A Few Memories*, she and Gilbert disagreed about her interpretation of the role, over which she had thought she would have more control. Anderson writes of her statuesque interpretation that:

During the rehearsals of [...] [*Pygmalion and Galatea*], I was frequently told that my reading of the character would not be tolerated by the London public. Galatea, the child of Pygmalion's art, a statue come to life, could not, it seemed to me, think, look, stand or speak like an earthly-born maiden; some remnant of the inanimate marble would inevitably linger about her, giving to her movements a plastic grace, and to her thoughts and their expression a touch of the ethereal. Mr. Gilbert did not agree with my conception of the classic meaning of Galatea's character – which seemed to me its strongest and most effective side. [...] painful and embarrassing as it was for me not to be versatile enough to carry out the brilliant author's wish that Galatea should speak certain comic speeches with a visible consciousness of their meaning, I felt convinced that my only hope of success was to stamp every word, look, tone and movement with that ingenuousness which seemed the keynote of her nature.[22]

---

[21] Anon., *The Stage Life of Miss Mary Anderson* (London, 1884), p. 16. The above comments are attributed to 'Clara Belle'.

[22] Mary Anderson, *A Few Memories*, pp. 148–149.

The comic speeches alluded to by Anderson are likely to be the passionate, yet innocent, love scenes in which Galatea displays ignorance of the etiquette required by Victorian society. Gilbert admitted to Clement Scott that there was a 'discrepancy between Miss Anderson's conception of the part and [...] [his] own', though he regarded it as 'artistically – if not dramatically – justifiable'.[23] Furthermore, Moy Thomas, writing to Clement Scott, quotes from a letter of Gilbert's according to which the playwright had said that Galatea 'should be more human than Miss Anderson makes it'.[24] Thomas adds that he did not himself regard Anderson's performance as cold and artificial, but nevertheless agreed with Gilbert's judgement that the part should be played in a more womanly way on the grounds that Gilbert was the author and 'what he intended he *must* know'.

Pygmalion and Galatea was produced ten times in London from 1871 to 1919. It is very likely that Shaw knew of it, or at the very least, his audience did. The play was such a success that it spawned a burlesque or travesty of its own. Henry Pottinger Stephens's *Galatea; or Pygmalion Re-versed*, acts as another variant and commentary on Gilbert's play.[25] This one-act comedy opened at the Gaiety on 26 December 1883 (during the third production of Gilbert's play). The play's title uses a pun to suggest both that the roles of Pygmalion and Galatea have been reversed (i.e. swapped) and that Gilbert's subject has been put into new verse. Stephens's travesty played at the Gaiety under the management of John Hollingshead. It was the intention of the Gaiety Theatre, during the time of Hollingshead's successor, to draw audiences away from Gilbert. We may be seeing the start of this practice in the form of Stephens's burlesque, which would have drawn its audience from those who had seen Gilbert's *Pygmalion and Galatea* at the Lyceum in 1883 or at the Haymarket in 1871 and 1877. George Rowell writes:

> Hollingshead's sacred lamp burnt brightly for the male playgoer, at whom the lavish display of tights by the gaiety chorus was firmly directed, but it is doubtful whether the ladies who made up so large a section of the Savoy audience ventured further east along the Strand to the Gaiety. When George Edwardes became manager of the Gaiety, therefore, he made it his mission to woo the audience whom Gilbert had coaxed into the Savoy. This he achieved by refining the burlesque element and developing the romantic side of the Gaiety's entertainment (Rowell, pp. 143–144).

---

[23] Pierpont Morgan Library, MS letter from W. S. Gilbert to Clement Scott, 10 December 1883.

[24] Letter from Moy Thomas to Clement Scott, 11 December 1883 (Copy in *TML*, Lyceum, 1883).

[25] Henry Pottinger Stephens and W. Webster, *Galatea; or Pygmalion Re-versed* (London, 1883).

The tights were a draw for Stephens's play, but they were not on the statue. Here, the statue is male and called Pygmalion. Pygmalion is an innocent who bears a close resemblance to Gilbert's Galatea: he is beautiful, oblivious to his vanity, has a restricted vocabulary and has to undergo a learning process (though here considerably truncated). Whilst Stephens retains the major elements of the situation, the switch in gender changes the focus to the topic of the working woman. Galatea, now a sculptor married to Cyniscos, is shown to be fickle in her choice of occupation and neglectful of her husband. Her views are modern: she argues that contemporary gentlemen are out of date in not taking her work seriously; yet ultimately this New Woman is tamed. The burlesque noticeably avoids the whole question of double-edged innocence. Pygmalion neither openly states that nor acts as if he returns the love that the leading women have for him (Galatea, Daphne and Myrine). He sees them, rather, as pleasant company. Pygmalion decides that he would not want to support a woman financially:

> Such pleasant girls – so frolicsome, so jiggy!
> They didn't *bore* me, and they called me 'Piggy!'
> Piggy, indeed! I don't know what they meant;
> I'm not the pig that means to pay their rent (p. 20).

Though he is regarded as a rival lover by their menfolk, Pygmalion is not romantically interested in his creator. Stephens's play is a further case of the suppression of the tensions that exist in Gilbert's play.

Gilbert's reviews and Stephens's burlesque highlight just how problematic the tension between Galatea's innocent character and her not-so-innocent situation was. Like Eliza, the statue's character was in danger of being misconstrued. By emphasizing the innocence and otherworldliness of Galatea, actresses played down the indelicate side of the play; as a result, Galatea was transformed from the womanly character we see on the page to a walking work of art on the stage. The playing-down of the sexuality of Galatea is read by Gail Marshall, nevertheless, as an instance of the 'Galatea-aesthetic' (p. 61). For her, Galatea is a 'highly charged icon of sexual desirability' (p. 4) who manages to realize 'self-conscious female sexuality on stage' (p. 61). I argue on the other hand, that this sexuality is dampened by the statue-simulation – a situation which troubles Gilbert, and on which many contemporary critics comment. In some responses to the play these changes altered the physical realism of Galatea's situation, as she is no longer a passionate character. For others, the play became more palatable to the audience.

Higgins's role as Eliza's teacher, and his enigmatic relationship with her, also have precedents in the nineteenth-century Pygmalion plays. Higgins, like Eliza has an ambiguous innocence. When Pickering asks him: 'Are you a man of good character where women are concerned?' (p. 229), Higgins ironically employs a Pygmalion-like metaphor: 'They might as well be blocks of wood' (p. 230).

Again, in this statement is the seed of its opposite: Pygmalion's block was transformed into a lover. Furthermore, Higgins's bad manners, swearing, bachelor status, and unconventional domestic arrangements, in placing Eliza under his protection, all mark him out to be someone who does as he likes. This unconventionality can be seen both as a kind of innocence (in that he is, for example, as unaware as Eliza is that he swears) and as a lack of restraint. Gilbert's Pygmalion likewise occupies an ambiguous position. Though he is clearly attracted to Galatea, and is temporarily punished with blindness for his interest in her, it is left unclear as to whether he has fallen in love with her. He tells her to regard him as a father-figure rather than a lover, but betrays his love for her on more than one occasion. Despite the ambiguities, Pygmalion posed less of a problem for critics, though some of them commented on the unpleasantness of his character. One review calls him: 'a selfish and cruel egotist who ruins the life of the being he has created' and asserts that 'Pygmalion treats poor Galatea very shabbily indeed'.[26] Higgins also has his unappealing side. He seems relatively unconcerned about what is to happen to Eliza after the experiment and does not consider the emotional impact that this metamorphosis will have on her.

Gilbert's Pygmalion, like Higgins, takes the role of the statue's teacher by improving her vocabulary and manners, and helping her to understand the complexities of society. Galatea is in need of education in all of the Victorian plays, though the learning process is handled in slightly different ways. Gilbert, like Shaw, explores the issue of how a woman should behave: for Gilbert she should be the 'angel in the house'; for Shaw she should be independent. Gilbert's ultimate goal is to use Galatea to teach Pygmalion's wife to have mercy on her husband and revoke her curse. As a pupil, Galatea eventually comes to understand that she must put right the chaos she has caused and change back into stone.[27] Despite the tensions, Gilbert, like Shaw, ultimately keeps his pupil-teacher relationship professional: the barrier to the union of the protagonists presents itself in the form of Pygmalion's wife. In *Pygmalion*, the reason for the platonic relationship of Higgins and Eliza is ambiguous. Despite clear statements from Shaw that his protagonists are not in love ('I am determined not to allow Higgins to be represented as the lover of Eliza'; 'I absolutely forbid [...] any suggestion that the middle-aged bully and the girl of eighteen are lovers.'), audiences and actors have supposed otherwise.[28] Herbert Tree's Higgins famously threw flowers

---

[26] *TML*, Haymarket, 1877.

[27] In A. J. Talbot's play, the innocent transformed statue, Galatea, also causes problems for her 'Pygmalion', known here as Percival Houghton, who has already pledged his affection to another woman. As in Gilbert's play, Galatea returns to her statue state. A. J. Talbot, *The Passing of Galatea. A Fantasy in One Act* (London, 1930).

[28] George Bernard Shaw, *Collected Letters 1926–1950*, ed. by Dan H. Laurence, 4 vols (London, 1965–1988), IV (1988), 447 and 815.

at Mrs Patrick Campbell's Eliza before the final curtain, implying that their characters were in love.²⁹ Shaw, who was furious with Tree for this, affirms that:

> It does not follow in the least that Eliza and Higgins were sexually insensible to one another, or that their sensibility took the form of repugnance, or that her combination of hatred and rebellion with dog-like fidelity was exactly what it would have been had her instructor been a woman, but the fact stands that their marriage would have been a revolting tragedy; and that the marriage with Freddy is the natural and happy ending to the story.³⁰

The confusion arises from the conflicting signals Shaw gives in the play. Setting aside the Pygmalion context (which I shall come back to later), Shaw raises the expectation of a different ending by questioning Higgins's honourable nature and Eliza's innocence; this creates a frisson between the two characters. Pygmalion-like, Higgins provides for Eliza's material needs, and teaches her to become his social equal, leading us to expect a love-relationship.

Higgins does not, however, regard women as property, as his disregard for Alfred Doolittle's sale of his daughter shows. Both Gilbert and Brough highlight this ownership issue. Gilbert's statue represents woman as a property that can be bought and sold, and married off. She is almost given to the art-patron, Chrysos. Chrysos's wife is horrified by the social chaos that would be caused if all wives could be made from marble. She says of her husband's art collection: 'They're bad enough in marble — but in flesh!!! / I'll sell the bold-faced hussies one and all' (p. 36). She is horrified by the competition, rather than the slavery or prostitution, that this would cause. Galatea even refers to herself as being owned by Pygmalion: 'I am made *by* thee *for* thee [...] I've no will that is not wholly thine / [...] I've no thought, no hope, no enterprise / That does not own thee as its sovereign' (p. 57). This does not seem to be a concept that Pygmalion rejects of itself, but rather one which his circumstances (as a married man) force him to shun. When Brough's statue is brought to life, money is immediately an issue. She is 'made for sale by the Sculptor, but really *soul'd* by Psyche'. This statue also regards herself as owned by Pygmalion and expects him to take financial responsibility for her. Higgins, however, separates ownership and love. He prefers Eliza to be emotionally independent of him even though he supports her financially.

Although Higgins and Eliza are separated by class, Shaw settles on personality as a barrier between his protagonists: they are unsuited in temperament and age. Shaw's inclusion of a social barrier is reminiscent of the Victorian plays; these,

---

[29] Michael Holroyd, *Bernard Shaw: The One Volume Definitive Edition* (London, 1997), p. 444.

[30] Laurence, IV, 311.

however, depict Galatea as socially clumsy, but not inferior in rank. The use of a class barrier draws, instead, on the Cinderella story, which stresses the heroine's social inferiority.[31] Furthermore, this element is also suggestive of a new late-nineteenth-century element in the poetic interpretation of the Pygmalion myth seen in the poetry of A. J. Munby, Thomas Sturge Moore and William E. Hurrell.

Munby restyles Galatea as a servant in his poem *Susan* (1893). Like Shaw, Munby frequently explored class issues.[32] *Susan* is based on the poet's unusual domestic arrangements. His fascination with Victorian women servants, and the contradictions which their lives posed for preconceptions about the abilities of women to do physical work, crossed over into his private life. Munby had a secret relationship with his servant, Hannah Cullwick, for eighteen years and later married her. Hannah continued her domestic work after their marriage, and Munby's diaries reveal his obsessive interest in her physical labour. His poem identifies the Pygmalion story with that of Cinderella, and suggests, moreover, that working women are the most noble and most feminine examples of the sex. Arundel, the gentleman-narrator, marries Susan, a 'maiden of the poor' (p. 9) who prefers to remain in her station after the wedding: '"Wife or no wife, / I are the master's servant, all my life"', she says (p. 12). Susan is devoid of ambition to rise up the social ranks. She resolves

> to be the servant still,
> And not the equal, of the man whose will
> Had long become her own will, and whose love,
> Pure as herself, had raised them both above
> The very notion of equality (p. 17).

Instead of threatening the gentility of the angel in the house, the working woman's domesticity is here represented as an ideal of 'virtue' (p. 16). She is a 'fair Cinderella' (p. 36), an Eliza Doolittle who can pass for a lady when dressed in genteel clothes; but, at the same time, she knows her place. When Susan is 'in her own guise', she is 'a simple country maid' (p. 36). Arundel worships his wife because of this ambiguity: 'she was so low / And yet so lofty' (p. 17). He appreciates her genteel beauty yet has a 'passion for the labourer in her' (p. 46). For the sake of form, Arundel attempts 'to make a lady of her' (p. 47) so that the people of his own class could understand and appreciate her qualities; Susan, however, prefers 'her own home – underground!' (p. 47), and the enterprise is abandoned.

---

[31] See Charles A. Berst, *Pygmalion: Shaw's Spin on Myth and Cinderella* (New York, 1995).

[32] A. J. Munby, *Susan* (London, 1893).

> Perhaps this Susan was of such a kind;
> A woman form'd and fashion'd to his mind
> By him, the new Pygmalion – but who wrought
> Unwisely at the model of his thought;
> For the rough marble, so constrain'd to live,
> Refused that polish he had wish'd to give? (*Susan*, p. 44).

Munby's Pygmalion rejects society's understanding of the role of a gentlewoman in favour of his own ideal. For Arundel, Susan's rank does not distract from her appeal and Munby abandons the exercise in social improvement, arriving at the same conclusion as Higgins, that class is merely a veneer.

Although Higgins does not work for a living, it is everywhere implied that he has undergone many years of hard study. His moulding of Eliza takes considerable skill and many weeks of repetitive work. Higgins is dismayed that Eliza could assume that she could teach phonetics merely on the basis of having received his elocution lessons. While the skill comes easily to the classical artist of the nineteenth-century plays and is not dwelt upon, Pygmalion's creative process is, at the turn of the century, considered in much more detail. Thomas Sturge Moore's 'Pygmalion' (1892) and William E. Hurrell's 'Pygmalion; Or the Worker and his Work' (1898) contemplate the physicality of Pygmalion's exertion with an enthusiasm also seen in the arts and crafts movement of the latter part of the century.

Moore, a poet, wood-engraver, and critic, was the older brother of the Cambridge philosopher G. E. Moore. His poetry depends on 'mythological subject matter, moralistic impulse, and traditional poetic diction'.[33] Moore had much contact with the Decadents during their heyday. While studying art he shared a house with Charles Hazlewood Shannon and Charles Ricketts in a small road of artistic residents in Chelsea, and his early career was influenced by the Pre-Raphaelites. He came to believe in a doctrine in which they had some interest: *ut pictura poesis*, or as the picture is, so is the poem. He helped to stage the first production of Oscar Wilde's *Salomé* in 1906, and wrote an opening scene to Wilde's unfinished play, *A Florentine Tragedy*, in the style of Wilde, in order that it could be performed. Moore's poetry, however, is not usually categorized as decadent, and even during his lifetime there was some confusion as to how it ought to be understood. Edward Marsh, the editor of *Georgian Poetry*, includes some of his poems in the first volume of his series, as does Martin Secker in his anthology, *The Eighteen-Nineties*.[34]

---

[33] Frederick Landis Gwynn, *Sturge Moore and the Life of Art* (Kansas, 1952), p. 1.
[34] Martin Secker, *The Eighteen-Nineties. A Period Anthology in Prose and Verse* (London, 1948), pp. 436–438.

> The literary historians of the nineteenth and twentieth centuries have given scant attention to Sturge Moore's work as a whole. When his name does occur in the surveys, it flashes sporadically as that of a latter-day Pre-Raphaelite, a Bridgean traditionalist, a trans-channel cousin of the symbolists, or simply an artistic unicorn (Gwynn, p. 81).

Moore's place in the literary movements of the turn of the century is hard to pin down, as his career is made up of different phases. His Pygmalion poem belongs to a period of dalliance with 'the spiritual impulses and diverse manifestations of Dandyism' (Gwynn, p. 84). It is one of Moore's earlier works, and was first published in *The Dial* (edited by Ricketts and Shannon).

> To work at sunrise nor till sunset rest,
> Week's end spliced in week's end: 'twas thus he wrought;
> And I have often seen him in my thought
> With eager bare arms leant across her breast
> To chisel chin or cheek, while, where they pressed,
> His labour's sweat made bright the marble bust.
> Till lo! she stands amid the work-shop dust
> In proudest pose of loveliness undressed.
> His work once stayed, he, weakened by long strife,
> Falls like a swathe from summer-heat's keen scythe:
> So sees he, waking at the day's decease, –
> Not the sea-mothered Mother of all life,
> Then vanished – but, alone, alive, he sees
> A naked woman quailing at the knees.[35]

Pygmalion's 'labour's sweat' glistens on the statue, and he works so hard that each week runs into the next. On finishing his sculpture Pygmalion faints from exhaustion. His loss of consciousness reveals a connection with the Pygmalion of the post-romantics. The quailing woman Pygmalion has created contrasts with the image of the powerful goddess. 'Aphrodite, in all her sensual manifestations, is never long absent from [Moore's] poetry' (Gwynn, p. 77). Moore's emphasis on work is reinforced by the nautical (splicing) and farming images. Here Pygmalion is a hard-working sculptor of a statue of Aphrodite which happens to come to life when he faints through overwork. No indication is given that Pygmalion wants the statue to be brought to life, or that the she is an embodiment of his ideal. She is sculpted in the image of Venus as Mother (creator), rather than as lover. Moore introduces a striking new element to the story, an element which twentieth century writers are keen to explore: pathos. The final scene of his newly transformed statue-woman naked and 'quailing at the knees' is unexpected and poignant.

---

[35] Thomas Sturge Moore, *The Vinedresser and Other Poems* (London, 1899), p. 56.

Shaw's Eliza likewise displays this uncertainty about what she is to do after her transformation.

William E. Hurrell's 'Pygmalion; Or the Worker and his Work' (1898) also characterizes Pygmalion as a sculptor-worker. Hurrell's Pygmalion dedicates himself to producing perfection.[36] In the preface, Hurrell explains his interpretation of the myth: the reader should understand that 'by the force of his Idealistic passion', Pygmalion became a 'demi-god, – a master workman affiliated to the gods themselves' (Hurrell, p. i). Pygmalion, the artisan, is an old 'workman in a smock' (p. 13). Some time after Galatea has come to life Pygmalion rediscovers a discarded statue of a limbless male torso. The torso grows limbs and turns into an old man. Pygmalion suffers 'pain when Work and Worker meet' (p. 19). The old man (called by his creator a 'horrible abortion' [p. 14]) echoes Frankenstein's monster, crying out in resentment '"Why hast thou made me thus?"' (p. 18). Before smashing 'the thing to tiny particles' (p. 18), Pygmalion responds:

> 'Must there then ever be
> Perpetual war betwixt creator and
> The work he, misconceiving, executes?' (Hurrell, p. 18).

Those who 'fall short of that perfection they desire' and those 'who feel themselves misshaped' (p. 19) are shown as afflicted and undeserving of life. Hurrell addresses problem of the idealist who has realized his ideal (in the form Galatea), and has gone on to fail in future projects. Higgins's experiment with Eliza, is likewise seen as the pinnacle of his career. Hurrell stresses that his tale is to be read as a parable instructing that human nature should be passionate about physical perfection. His conception of God and the artist as craftsmen-workers has Masonic overtones. His smock-wearing Pygmalion is an allegory for God (as craftsman) and he explores the Creator's difficult relationship with his creature.

Shaw's Nineteenth-Century Context: Cinderella-Pygmalion

Part of Vesonder's argument concerning the theatrical precedents for Shaw's *Pygmalion* centres on the Cinderella story. The confusion over Shaw's ending, he suggests, partly results from the multiplication of mythical allusions at this point – that is, the combination of Cinderella and Pygmalion. The Cinderella and Pygmalion stories both involve the transformation of the heroine and the marriage of the protagonists: 'Just as the poor and mistreated Cinderella becomes a princess through the intervention of her Fairy Godmother, Shaw's flower girl is elevated

---

[36] William E. Hurrell, *The Passionate Painter and Other Verse* (London, 1918).

briefly into the aristocracy and permanently into the middle class' (Vesonder, p. 40). Maurice Valency and Martin Meisel explore the nineteenth-century theatrical antecedents of Shaw's *Pygmalion* through variations on the Cinderella theme.[37] Meisel argues that although Shaw's play is dependent on a union between the Pygmalion and Cinderella stories, the playwright 'relies so heavily on its [the Cinderella-Pygmalion theme's] fundamental appeal throughout *Pygmalion* that his refusal to end with a match between Higgins and Eliza was considered mere perversity' (Meisel, pp. 176–177). It is clear from the contemporary reviews that the ending was indeed felt to be inappropriate. The *Westminster Gazette* notes that the closing scenes were 'very puzzling to an audience trying desperately to make out to what it is leading'.[38] The reviewer suggests, furthermore, that we are 'cheated at the end!' and that Shaw's ascription of his play the genre of '"romance" obviously is a joke' (p. 224). Although it is certain that audiences experienced confusion at the end of the play, it is unlikely that it is the amalgamation of the two stories that causes this. The tales are consistent on the marriage point: Cinderella, Galatea and Eliza do not marry the agent who actually brings about their transformation. Rather, the confusion stems from the insufficient distinction between the Pygmalion love role and the central transformatory role of Venus.

Ovid's myth presents man as an unsuccessful transformer of the raw materials, and the goddess as the successful transformer. Pygmalion can create beauty, but he cannot create life; Pygmalion, the sculptor, moulds the heroine, but he does not have the power to cause the central transformation of the tale. The removal of the central magical agent leaves Shaw with a gap in his renarration. The nineteenth-century Pygmalion plays retain the supernatural character, thus keeping the two transformatory roles separate. Their Pygmalions are not responsible for the central metamorphosis: the vivification. Shaw creates a difficulty in making Pygmalion responsible for the main transformation of the play.

Similarly, Cinderella's supernatural Fairy Godmother is the sole agent responsible for her transformation. Shaw follows Cinderella in this respect. Higgins is the only pertinent transformer (if we discount Colonel Pickering's occasional assistance), and he performs the central transformation of the Cinderella tale: 'It is a story of a poor girl who meets a gentleman at a church

---

[37] Valency, pp. 315–319, Martin Meisel, *Shaw and the Nineteenth Century Theater* (London, 1963), pp. 411–412. Charles A. Berst also argues that *Pygmalion* is an 'updated combination' of Cinderella and Ovid's *Pygmalion* (p. 14).

[38] Unsigned notice (initialed E. F. S.), *Westminster Gazette*, 43 (14 April 1914), p. 3. Cited in *George Bernard Shaw The Critical Heritage*, ed by T. F. Evans (London, 1976), pp. 223–225 (p. 224).

door, and is transformed by him, like Cinderella, into a beautiful lady'.[39] Higgins takes Eliza out of the gutter in the same way that Cinderella is rescued from her life of drudgery. Though we might not think of Higgins as a Fairy-Godmother-Venus character, it cannot be denied that his transformatory powers make the ensuing relationship between Eliza and Freddy possible. Yet if we see Higgins in this way, then the lack of love-interest between him and Eliza should not come as a surprise. The difficulty arises from the features of his character which mark him out as a Pygmalion figure: his solitary life, his gender, the nature of his skill, his gifts to Eliza, and, furthermore, specifically in the nineteenth-century context, his role as an educator and his interest in Galatea's social deficiencies. If Higgins is a Pygmalion figure, then we expect a love interest. The problem is, then, that Pygmalion is not the Fairy Godmother. Recasting the central transformation as Higgins's responsibility forces him to function as a Venus or the Fairy Godmother type, while his character suggests that he is a plausible Pygmalion-like husband. If, however, we are prepared to see Higgins as the successful transformer of the Pygmalion story (i.e. like Venus, rather than like Pygmalion), then there is no difficulty with regard to love-interest. The problem lies not with the conflation of the two tales, but with the amplification of the role of Pygmalion into that of Venus, or as Shaw implies, the Fairy Godmother.

A similar amplification occurs in George du Maurier's novel *Trilby*. Here Svengali, turns tone-deaf Trilby, whom he marries, into a singer through mesmerism. *Trilby*, like Shaw's *Pygmalion*, expands the role of Pygmalion (as secondary transformer) into that of the primary transformer. In this case, Svengali's use of mesmerism gives him a mystical and quasi-supernatural side too. The devil-like mesmerist possesses Trilby's soul in way that contrasts with the simpler more natural love that Billee has for her. The love interest between Svengali and Trilby, as a marriage of natural and supernatural, is shown in a sinister light. Svengali's role, however, is fundamentally that of an educator; like Higgins, he teaches the heroine. Trilby is ultimately punished for succumbing to Svengali's potency. The rights for the stage version of *Trilby* (adapted by Paul Potter in 1895) were bought by Herbert Beerbohm Tree, who went on to play Higgins for Shaw. It is likely that Shaw's audience may have remembered Tree in the role of Svengali, one of the parts for which he was renowned, and that this, too, may have effected the audience's perception of Higgins. Tree, known for altering his roles, greatly enhanced the role of the Svengali, and, as he went on to do in *Pygmalion*, made free with the ending. He concluded Potter's play at the curtain of the third act when Svengali, the villain of the piece, dies from a heart attack and Trilby falls into the arms of Billee, who loves her. Tree leaves the

---

[39] Shaw cited in Archibald Henderson, *George Bernard Shaw: Man of the Century* (New York, 1956), p. 616.

audience with a sense of hope, rather than ending with Potter's sketch of Trilby's possibly-fatal brain-fever. The expectation of a marriage between Higgins and Eliza may arise from the influence of *Trilby*, whether through Tree's production or du Maurier's novel.

When Shaw came to adapt the Cinderella theme, as Valency notes, there were countless stage versions of it, some of which he may have drawn on: 'The fable offered an excellent basis for plays of *déclassement*', and the class issue was extremely popular in the romantic comedies of the nineteenth century' (p. 315). Like Shaw's *Pygmalion*, these romances eschew the marriage of the main transforming agent and the heroine. *Déclassement* characterizes the Cinderella tale, but it is not, until the late nineteenth century, a feature of the Pygmalion myth. Shaw is the first playwright to add the theme to the Pygmalion narrative and thereby integrate Cinderella with Pygmalion. Many mid-century plays employ Shaw's Pygmalion themes (such as the education of a young woman), although none of these plays explicitly identify their subject with the Pygmalion tradition.

Perhaps the closest of the Cinderella romances to Shaw's *Pygmalion* is Dion Boucicault's *Grimaldi; or the Life of an Actress* (1855).[40] *Grimaldi* is a *Trilby*-like melodrama in which Violet, an orphaned Covent Garden flower-seller, is put on the stage by an obsequious poverty-stricken impresario, who later turns out to be a French-speaking Italian duke. Grimaldi adopts her, teaching her French and acting; Pygmalion-like, Grimaldi 'polishes' Violet's social veneer (p. 14). She quickly receives several proposals of marriage, but is a Galatea-like innocent and knows nothing of love: 'Love – love! I have read of it, papa has shown me how to act it, but I don't know what it is' (p. 13). Shaw's depiction of Eliza's innocence is extremely resonant in this context. Grimaldi stresses that Violet, despite being an actress, is ingenuous. He says to Lord Arthur:

> GRIMALDI I give you in trust de only fortunes she possess – her innocence. It is all to her, it gives freshness to her voice; grace to every limb; it covers her like a charmed robe; it shall be de secret of her success. De publique shall say 'She is not great artiste – She has not force – but – but, she has something dat touch us dere in de heart – we cannot tell. Eh, bien! it is her innocence' (p. 17).

Violet is a runaway success and men are even seen wearing violet trousers in homage to her. The play ends with the heroine's rescue, having been kidnapped and drugged by the evil Maltravers. Violet's virtue is saved in the nick of time by Grimaldi and by Lord Arthur, who is shot by the villain. Arthur disappears from society to recover, and is assumed to be keeping Violet as a mistress. Violet, who

---

[40] Dion Boucicault, *Grimaldi; Or The Life of An Actress. A Drama, in Five Acts* in Dion Boucicault, *35 Plays*, Popular Nineteenth Century Drama on Microfilm (Canterbury, 1982).

has secretly married Lord Arthur, risks her reputation in order to hide the marriage from his family, whom she expects will disapprove. Lord Arthur reveals to his mother, the Countess, that rather than wound her 'pride, this weeping angel [Violet] consented to a disgraceful secrecy' (p. 34). Grimaldi confesses to his identity as the Duc de Saint Elmo, who was in love with the very same Countess thirty years ago, and she recognizes him. It is revealed that, as his adopted daughter, Violet is heir to Grimaldi's title and is therefore a fitting wife to Lord Arthur. *Grimaldi* is true to the Cinderella-Pygmalion theme in that the transformer (Grimaldi) does not marry his protégé.

Shaw may indeed have been indicating a connection with Boucicault's play in showing Eliza sell violets in Covent Garden. There are other points of similarity. The relationship between Higgins and Eliza is, likewise, that of father and daughter, teacher and pupil. *Grimaldi* ends with an important verification scene, reminiscent of the Ambassador's party in *Pygmalion*. When the transformation is a gradual process (as in Shaw's *Pygmalion*) rather than instantaneous (as in Cinderella and Pygmalion), a scene of this type is often used as confirmation that the metamorphosis is complete. Violet's transformation into an acceptable wife is established at an aristocratic garden fête. Violet is also shown to be a moral woman (having married Lord Arthur and refusing to accept money to marry someone else); furthermore, she enjoys adopted aristocratic status (through Grimaldi), and becomes a fashionable lady who has been presented to the Queen. She acquits herself admirably and with modesty when she is called upon to describe her audience with the Queen. This verification scene acts as a climax in plays of this type, and in the case of *Pygmalion*, is the goal towards which Higgins and Eliza work. Shaw is aware of the tradition of including such a scene, calling it 'obligatory'.[41] The scene also features in Thomas and John Maddison Morton's *All that Glitters is not Gold* (1851), where Martha Gibbs, the mill-worker, conducts herself appropriately at a ball, and in Tom Taylor's *An Unequal Match* (1857), where Hester Grazebrook impresses a Grand Duke.

T. W. Robertson likewise makes Cinderella an heiress in *School* (1869).[42] Robertson frequently treats class themes: *Society* (1865) is a satire which contrasts the *nouveaux riches* with the well-born poor, *Caste* (1867) is a social comedy about breaking class barriers, and *Birth* (1870) treats the theme of changing social structures. *School* is conspicuously on the Cinderella theme. Bella, an orphaned pupil-teacher reads the story of Cinderella to her pupils. Her prince is Lord Arthur Beaufoy, who wishes to marry a clever woman, 'not a regulation doll of the same pattern as the other dolls – the same absence of thought, the same simper, same stupid dove-like look out of the eyes' (p. 245). Like Pygmalion, he expresses a

---

[41] Cited in Meisel, p. 172.
[42] T. W. Robertson, *Six Plays*, ed. by Michael R. Booth (Ashover, Derbyshire, 1980).

distaste for marriage. When Bella is seen leaving her shoe behind, having been frightened by a startled cow, Beaufoy claims the shoe and falls in love with its owner. Though clever, Bella's simplicity is also emphasized. She is intercepted by Beaufoy in the grounds of the school when on an errand to fetch a jug of milk and is also seen shelling peas. The other school-girls catch Lord Beaufoy with his arm around Bella's waist and denounce her. She is dismissed from the school and, as in Boucicault's *Grimaldi*, it is assumed that she has become the lord's mistress. Bella is revealed to be the granddaughter of Lord Faringtosh, Beaufoy's uncle, and the play ends with Lord Beaufoy presenting Bella, as his wife, to the school. The girls take up the story of Cinderella again and compare it with Bella's situation. Faringtosh is declared the 'godmother' (p. 282) and Lord Beaufoy presents his wife with a pair of glass slippers.

Like the Pygmalion myth, the Cinderella tale depends on the double-nature of its heroine: Cinderella is poor but appears to be rich at the Prince's ball. She is, like Eliza, perceived by some to be insignificant, by others to be worthy of admiration. The Cinderella romances take this further, implying a moral ambivalence in the heroine's character. The double perspective of Cinderella's character is a component of Edward Bulwer Lytton's *Money* (1840), another possible precedent for Shaw (the double-natured heroine is also part of *Grimaldi*, *School*, *Pygmalion* and *Pygmalion and Galatea*).[43] In *Money*, the poor but well-connected Alfred Evelyn secures a legacy from a relative who suggests that, as heir, he has a moral obligation to marry either his penniless cousin Clara Douglas, whom he loves, or his worldlier cousin Georgina Vesey, who has £10,000. Evelyn wishes to marry the woman who cares for him the most and for whom he has the highest esteem. Before inheriting, he importunes Georgina for a charitable donation to his former nurse; the money is given anonymously, and he thinks, because Georgina is the only person who knows where to send it, that the act of charity is hers, but hopes that it is Clara's. He sets his heart on marrying the woman who claims the charitable act. Georgina's money-grabbing father, Sir John, tells Evelyn that his daughter has sent the money, and they become engaged. Clara, who loves Evelyn, is mortified. To confirm his assessment of Georgina's character, however, Evelyn pretends that he has lost all his money and it quickly becomes clear that Georgina no longer wants to marry him. Clara, to whom Evelyn has secretly given £20,000, sends £10,000 to Evelyn to clear his supposed debts, implying that the money has come from the nurse's anonymous benefactress. Georgina accidentally reveals she has not sent the money, and Evelyn and Clara are reconciled.

Bulwer's play contains Cinderella-like transformations which largely concern circumstance. Clara is impoverished but not socially inferior to Evelyn. Her

---

[43] Edward Bulwer Lytton, *Money* (London, 1840).

situation is altered by the money she is given. Evelyn, however, perceives her to be more worldly and materialistic than she is; furthermore, her innocence is misconstrued by him. The acquisitive Georgina, on the other hand, is thought to be modest and generous, but is neither. Clara passes both of the tests, by willingly donating her money, and good eventually triumphs. Evelyn's image of Clara is transformed even though her real nature remains constant, and it is Clara who manages to transform his opinion of her. Evelyn, who has a substantial fortune, is the prince-like character who marries Clara at the end of the play. Shaw's Eliza is, similarly, scrupulous about money matters, preferring to marry for love and even support her husband financially if necessary.

Tom Taylor's *An Unequal Match* (1857) also emphasizes the double-nature of Cinderella. Taylor highlights class, rather than the financial and ethical barriers between the protagonists seen in Bulwer's *Money*.[44] Hester Grazebrook, a simple Yorkshire milkmaid, marries Sir Harry Arncliffe, an artistic gentleman who regards her as a 'pretty Perdita' (p. 12). Initially Harry disregards their unequal stations, professing that Hester is above him in 'innocence and truth' (p. 16). When they first become acquainted, they are both unaware that he is on the point of inheriting a title and money from an uncle. The inheritance changes everything. After marrying, Hester quickly tires of 'fine ladies, and affectation, and idleness' and longs for her working life (p. 22). She feels like a caged bird in 'a very grand aviary, with golden wires and freshest water, and the choicest seed, and the largest lumps of sugar, and the kindest keeper; but the bird must long for the woods now and then' (p. 41). Her new acquaintances find fault with her behaviour and ancestry. Hester's working-class father, a blacksmith, is wholly unacceptable to her husband's relatives, and Arncliffe comes to the conclusion he 'shall be a laughing stock for the whole county' (p. 32). Grazebrook is not the rogue that Doolittle is, but his unexpected arrival, when the Arncliffes are entertaining, acts in a similar way to Shaw's scenes with the intrusive dustman.

Hester recognizes her social deficiency ('I am so ignorant and so uninformed' [p. 34]) and worries about the comparison she feels her husband must be making between herself and the elegant Mrs Topham Montressor, the companion her husband has provided (who also has designs on Sir Harry). Arncliffe's health forces him to the spa at Ems and Mrs Montressor contrives to make her doctor send her there too. Hester is horrified and thinks, incorrectly, that her husband meets Mrs Montressor by design. The final act takes place in the German spa. Mrs Montressor flatters herself that she has attracted the attentions of the Grand Duke of Seidlitzstinkingen. In fact it is Hester, having secretly followed them to Germany, who is the 'schöne Engländerin' (p. 46) he admires. Arncliffe begins to tire of Mrs Montressor's 'coquetry' (p. 47) and her satirical recollections of

---

[44] Tom Taylor, *An Unequal Match* (Manchester, 1874).

Hester's behaviour. The 'schöne Engländerin' arrives and is, to everyone's astonishment, the newly improved Hester. Hester criticizes her husband's new beard and pipe, and his unfashionable dress, declaring ironically 'What a task I shall have to civilize you' (p. 56). Arncliffe, though initially dazzled by his wife's new charms, realizes that he prefers the 'natural loving girl' to the 'artificial, self-confident coquette' she has become (p. 58). He is even troubled by her new-found snobbery and 'coldness' towards her father (p. 62).

In her transformed state, Hester, like Eliza and Violet, is an actress: 'I've developed quite a talent for acting since you've been away' she says (p. 59). Her summary of her talents points to Shaw's later understanding of the superficialities of the social veneer:

> HESTER I've learned to suppress my real feelings, to laugh at my rivals, to be tolerant of bores, lightly to accept attentions lightly offered – nay, even to turn my back on my own father. In short, I have tried in all things to take Mrs Montressor as my model (p. 64).

Her husband shows some concern over Hester's relationship with the Grand Duke, but, on reading her correspondence to him, discovers the Duke's attentions to have been politely declined by his wife. Arncliffe declares to Mrs Montressor that he has 'learned at length how to estimate' his wife 'at her real worth' (p. 64) and Hester eventually reveals that she is still the same person beneath this new veneer.

The play has much in common with Shaw's *Pygmalion*: both emphasize the inadequacy of class as a guide to character. For Taylor, however, the onus is on Hester to transform herself through observation rather than through her education by a Pygmalion or Svengali figure. Hester is more sophisticated than the innocent Galatea-like milkmaid of Gilbert's *Patience* (1881); she knowingly understands her ironic statements and manages successfully to humiliate Mrs Montressor and retain her husband's respect at the same time. Hester's hurried self-induced transformation is perhaps a little implausible, but what makes her like Eliza is her consciousness of what she is doing. Theirs are deliberate attempts at self-improvement which result in them both understanding that fundamentally the only thing that has changed is how society views them.

Shaw's *Pygmalion* may also owe something to Somerset Maugham's highly successful first novel, *Liza of Lambeth* (1897).[45] Set in the downtrodden world of south London factory-workers, this variation on the Cinderella theme ends in tragedy. Liza is a cockney girl who has some pretensions to gaining a higher social status, but is unable to effect this. She is first seen dancing and showing off a new dress to bystanders in a London street, and her hauteur wins her the soubriquet

---

[45] W. S. Maugham, *Liza of Lambeth* (London, 1897).

'your lidyship' (p. 36). Maugham describes the drudgery of Liza's daily life: 'Cinderella herself was not more transformed [...] but Cinderella even in her rags was virtuously tidy and patched up, while Sally had a great tear in her shabby dress, and Liza's stockings were falling over her boots' (pp. 86–87). Liza escapes this world only briefly by visiting the theatre and watching plays. Her trips to the theatre with the slightly sinister Jim Blakeston lead to her being drawn into an amorous relationship with him, and eventually to her ruin. She is accused by his wife of being little better than a prostitute and is physically attacked by her. Liza falls ill and dies after this confrontation. Jim is remorseful and blames himself for her death.

Maugham never lets Liza rise beyond the social scene in which she is placed, being more interested in the realism of her situation. He describes deprivation, physical abuse within marriage, and the unglamorous escapes for those who are imprisoned by poverty. The one ray of hope for Liza is a marriage proposal from her friend Tom, but she rejects him because she does not love him. Liza's relationship with Blakeston is never fully explained. He lunges threateningly at her when she is first seen dancing in the street and laughs at her along with the other bystanders. He deliberately gets her drunk in order to kiss her and is unconcerned with the effect that their relationship has on his family or on Liza's reputation. His only redeeming feature is his remorse at the end of the novel. Maugham's Liza is a Cinderella who is neither transformed nor finds her prince. Shaw may be indicating a link with this text through his use of a variation on the heroine's name and the London setting.

Unstaged Pygmalion plays of the Nineteenth Century

The unstaged Pygmalion plays of the nineteenth century interpret substance of the myth more along the lines of contemporary poetry than contemporary drama. These plays do, however, confirm that there is a fashion emerging for the use of an extra transformation scene, whether it be a reversal of the first metamorphosis or an additional gift to the statue. Written in the 1880s, these plays are a miscellaneous group. Andrew Lang's 'lyric drama', *The New Pygmalion; or The Statue's Choice* (1883), is a magazine piece published while he was a Fellow of Merton College. Ronald Ross's *Edgar or the New Pygmalion* (1883) was published in Madras, and Agnes Rous Howell, *Euphrosyne; or The Sculptor's Bride* (1886) was intended as a libretto. All, except Lang's which is short, depict the statue as deficient in some respect, and all, except Lang, provide the statue with a large speaking part.

Lang is better known as a classical scholar, anthropologist and poet than as a playwright; he seldom used the dramatic form, writing only one full-length play:

The Black Thief (1882).⁴⁶ He took little interest in theatre and confessed that he was 'conscious of an entire ignorance of the stage', though he co-wrote an amusing parody of Rider Haggard's *She* (entitled *He* [1887]) with W. H. Pollock in the burlesque style.⁴⁷ The action of Lang's *New Pygmalion*, like Rousseau's scène lyrique, takes place in one scene: the sculptor's studio. When the curtain rises, Pygmalion is in the process of heaping incense on to an altar at the base of the pedestal beneath a 'chryselephantine statue' of Galatæa (p. 299). Pygmalion prays to Aphrodite, before the shrine, to make his statue of her come to life; in return, he says he will build her a golden altar. After throwing incense on the flame he leaves and the ghost of a sculptor arrives and prays to Aphrodite that Pygmalion's prayer should not be answered, and that the image be brought to life and given to him instead. He claims that the statue is the work of his own hand and not Pygmalion's. The ghost throws incense on the flame and leaves through a trap-door. Aphrodite appears, 'floating among her doves' (p. 300) and brings the statue to life. On coming to life the statue, like the others on the nineteenth-century stage, reveals herself to be inexperienced. She asks, Miranda-like, 'What world is this I know not of, / What flutters in my breast?' (Lang, p. 301). She is 'a woman with a child-like heart' (p. 301). Aphrodite explains that Galatæa is to marry the man who made her. Both Pygmalion and the ghost claim to have made the statue, and the statue is made to choose between them. Her choice is dictated by her vanity, perhaps echoing Gilbert's play. The ghost-sculptor reveals that he could make another image as fair as herself; Pygmalion, on the other hand, reveals that he could not make another as beautiful as she, and would not if he could. The disappointed ghost leaves 'swearing in Greek, Etruscan, and Hittite' (Lang, p. 302). The play's humour lies in Pygmalion's power to unexpectedly outwit both the statue and the ghost-sculptor.

Agnes Rous Howell's *Euphrosyne; Or The Sculptor's Bride* (1886) is the only Pygmalion play of the nineteenth century written by a woman.⁴⁸ The play possesses, at times, the intensity of Rousseau's monodrama. The opening scene echoes Stephens's burlesque of Gilbert: Pygmalion's friends accuse him of being in love because he is neglecting them. When pressed for the name of his beloved Pygmalion exclaims 'Art is my mistress, and Art alone' (p. 7). Pygmalion's prayer to Zeus brings Euphrosyne, his statue, to life: 'O Zeus! who hast enabled me with these unworthy hands to create this fair form, aye, and to make it life-like, wilt thou not complete my work, and endue it with Promethean fire?' (p. 18). Echoing the 'Adam's dream' figure, Urania answers Pygmalion's prayer while he dreams that she comes to life. Atropos, one of the fates, reveals that Euphrosyne will only

---

⁴⁶ Andrew Lang, 'The New Pygmalion; or The Statue's Choice. A Lyric Drama', *Longmans' Magazine*, 1 (1883), 299–302.
⁴⁷ Roger Lancelyn Green, *Andrew Lang: A Critical Biography* (Leicester, 1946), p. 63.
⁴⁸ Agnes Rous Howell, *Euphrosyne; Or the Sculptor's Bride* (Norwich, 1886).

be alive for a day, and during the marriage ceremony she begins to turn back into marble. Unable to bear her departure, Pygmalion embraces Euphrosyne, and they both turn to marble. Finally Urania appears from the temple of hope and brings the lovers back to life. The play, like the first three of this century, contains the now obligatory second transformation scene, which prolongs the action and creates suspense. Like the other transformed statues of this period, Euphrosyne is perplexed by her birth. She tries to understand her new bodily state: 'What is this warmth which through my veins / Doth upward creep' (p. 25). She asks what names she should give to what she feels and sees, and is taught by Pygmalion. Again, her knowledge is shown to be selective. She does not know what or who she is, but she is capable of asking Pygmalion whether he is her father or her brother.

Ronald Ross's *Edgar Or the New Pygmalion* (1883) also explores the nature of the new-born statue and her learning experience.[49] The statue, Niobelle, is brought to life when Edgar, a sculptor and nobleman, hears God's voice in a dream telling him that he 'should have that which I wished' (p. 64). The humour of the play is often erudite and occasionally dark. The new Pygmalion's talents are compared with those of a less-able sculptor of inappropriate and 'unsavoury' themes (p. 60). This man has sculpted Judas after his hanging, and Ariadne with sea-sickness, about which he says 'It took me five years to reach the consummation of that vomit' (p. 60). All this is justified by the sculptor as 'art for art's sake', rephrased by another character as 'Filth for filth's sake' (p. 60). The play, like the literature of the fleshly debate, expresses concern about the moral rectitude of sculpting the human form: 'There is too much grossness in them. The soul is the one thing admirable; bodies are coarse. I hate sculptures' (p. 61). Edgar ignores these sentiments and petitions the statue to come to life:

> Oh! that these frozen veins might swell with life;
> This thick amorphous stone turn into flesh
> And teem with thronging blood (Ross, p. 68).

When the statue appears as a woman, Edgar faints with shock. Niobelle's education immediately becomes an issue. Edgar teaches her about God and nature and treats her as a child. His confidence in his intellectual ability is unquestioned as he contemplates revealing to her the 'infinite movings of this intricate world' (p. 75). Like her counterparts on the stage, Niobelle is inconsistent in her knowledge: she knows Edgar's name without being told, but does not know that a lamp is not a star.

The education issue fades into the background when Edgar's cousin, Julian, falls in love with Niobelle and the sculptor loses his influence over her. Julian has

---

[49] Ronald Ross, *Edgar Or The New Pygmalion* (Madras, 1883).

promised to marry Clissa, who kills herself with his dagger when she discovers that she has been abandoned. The climax of the play is a fancy-dress ball at the Marquis of Amaralza's palace. Edgar warns Niobelle, who dresses as Helen of Troy, that her beauty and actions might be misunderstood, and her vanity echoes that of Gilbert's Galatea.

> Sweet child, sweet child,
> I love the word! What are you still but a child?
> Your pouts, your vanities, your ways, your whims
> Subscribe you infant still; but now your toys
> Are the hearts of men. Beware, my Niobelle,
> They who run blindly meet a fall (p. 123).

At the ball, Julian and Niobelle agree to elope. Edgar, who is angry with his cousin for remaining unaffected by Clissa's suicide, discovers their plans and tricks them into going to his studio. Charging Julian with responsibility for Clissa's death and stealing Niobelle's affection, Edgar kills him with a sword. Niobelle is compelled to mount her pedestal and become marble again. Edgar smashes the statue with a mallet. The play ends with him journeying to the mountains and declaring that 'man makes his own misery, not God' (p. 150).

Although it is doubtful that the unstaged plays link directly to Shaw, their content serves as a wider dramatic context. Unlike the poetry of the period, the demands of this genre require a decent speaking part for the statue. The influence of Gilbert leads to a tendency towards treating the theme as a comic subject. Even Ross's play, with its tragic ending, contains many comic interludes, and its main subject points up the humour of the innocent abroad: the eclectic nature of Galatea's knowledge often makes her comments unexpected as she exposes the inconsistencies of society. The persistence of this element in the unstaged plays may also derive from Gilbert, and it is unsurprising to see it used by Shaw a few decades later.

Conclusion

The notion that Shaw's *Pygmalion* is a dramatic departure from Ovid has to be qualified by the acknowledgment that it bears some resemblance to the Victorian plays on the Pygmalion and Cinderella themes, and in particular to Gilbert's play. For Ovid, the Pygmalion story is about a man who creates a woman, giving her the qualities he finds attractive. In Ovid she is everything he desires. In the nineteenth-century plays, the statue is more than Pygmalion bargains for. Gilbert's *Pygmalion and Galatea*, clearly the most successful, highlighted, through its successive productions, the problems of combining serenity and classical poise with passion.

This difficulty was overcome by the actresses of the period, who chose to play Galatea in a child-like and emotionally tame way. Her innocence and inexperience is a focus for most of the plays and is also an issue for the Cinderella variants. Pygmalion in the role of the lover *and* the educator of the innocent poses a problem in the nineteenth century. Brough's mind-less innocent has to be transformed a second time before she can love, as love and innocence are incompatible.

When Eliza's character is placed in the context of Gilbert's Galatea we can see a precedent for Shaw's development, firstly, of the tension between Eliza's innocent cockney character and the way in which she is perceived by the middle classes, and secondly, of the tension between Eliza as an actress who knowingly deceives, and at the same time retains her innocence. Gilbert's exploitation of a similar duality in his characterization of Galatea, a duality highlighted by its obvious suppression in performance (and in Stephens's burlesque), makes him a more relevant context for Shaw than Ovid. It is a feature which is also present in the Cinderella variants of the Victorian period. The popularity of the *Cinderella-déclassement* theme on the nineteenth-century stage, and Shaw's direct allusions to the tale, makes it another likely context for understanding Shaw's development of Eliza. These plays similarly depend on a dual perspective of the heroine. Such tensions resemble the moral questioning already seen in the mid-Victorian poetry on the subject. In the way in which the Pygmalion plays focus on the expanding role of Pygmalion as educator, and in the way in which Galatea's innocence and inexperience are portrayed effectively as obstacles to their union, these plays are the precursors of Shaw. Contextualising Shaw in this way, we must acknowledge that his work is not a dramatic departure from the Pygmalion story as it was developed on the nineteenth-century stage, or even an unsuccessful marriage of the Cinderella and Pygmalion stories. Rather, we should see it as a genuine variant of the Ovidian myth, at least as reinterpreted by the nineteenth century.

Chapter 6

The Twentieth Century: Towards a Conclusion

The Galatea Story

The Pygmalion story prior to the 1880s predominantly represents Galatea in two ways: she is either accepting and appreciative of her lot as a wife, demurely fulfilling Pygmalion's ideal, or she is a disappointment to Pygmalion, who views her with disgust. Prior to the eighteenth century, Galatea is consistently portrayed as inferior to Pygmalion, inconstant, dependent, immodest, criminal, and an easy prey to temptation. Rousseau's *Pygmalion* helped to disseminate a less negative view of Galatea, although his sculptor reduces the statue to a projection of himself. In forging his own fantasy around the statue-like Sara, Hazlitt's Pygmalion similarly forgoes interaction with another in favour a narcissistic replica. Concurrent with this is Hazlitt's desire to treat the woman as a goddess, and thus make her something untouchable and incapable of responding.

From the 1820s until the end of the nineteenth century we find a number of recurrent themes which express standard male views of women's bodies. Galatea is like a flower or a child and is immobilized by her heavy hair. For James Payn she is 'as fair and flawless as the lily's grace' (p. 11). Joseph John Murphy's statue-woman has 'a flower's soft bending grace'.[1] Writers emphasize the whiteness of the statue and of the woman she becomes. Beddoes writes: 'all her marble symmetry was white / As brow and bosom should be' (*Plays and Poems*, p. 101). This, of course, reflects her statue state, but it is also an reflection of the purity and beauty required (by men) in womankind. Galatea's voice and actions are often child-like: Beddoes's Pygmalion calls her 'my delicious child' (p. 102), Buchanan's statue-woman has 'prattled infants' speech',[2] and George Eric Lancaster's Pygmalion asks his statue to lift up her arms to him 'like a child'.[3] Joseph John Murphy talks of her possessing 'the purity of childhood' (p. 66), as does Andrew Lang's Pygmalion, who wants 'a woman with a child-like heart / "And passionately pure"' (p. 301). Galatea is without rights and exists only as a dependant. Ronald Ross's Galatea occupies the uneasy position of being both child and woman.

> What are you still but a child?

---

[1] Joseph John Murphy, *Sonnets* (London, 1890), p. 66.
[2] Robert Buchanan, *Undertones* (London, 1863), p. 178.
[3] George Eric Lancaster, *Pygmalion in Cyprus* (London, 1880), p. 5.

> Your pouts, your vanities, your ways, your whims
> Subscribe you infant still; but now your toys
> Are the hearts of men (p. 123).

Pygmalion, as conceived by John Hooley, regards grace as naturally incompatible with childhood, but nevertheless requests Galatea to be a child who is at the same time 'gifted with graces girlhood lacked'.[4] Part of the infantilization of Galatea is the restriction of her knowledge; her naivety epitomizes the simplicity regarded as appropriate for both classical beauty and for women. The child-like woman is so overwhelmingly the Victorian conception of Galatea on the stage that it is not surprising that this theme is continued by George Bernard Shaw in his *Pygmalion*.

The emphasis on purity and the infantilization of Galatea contrasts with the eroticism of some of her incarnations. Robert Whitehouse's Galatea begins as 'a ripened bud / That knows not that the summer is at hand' and ends as a 'surrendered woman [...] / Close nestled in his [Pygmalion's] strong arms'.[5] Emphasis is often placed on descriptions of Galatea's hair. These occasionally have negative or oppressive overtones. William Cox Bennett's statue has man-catching hair: 'nets of gold, / Fit as lorn Ariadne's streaming hair / To catch flush'd Dionusus' [sic].[6] Ernest Hartley Coleridge's Pygmalion sculpts her with 'great locks, such as no breath / Of living breeze could nestle in and stir'.[7] J. J. Murphy's statue has hair that turns 'dark, and flow[s] / In waves of raven blackness / Like clouds of lingering night' (p. 67) and when G. E. Lancaster's statue is transformed, she requests that Pygmalion free her heavy locks: '"Pygmalion, loose my hair; / Unbind it; let it fall!"' (p. 13). These later become a bed as Pygmalion offers to lie with Galatea 'among thy hair'(p. 26). Frequent reference to Galatea's blood red lips, blue eyes and rosy cheeks conform to Victorian conceptions of female beauty. Rather more disturbing, perhaps, is the frequent reference to Galatea as chained or captive. James Payn's statue is bound by her form: 'This statue [...] needing not the chain / On those fair wrists to mark the fetter pain – is *but* a statue' and his Pygmalion is a 'slave-sculptor' (p. 13). Robert Buchanan's Pygmalion girdles the waist of his animal-like Galatea 'with clasp and cord of gold' (p. 178) and Frederick Tennyson's Pygmalion throws a 'chain of gold [...] round the fair cold marble neck' (p. 45). These seem to be incidents used for no purpose other than to demonstrate Pygmalion's superiority.

The Pygmalion story is largely perpetuated as an instance of male definition of the female: Galatea's body and her identity are created to his specifications. The statue is a living doll who embodies the fantasies of the sculptor; the story

---

[4] John Hooley, *Pygmalion and Other Poems* (Calcutta, 1874), p. 114.
[5] Robert Whitehouse *Pygmalion and the Statue* (London, 1910), p. 32 and p. 37.
[6] William Cox Bennett, *Poems* (London, 1862), p. 109.
[7] Ernest Hartley Coleridge, *Poems* (Chertsey, 1881), p. 4.

culminates in the usurpation of woman's biologically creative role when Pygmalion creates her. The nineteenth century retells the story either using Pygmalion as the narrator, or through a narrator whose concerns were closely identified with the sculptor. Pygmalion's story, his personality, and his creativity are explored in great depth, while Galatea is, to a large extent, a speechless physical form. Her mental capacity and the question of her freedom of choice were ignored until the burlesques and comedies of the mid-nineteenth century developed her role (largely because of the necessity and value of having actresses on the stage). In these comedies, nevertheless, Galatea remains a child-like innocent, or is an innocent flirting with the possibility of understanding the daring things she says. It is tempting to conclude that the Pygmalion story cannot be told in any way other than to reflect male fantasies. The story is, however, reclaimed by women writers in the latter part of the nineteenth century – a practice that continues into the twentieth century.

Feminist interpretations of classical stories involve subversion of traditional perspectives, provoked by a need to redefine and appropriate androcentric literature.

> For feminists, the rewriting of myths denotes participation in [...] the struggle to alter gender asymmetries agreed upon for centuries by myth's disseminators. When feminists envisage that struggle, they often think of the rewriting or reinterpretation of individual stories: for example, by changing the focus of the narrative from a male character to a female character, or by shifting the terms of the myth so that what was a 'negative' female role-model becomes a positive one.[8]

Furthermore, as Jane Caputi writes, 'Feminist thinkers have continued to expose the patriarchal bias of mythographers (past and present) and the ways that these entrenched mythic symbols and paradigms construct and maintain phallocentric reality'.[9] Feminist interpretations of the Pygmalion story offer a new kind of focus on the statue. They concentrate keenly on Galatea's rights, her choices and her reaction to being created by Pygmalion. She is permitted to regret her transformation and to display anxiety at the purpose for which she has been created. This revolution in viewpoint is explored briefly by Robert Graves in his sonnet 'Galatea to Pygmalion' (1938).[10]

---

[8] Diane Purkiss, 'Women's Rewriting of Myth', in *The Woman's Companion to Mythology*, ed. by Carolyne Larryngton (London, 1997), pp. 441–457 (pp. 441–442).

[9] Jane Caputi, 'On Psychic Activism: Feminist Mythmaking', in *The Woman's Companion to Mythology*, pp. 425–440 (p. 425).

[10] Robert Graves, *Collected Poems* (London, 1938), p. 109. Charles Martin's comment that Robert Graves did not 'engage Ovid explicitly in his own poetry' cannot be correct as Graves's two Pygmalion poems show (Charles Martin, *Ovid in English* [London, 1998], p. 333).

> Galatea, whom his furious chisel
> From Parian stone had by greed enchanted,
> Fulfilled, they say, all Pygmalion's longings:
> Stepped from that pedestal on which she stood,
> Bare in his bed laid her down, lubricious,
> With low responses to his drunken raptures,
> Enroyalled his body with her demon blood.
>
> Yet young Pygmalion had so well plotted
> The art-perfection of his woman monster
> That schools of eager connoisseurs beset
> Her famous person with perennial suit;
> Whom she (a judgement on the jealous artist)
> Admitted rankly to a comprehension
> Of themes that crowned her own, not his repute.

Graves sees Pygmalion as a man overshadowed by his Frankensteinian 'woman monster'. This Dionysian Pygmalion is endowed with a passion and carnality ('furious', 'greed', 'lubricious', 'drunken', 'jealous') which lessens his reputation. Galatea fulfills Pygmalion's fantasies, yet she is brought down to base behaviour; she is both queen and 'demon'. Pygmalion, Graves says, has created such a perfect art-work that writers ('eager connoisseurs') have 'beset / Her famous person with perennial suit' in their renarrations of her story. Galatea has usurped Pygmalion's royal power and 'crowned her own' reputation. The 'suit' echoes Pygmalion's own, and their carnal knowledge of Galatea is implied in the second stanza when she 'rankly' reveals her 'themes' to them (this mirrors the 'lubricious' scene of the first stanza). The sonnet illustrates the new emphasis in the story: the empowerment of Galatea. Her empowerment is double-edged. Galatea is both regal and low, perfect, yet rank. 'Schools of eager connoisseurs' have indeed paid tribute to Galatea in the past, but in the late nineteenth and early twentieth century, the emphasis in the story moves towards revealing her themes in a new way. The twentieth century perpetuates some of the traditional characteristics of Galatea, but much time is spent on understanding the implications of her gender and sexuality.

Irish and American Feminist Versions: 1880s–1920s

Versions of the Pygmalion story by women with feminist agendas belong to the 1880s and the 1920s and they protest, in particular, their concerns for Galatea's welfare. These versions of the Pygmalion myth involve considerable alterations to the narrative. They confront the antecedent androcentric morphology of the tale through their recognition of the victimhood of Galatea. By repositioning the story, using Galatea as the narrator, Emily Henrietta Hickey, Elizabeth Stuart Phelps,

Genevieve Taggard and Roselle Mercier Montgomery bestow a new voice upon her with which she can express the anxieties of womanhood. These turn of the century poems are innovative in terms of their content, but their form is traditional, the sonnet being the preferred genre. There is great variety of approach in the myth-revisionist endeavour, but the feminist writers who revise the Pygmalion myth principally explore Galatea's experience as a disempowered woman, with H. D.'s Modernist version of the tale, 'Pygmalion' (1917), standing quite apart from the others through its concentration on the sculptor's creative crisis and its experimental form. H. D., despite her usually conspicuous feminism, avoids a direct contention with the problematic nature of the myth for women. Instead, she recasts the myth by imposing layers of meaning which imply a questioning of masculine certainties about artistic creativity. The story seems to have attracted little attention from British women writers of the period, being retold by Americans and the Anglo-Irish writer, Emily Hickey.[11] Speaking from Galatea's point of view is not exclusive to women writers, however. Charles J. Rowe's 'Galatea' (1947) is devoted to the statue's experience of her metamorphosis. Pygmalion opens the poem with 'Speak, Galatea, tell me of your dream / About your coming, ere your vision woke' (p. 414). While this Galatea does not question Pygmalion's motives for wanting her to come to life, and Rowe depicts her as utterly dependent on him ('I have no life but yours' [p. 414]), he nonetheless attempts to give Galatea a perspective on the story.[12]

Emily Hickey's 'Sonnet' marks the beginning of a significant increase in the interest in the Pygmalion story shown by women writers. An Anglo-Catholic Irishwoman, and the daughter of an Anglican priest, much of her work is devoted to Christian thought and the Irish Question. She joined the Catholic church in 1901, the church which she associated with the servants who attended her household during her childhood in Ireland. Hickey was an academic and a poet who believed strongly in higher education for women and helped to bring this about. She taught English language and literature at the Collegiate School for Girls and later at the London Collegiate School.[13] Hickey is perhaps best known for her connection to the Brownings. She was the first honorary secretary to the Browning Society (the organization formed to promote the works of Robert Browning), edited some of Robert Browning's work, and corresponded with him. 'Sonnet' is part of *A Sculptor and Other Poems*, a work devoted to aesthetic issues. The principal poem of the collection, 'A Sculptor', advocates life above art when the

---

[11] In this chapter I have drawn on the work of American and Irish writers, given the increasing globalization of the literary market. The work of these writers was available in Britain, and is reviewed there.

[12] Charles J. Rowe, 'Galatea', *Poetry Review*, 38 (1947), 414.

[13] Enid Dinnis, *Emily Hickey: Poet, Essayist – Pilgrim. A Memoir* (London, 1927), pp. 21–24.

protagonist, a sculptor, neglects his wife in favour of his art and is punished with the failure of his skill. Hickey's Galatea sonnet likewise contrasts art and life in a brief monologue spoken by the statue-woman after her transformation. Hickey is fascinated by the statue's predicament both as a woman and as an art-work: something to be gazed at and appreciated for its visual qualities, but not known or understood.

> I was Pygmalion's handiwork; I grew
> Into that beauty he had bidden be;
> He saw, and gaz'd, and lov'd exceedingly,
> Yea, lov'd me into life. He little knew
> I, who was his and he and myself too,
> Had other life in store for him and me,
> Art's life of splendid immortality,
> A meed for ever paying, for ever due!
> Why did he win for me this mortal breath
> Why did the ivory sheen of face and limb
> Flush into tender ruddiness for him?
> O fateful praying love that quickeneth!
> Alas for the perisht pride, the frame-gold dim,
> The gift, my life, that to his name was death.[14]

Here, Galatea laments Pygmalion's removal of her immortality and sees life only in terms of what she has lost. Pygmalion assumes that his love will be returned. In a cryptic sentence 'He little knew / I, who was his and he and myself too, / Had other life in store for him and me' (Hickey, p. 138), Galatea shows a reluctance to become the object, emphatically retaining her subject positioning by using 'I' at the beginning of line 5. Her excessive pronominalism enacts the new power struggle between her and Pygmalion. She does not easily succumb to objectification, and instead suggests that they have separate viewpoints, both having their own plans for each other. Hickey concentrates on Galatea's feelings, avoiding the usual nineteenth-century emphasis on visual classical details and descriptions of Galatea's beauty.

Emily Hickey's sonnet was soon matched by a longer poem by the American poet Elizabeth Stuart Phelps. 'Galatea', in *Songs of the Silent World and Other Poems* (1885), assumes the statue is conscious before her metamorphosis, and has Galatea consider the disadvantages of undergoing the transformation from art to life.[15] Phelps, a significant poet, novelist and short-story writer, campaigned tirelessly for women's rights during the 1870s and 1880s. Writing countless articles on reform, she argued strongly for women's right to enjoy complete

---

[14] Emily H. Hickey, *A Sculptor and Other Poems* (London, 1881), p. 138.
[15] Elizabeth Stuart Phelps, *Songs of the Silent World* (Boston, 1885), p. 69.

equality with men. In *The Independent*, a liberal newspaper, she hypothesizes that

> when women are admitted to their rightful share in the administration of government [...] [and are able] to represent, in their own characters, the interests of their sex; when every department of politics, art, literature, trade is thrown open, absolutely, without reservation, to the exercise of their energies; when the state ceases to expend a dollar more for the education of its boys than of its girls [...] when marriage and motherhood no more complete a woman's mission to the world than marriage and fatherhood complete a man's [...] only then can we draw the veil from the brows of the TRUE WOMAN.[16]

'Galatea' acts as a vehicle for her feminist thought. The poem opens with Galatea begging Pygmalion for 'a moment's grace' before she decides whether to come to life:

> A moment's grace, Pygmalion! Let me be
> A breath's space longer on this hither hand
> Of fate too sweet, too sad, to mad to meet.
> Whether to be thy statue or thy bride –
> An instant spare me! Terrible the choice,
> As no man knoweth, being only man (Phelps, p. 69).

No longer the naive of the burlesques, Galatea quickly weighs up the options ('Shall I dare exchange / Veins of the quarry for the throbbing pulse?' [p. 69]), and she is aware that if she comes to life, she will have to submit to Pygmalion's will, like 'a wave tossed up the shore of his desire, / To ebb and flow whene'er it pleaseth him' (p. 69). Despite her reluctance to undergo the change, Galatea confesses that she loves the sculptor. Nevertheless, she is apprehensive about becoming a woman. Man's love for woman is fickle, she says; women are 'Remembered at his leisure, and forgot, / Worshipped and worried, clasped and dropped at mood' (p. 69). The statue observes that any one who knew in advance what a woman's life was like would never choose to become one: 'What woman out of all the breathing world / Would be a woman, could her heart select' (p. 70). She is, nonetheless, compelled to come to life by an 'awful Law' (p. 70) and in doing so she makes a 'sacrifice supreme' (p. 70). Ultimately, Galatea is ambivalent about womanhood: to love a man is both a 'Paradise' and a 'Hell' (p. 70). As she is removed from her high pedestal, so she accepts her inferior role:

---

[16] 'The True Woman', *The Independent*, October 12 1871, p. 1. Quoted in Lori Duin Kelly, *The Life and Works of Elizabeth Stuart Phelps: Victorian Feminist Writer* (Troy, New York, 1983), p. 62.

> Pygmalion! Take me from my pedestal,
> And set me lower – lower, Love! – that I
> May be a woman, and look up to thee;
> And looking, longing, loving, give and take
> The human kisses worth the worst that thou
> By thine own nature shall inflict on me (p. 71).

Love is to be Galatea's consolation.

Hickey and Phelps both highlight the difficulty of choosing between love and independence. Genevieve Taggard's 'Galatea Again' (1926) goes further than this in asking to be changed back into marble.[17] Taggard, a biographer of Emily Dickinson and a left-wing protest-poet, characterizes Galatea's womanhood as a life of 'wild crying face and frantic eyes' and of being pursued by the infantilized male who tries to appeal to her maternal instincts (p. 39).

> Let me be marble, marble once again:
> Go from me slowly, like an ebbing pain,
> Great mortal feud of moving flesh and blood:
> This month so bruised, serene again, – and set
> In its old passive changelessness, the rude
> Wild crying face, the frantic eyes – forget
> The little human suffering interlude.
>
> And if you follow and confront me there,
> O Sons of Men, though you cry out and groan
> And plead with me to take you for my own
> And clutch my dress as a child, I shall not care,
>
> But only turn on you a marble stare
> And stun you with the quiet gaze of stone (p. 39).

Taggard's Galatea rejects Pygmalion and the 'Sons of Men', dismissing their curtailment of her identity to that of wife and mother. The return to marble is an escape from the harshness of the married-woman's life. The marble refuge both protects and avenges her, and her Medusa-like stare threatens any man who would prevent her escape. The life she flees is depicted here, as in Charlotte Perkins Gillman's 'The Yellow Wallpaper' and Charlotte Brontë's *Jane Eyre*, as an hysteria brought on by patriarchal oppression.

The American writer, Roselle Mercier Montgomery shows a defiant Galatea in 'Galatea to Pygmalion' (1929) admonishing the sculptor for daring to cause her transformation:

---

[17] Genevieve Taggard, *Words for the Chisel* (New York, 1926), p. 39.

> It was a male intrusion to evoke
> Me from the marble with a chisel stroke.
>
> Alone there in my virgin tenement
> I was serene, untroubled, quite content –
>
> With no possessive one to say, 'Do this!',
> 'Stay here!', 'Go there!', or, 'Come, my love, a kiss!' [...]
>
> It was a gesture of male arrogance
> To break my dream, to wake me from my trance.
>
> You were a daring and intrusive one (Montgomery, pp. 39–40).[18]

Again the marble state is associated with unmarried freedom and Galatea looks back on it as a haven. Montgomery highlights the differences between the lives of powerful men and powerless women: 'It is a great adventure to be human, / A greater venture still, to be a woman!' (Montgomery, p. 39). As in Phelps's poem the statue feels indignant about having to submit to Pygmalion's will. Montgomery is ambivalent, however. A second voice argues that the marble life cannot 'match the bliss / Of lips, warm lips, beneath a lover's kiss' (p. 40), echoing Keats's 'Ode on a Grecian Urn'. Galatea concludes that 'it was a gesture of male arrogance' to take her from her marble 'dream', but, in her second voice, she blesses the phallic chisel.

Pygmalion's Artistic Crisis and Disappointment: the 1900s to the 1930s

The Pygmalion story was unattractive to most of the British and American avant-garde writers of the early twentieth century. Classical subjects are not, however, abandoned by Imagists and Modernists, who present an ambivalent view of its merits at the beginning of the century. Imagist principles rely on a fragmentation of narrative, but not an outright rejection of the classical subject; classical stories are frequently drawn upon through allusion rather than renarration. Richard Aldington, a key member of the Imagist group, states that although the Imagists 'believe passionately in the artistic value of modern life', it is nevertheless important that they retain 'absolute freedom in the choice of subject'.[19] To affiliate oneself with classicism, then, is not necessarily an endorsement of the past as

---

[18] Roselle Mercier Montgomery, *Many Devices* (New York and London, 1929), pp. 39–40.

[19] Richard Aldington, in *Some Imagist Poets* ed. by Amy Lowell (London, 1915), pp. vi–vii.

glorious, but an exercise of freedom. Aldington defends his own classicism against the accusation that it is a mere 'parade of eruditon':[20] 'When I use the word "god" or "gods", or the name of some Hellenic deity, I am not indulging in a mythological flourish but refer to the actual experience of some "potency"' (*Complete Poems*, p. 16). Aldington gives an idiosyncratic and fragmentary view of the classical subject, as Eliot and Joyce do in their own distinctive ways. Aldington's 'Evening', 'Church Walk, Kensington' and 'Eros and Psyche' depict a modern world integrated with glimpses, and often relics of the classical:

> In an old dull yard near Camden Town,
> Which echoes with the rattle of cars and 'buses
> And freight-trains, puffing steam and smoke and dirt
> To the streaming sooty sky –
> There stands an old grimy statue,
> A statue of Psyche and her lover, Eros [...]
> What are they doing here in Camden Town
> In the midst of all this clamour and filth? (p. 53).

The city stifles the classical beauty of the statues which are a poignant echo of a former glory. As Aldington's 'Faun Captive' says: 'Who now regards me or who twines / Red wool and threaded lilies round the brows / of my neglected statues?' (p. 69). The traditional myth retold as narrative is in decline as classicism is reinterpreted for modern use. Although his work is littered with decaying statues, Aldington does not retell the Pygmalion story; his American wife, H. D. (Hilda Doolittle), however, gives the story new vigour. H. D.'s poetry reanimates the classical world through altering perspectives. Her agenda is not as remote from the imagists as it might seem. Under the influence of H. D., Ezra Pound's early conception of the imagists is of a band of 'ardent Hellenists' writing in '*vers libre*'.[21] The classical tradition is not discarded; it is entered into with an almost mystical wish to understand the mythological and the religious 'potency' on a level which is more psychological and anthropological than it is literary.

H. D.'s 'Pygmalion' avoids the Galatean perspective of her compatriots. Instead, the focus is on the sculptor's repeated questioning of his purpose. The poet reveals an insecure and perplexed Pygmalion. The sculptor is uncertain of whether he resides in deterministic universe or whether his actions are attributable to his own free will. This war-time Pygmalion is more worried about his freedom of choice than about his statues. The poem has proved perplexing, and there is some confusion over the sources of this version of the story.

---

[20] Richard Aldington, *The Complete Poems* (London, 1948), p. 16.

[21] Ezra Pound, *Poetry I* (November, 1912), p. 65. Cited in Vincent Quinn, *Hilda Doolittle* (New York, 1967), p. 21.

We may well ask where the poet found this Pygmalion who hurls questions at heaven. [...] Pygmalion while never a god, seems to have been an early priest-king of Cyprus who, like the Minoses of Crete, was as much concerned with the worship of the gods as with the rule of his people. Although she has portrayed him as a sculptor, H. D.'s Pygmalion reacts to the gods with such baffled awe as might have been felt by a conscientious priest-king. Once again the poet has looked behind a myth and resurrected a hero in his original state. By abolishing his love-affair with Galatea and by altering his orientation from Aphrodite to Athene, she has made her Pygmalion a fit companion of Adonis and Helios.[22]

H. D.'s omission of the love affair with Galatea does not return the myth to its origins, however; the affair is part of the earliest transcriptions of the myth. The only version which vaguely resembles that described above is the late classical account by Porphyry. Porphyry's King Pygmalion is concerned with the broken vows of his priests. Porphyry's Pygmalion is, however, neither a priest nor a sculptor; but of the classical accounts of Pygmalion, this is the closest to the above quotation. As Porphyry is post Ovid, his version cannot be seen as a return to an original state. H. D.'s poem bears little resemblance to Porphyry's account, or the version in the above quotation. Pygmalion's identification as a sculptor solidly associates the poem with the Ovidian and Aphroditean tradition. Rather than divorcing her subject from Aphrodite, as Swann suggests, the poet retains a connection to the goddess through Pygmalion's affiliation with Hephaestos (p. 71). Hephaestos (or Vulcan) is the Greek god of fire and the husband of Aphrodite. According to Roman myth, he is also the patron of artists who work in iron and metal.

> Many speak of his [Vulcan's] two golden statues, which not only seemed animated, but which walked by his side, and even assisted him in the working of metals. It is said that, at the request of Jupiter, he made the first woman that ever appeared on earth, well known under the name of Pandora.[23]

H. D.'s revisionism is not a rejection of Ovid in favour of an 'urtext'; instead, the poet unites the aphroditean myth of the sculptor-lover with vulcanian myth of the sculpting fire god. Pygmalion's anxieties do not arise from priesthood, but from his role as a sculptor, and are focused on his use of vulcanian 'fire': 'Am I the master of this fire, is this fire my own strength?' he asks (p. 71).

Throughout the poem Pygmalion casts doubts on his own creative abilities, questioning the certainties of a Coleridgean poetic 'secondary' imagination, which

---

[22] Thomas Burnett Swann, *The Classical World of H. D.* (Nebraska, 1962), pp. 95–96.
[23] Lemprière's *Classical Dictionary* (London, 1963), p. 666.

could confidently echo the primary imagination of God. Echoing Rousseau's self-destructive Pygmalion, H. D.'s sculptor toys with the idea of becoming a vulcanian sacrifice: 'Shall I let myself be broken in my own heat?' (p. 70). The complex fire symbolism knits together the Venus and Vulcan myths. Pygmalion thinks he may destroy the fires of inspiration and passion if he cleaves 'the rock as of old' (p. 70). The anxiety of destroying the fire leads to the failure of Pygmalion's work. Pygmalion goes on to compare the strength of his inspiration with a volcano 'which lifts the rock from the earth' (p. 70), yet he is unable to say whether he is the 'master of this fire' (p. 71), or whether he has created the fire. Pygmalion is, nevertheless, conscious that he makes 'god upon god / step from the cold rock' (p. 71) with the aid of Hephasetos-Vulcan. These cold sculptures of the god are, however, 'less than men' because they are the work of a man (p. 71). The new Promethean fire, however, changes everything: it makes Pygmalion's hand shake, hovers over his head and makes his live. The vivified statue-gods cry out at him before they melt 'into the light' (p. 72). The melting stone echoes Ovid's representation of the transformation of the statue as like softening wax. This loss of corporeality encourages Pygmalion to think that the gods have departed:

> they have gone;
> what agony can express my grief?
>
> each from his marble base
> has stepped into the light
> and my work is for naught (p. 72).

The apparent departure of the gods causes Pygmalion to consider whether his art has brought the gods to life:

> Now am I the power
> that has made this fire
> as of old I made the gods
> start from the rocks?
> am I the god?
> or does this fire carve me
> for its use? (pp. 72–73).

In his uncertainty as to where he fits into the scheme of things, Pygmalion examines his role and identity: is he the carved god or the divine Vulcan, he asks. Pygmalion does not know whether he is acted upon or acts, whether he makes or has been made by the gods: 'Which am I / the stone or the power?' (p. 70).

The slippage between subject and object orientations suggests a world of uncertainties as Pygmalion goes through both a religious and a creative crisis. At the end of the monologue, none of these questions is answered. H. D.'s

'Pygmalion' recalls the uncertainties of the Romantic imagination seen in Rousseau's sculptor. H. D.'s vacillating monologue is fragmented and unresolved; but it is not as Sarah Annes Brown suggests, the 'confused' offering of 'a female writer who is debarred from total identification with Pygmalion despite being herself an artist' (Brown, p. 196). The modern Pygmalion's self doubt has none of the posturing of Rousseau's, but the poem has none of the responsibilities to resolve the tension it creates. It is a critical commonplace that H. D.'s classical revisionism has a strong feminist agenda, and the poet usually focuses on the situations and experiences of women in classical myths. The absence of Galatea from the story points up the misogynism Pygmalion is famed for. This Pygmalion, like Rousseau's is concerned with himself and the nature of his own grand purpose. H. D.'s sculptor is even more self-involved than Rousseau's and the statue of Galatea is never mentioned. Pygmalion's central concern is his own creative crisis. He does not understand the purpose of his art, nor even whether he is in control of it. In this early piece, H. D. is more concerned with observing Pygmalion experiencing the trauma of aesthetic endeavour than with the feminist revisionism she was later famed for.

Pygmalion's crisis is often (though not by H. D.) intimately connected with his love for the statue and with the issue of whether Galatea matches up to the ideal he forms of her. In the 1920s, Pygmalion frequently regrets causing the statue's transformation. Cecil Day Lewis's early poem 'The Perverse' (1928) characterizes Pygmalion as an idealist who attempts to combine the human and the abstract.[24] Pygmalion's lover has denied him, and so he turns in despair to couch 'with the Absolute' (p. 33). Pygmalion recreates his beloved as an Hegelian absolute, and as such she becomes his companion all 'summer through' (p. 33). The intellectual ideal becomes unsatisfactory, however, because of its lack of body: 'He got small joy of the skimpy bedfellow – / Formulas gave no body to lay bare' (p. 33). Eventually Pygmalion's beloved returns and no longer denies him; but he finds that

> [...] No more denied
> Seemed no more ideal. He was unsatisfied
> Till he strained her flesh to thin philosophies (p. 33).

The real, by virtue of its not being the ideal, chases away Pygmalion's love. His dreams give him 'a chill enchanted image of her flesh' (p. 33); in his mind she becomes stone-like and perfect. Such dreams 'inflamed his waking wish' and his attention is drawn again to the real woman: 'the quick beauty no dream-chisels grave' (p. 33). Pygmalion concludes, though, that he 'would have changed her body into stone' (p. 33) if he had the power to do so. The perversity of the poem's

---

[24] Cecil Day Lewis, *Country Comets* (London, 1928), p. 33.

title lies in the circularity of the story: Pygmalion is unable to experience the real without wishing it to be the ideal.

Charlton M. Lewis, writing in the *Yale Review* in 1921, also reworks the tale as an exploration of idealism.[25] Lewis's Pygmalion creates a statue

> not of woman – for never woman wore
> Such perfect breathing beauty, nor shall forevermore –
> But of the highest grace to which our human thoughts aspire,
> When the immortal vision fires the mortal heart's desire (p. 727).

This post-romantic Pygmalion is possessed by his idealism, enshrining 'a dim ideal in the temple of his dreams' (p. 726). Lewis's Pygmalion desires what he ought not to want: 'But the moth desires the candle and a man desires a star' (p. 726); and as the moth image suggests, the result is ruin. The poem ends with what Lewis calls the 'sequel' (p. 727), which is clearly taken from Ovid's *Metamorphoses* and is a rare acknowledgment of the Pygmalion myth's position within a series of stories:

> To their aging eyes the sordid darkness of the times
> Was terribly illumined by their children's children's crimes;
> Till Myrrha's sin and Smyrna's sin, too loathsome to elate,
> Unnatural, unspeakable, filled the cup of fate,
> And one fair child, Adonis, last of Pygmalion's race,
> Avenged on Aphrodite her blundering act of grace (p. 727).

Lewis directs us to his 'moral': to seek the ideal is as 'the utmost end and aim of art', but 'ill it was' for Pygmalion to desire Galatea 'with mortal fleshly yearning' (p. 728). Pygmalion's rejection of the Dionysian 'lyric ecstasies' of the 'God of the vine-fed frenzy' (p. 728) and the cupidinous 'God of the golden bow' (p. 728), leads him to retire. The sculptor says of these gods: 'In glimpses still you visit me, and still I hear you calling' (p. 728), but he is forced to retreat into his own protective valley 'the true heart's homing-place for me and mine together' and the domestic ideal ('a candle's in the window, and the kettle's on the crane' [p. 728]) in order to keep them at bay.

Robert Graves's 'Pygmalion to Galatea' (1925–1926), the precursor of his 'Galatea to Pygmalion', attempts a restoration of Pygmalion's idealism and the accomplishment of his goal.[26] Pygmalion sings, to the newly transformed Galatea, of how he expects her character to develop. Galatea, confined to her pedestal for the duration of the song, is unsure of what her human nature means, and listens to

---

[25] Charlton M. Lewis, 'Pygmalion', *Yale Review*, 10 (1921), 726–728.
[26] Robert Graves, *Poems (1914–1926)* (London, 1927), pp. 201–203.

Pygmalion's wish that she should be 'lovely', 'merciful', 'constant', 'various' and modest. These qualities are shown to be the ideal of womanhood. Pygmalion also wishes Galatea to retain the mystery he associates with the ideal statue: 'keep our love aloof and strange, / Keep it from gluttonous eyes, from stairway gossip' (Graves [1927], p. 202). When the song ends Galatea replies:

> 'Pygmalion, as you woke me from the stone,
> So shall I you from the bonds of sullen flesh.
> Lovely as I am, merciful shall I prove:
> Woman I am, constant as various,
> Not marble-hearted but your own true love' (Graves [1927], p. 203).

Galatea promises to be faithful and to improve Pygmalion in a spiritual sense. A tension arises between Pygmalion's directive purpose and the freedom and active nature he suggests Galatea should have. He wants her to be as capable and mercurial as a society hostess, yet at the same time, he suggests that she should be 'unsubjected' (p. 202):

> 'As you are various, so be woman:
> Graceful in going as well-armed in doing.
> Be witty, kind, enduring, unsubjected:
> Without you I keep heavy house.
> So be woman!' (p. 202).

When she steps down from the pedestal, Galatea questions Pygmalion's power by requesting 'an equal kiss', yet ultimately she agrees to be the ideal he wishes for.

The Pygmalion poems of the 1930s have little to do with the political themes which dominate the mainstream poetry of the decade. Pygmalion is tucked away in magazines and collections by minor poets. Writers of this decade continue the pessimistic outlook of the early twentieth century. Frank Laurence Lucas (1894–1967), a Cambridge classics fellow, poet and playwright with Bloomsbury connections, published 'Pygmalion to Galatea' in 1930 – a poem also concerned with ideals of womanhood.[27] Lucas's Pygmalion, watching his wife sleeping, thinks back to the time when she was a marble statue and caused no 'heart ache' (p. 32). Pygmalion regrets having caused her to come to life, and he prays that she continues to sleep:

> Sleep on, cold eyes I once so longed to wake;
> Could it but be for ever, that were best.
> Sleep on; the lifeless face is loveliest,

---

[27] Frank Laurence Lucas, *Marionettes* (Cambridge, 1930), p. 32.

> Whose blind eyes sham no soul, bid no heart ache,
> Uncurst with life's unrest (p. 32).

He laments that mankind often requests his 'own worst torment' from the gods who 'with a smile [...] grant us our despair' (p. 32). The problem, for Pygmalion, lies in the comparison of the statue's perfect state with the imperfections of humanity. His prayer has led to the woman's beauty being spoiled by time. Furthermore, he has learnt that loving a woman is more demanding than loving an insentient stone: 'There are harder loves than stone', he puns. Pygmalion mourns the loss of his unchanging ideal, suggesting that life's rewards are meagre in comparison.

Fletcher Allen's short story 'Sequel to Galatea' (1932) published in *The Cornhill Magazine* under the editorship of Leonard Huxley, is likewise negative about the outcome of the relationship between Pygmalion and Galatea and opens with a comparable use of vindictive gods: 'There was laughter on Olympus' (Allen, p. 235). Allen's Galatea is a devoted beauty who has 'no mind apart from' Pygmalion's (p. 237). After her transformation, Pygmalion loses his ability to sculpt perfect statues, his income declines, and he quickly grows tired of Galatea's conversation and unappetising cooking:

> Galatea has killed all inspiration. When I speak, she echoes what I say. What I think, she thinks after me, but she will not quarrel with me. There is no motion to my life. [...] 'Would to the gods', he cried, 'that they had not heard me when I prayed that you might breathe and be alive' (Allen, p. 239 and p. 241).

The gods respond by changing Galatea back into stone. Pygmalion examines Galatea closely to make sure that she has returned to stone: he takes 'her hands and felt them cold, rang steel on her thighs, and was content' (p. 241). In the final scene, Pygmalion, now old and mad, is pitied by the younger generation for worshipping at the feet of the statue of Galatea everyday. He intends to sculpt another statue, but both he and his friends know that this will never happen.

This preference for the untransformed statue continues in 'To Galatea' (1934) by the Seattle-born poet Audrey Wurdemann. Here Pygmalion asks the statue to remain as she is: 'With unbowed head I pray: do not awaken, / Be marble, inviolate and inscrutable'. Pygmalion asks the statue to help him to preserve his ideal.[28] Lennard Gandalac's 'Galatea' of 1934, however, treats Galatea as a sinner who is left without a man to help her and dies. Her death is a punishment for her incestuous relationship with her father-creator; their unborn child also dies.[29] This

---

[28] Audrey Wurdemann, 'To Galatea', *Bright Ambush* (New York, 1934), p. 4.
[29] Lennard Gandalac, 'Galatea', *Canadian Forum*, 14 (1934), p. 268.

contrasts with G. J. D. Coleridge's classical 'Pygmalion' (1935) which retells the story along traditional lines, depicting the statue as 'a perfect woman exquisitely formed' (p. 18).[30] She is 'the best and sweetest wife / Man ever had vouchsafed to him' (p. 19).

New Pygmalions: The 1940s to the 1990s

Ovid's reputation reaches a low point in the poetry of the 1940s and 1950s, when classical mythology is no longer involved in the cutting edge. Philip Larkin's disapproval of the 'common myth-kitty' as an ideologically burdened irrelevance identifies classicism with the erudition, elitism and obscurity of the Modernists. The social agenda of the 'Movement' poets directed attention towards contemporaneity. In this period the Pygmalion story remains alive primarily in the work of American and other overseas writers of English. There has, more recently, been something of a revival in interest in Ovid. This resurgence of interest has produced several new versions of the Pygmalion story. C. H. Sisson's *Metamorphoses* (1968), the specially commissioned poems in Michael Hofmann and James Lasdun's *After Ovid* (1994), and Ted Hughes's *Tales From Ovid* (1997) have all gone some way to promoting the idea of Ovid's relevance for today.[31]

There are few poems on the Pygmalion subject during the forties and fifties. The conservative journal *Poetry Review* published 'Galatea' by Charles J. Rowe in 1947 and a poem of the same name by Malcolm H. Tattersall in 1948.[32] Rowe's account of the transformation seen through the eyes of Galatea is not radical like earlier feminist versions which use her perspective. Galatea views Pygmalion as a protector-king and declares that she has 'no life but' his (p. 414). Tattersall's sonnet sees Galatea as a vision caused by an overheated imagination. Alun Llewellyn's 'Galatea' (1956), in *Poetry Review*, is more positive.[33] He looks back to the certainties of a traditional perspective. The American poet and New Critic Richard Palmer Blackmur reads Pygmalion's creativity as an act inspired by the 'fiend'.[34] Galatea is a 'torso spoiled', 'the sweet too fine for flesh' (p. 150).

Australian poet and critic, Alec Derwent Hope composed 'Pygmalion'

---

[30] G. J. D. Coleridge, *Pygmalion and Other Poems* (London, 1935), pp. 7–19.

[31] *After Ovid: New Metamorphoses*, ed. by Michael Hoffmann and James Lasdun (London, 1994), p. xii. This is an anthology of specially commissioned versions of Ovid's stories from Ovid's *Metamorphoses*. Writers in the anthology 'translate, reinterpret, reflect on or completely re-imagine the narratives' (p. xii).

[32] Malcolm H. Tattersall, 'Galatea', *Poetry Review*, 39 (1948), 383.

[33] Alun Llewellyn 'Galatea', *Poetry Review*, 47(1956), 19.

[34] R. P. Blackmur, *Poems*, ed. by Denis Donoghue (Princeton, New Jersey, 1977), p. 150.

(1938–1941) early in his career.[35] His poem combines traditional subject matter with some taboo-challenging content. Pygmalion begins by hoping that the statue will be his ideal incarnate when it comes to life. Once they have embarked on their life together, however, Pygmalion and Galatea 'cannot wake back to those selves again' (p. 25), and the consummation of their love is seen in part as a loss. Pygmalion is unable to conjure up a mental picture of Galatea as once she was. Our memories of people are not stable, Hope suggests. When he thinks of Galatea, Pygmalion can only remember 'the surprise of unaccustomed hands, reluctant eyes, menstrual, remote' (p. 25). This image of her invades Pygmalion's mind and he imagines Galatea as a

> [...] cancer ripening in the will,
> pushing its intricate trespass furtively
> in the soft belly fibre . [...]
> This is my room, my mind. Get out of here! (p. 25).

Pygmalion experiences 'the horror of Love' (p. 25) and demands that Galatea take her 'damned clothes', her 'two-sex thoughts', and her 'laugh' (p. 26) and leave him alone to remember her silent simper. Pygmalion contemplates his future relationship with his wife, wondering whether she will try 'to build / a garden suburb of kindness' where they piled their 'terrible sexual landscape, heap on heap of raging mountains' (p. 26). The notion that their relationship has altered into a tame parody of what it once was is rejected as Pygmalion acknowledges his need to experience 'loss' of his idyllic vision of her (p. 26).

Hope gives the story a new context and modern scenery. Patrick Kavanagh, in the sixties, likewise changed the setting and the went further, in depicting Pygmalion as female. Kavanagh recasts Pygmalion as a stone-like Irishwoman working in a field. She has a twisted face deadened by hardship, and lips 'frozen in the signature of Lust'.[36] The speaker asks 'every man from Balladreen to grassy Boyle' for the name of the woman, and all reply that she is 'a stone Pygmalion' (p. 31). The men smile at the speaker's insistence that 'at dawn tomorrow she will be / Clay-sensuous' (p. 31). While retaining the essence of the story – love and stone – this version combines the role of the sculptor and the statue, presenting Pygmalion as the one who will soften into life and become submissive.

Pygmalion's disillusionment with Galatea continues into the 1960s. C. H. Sisson's humorous and cynical version in 'Metamorphoses' (1961) retells the myth as part of a rendering of several tales from the *Metamorphoses* and follows Ovid quite closely.[37] Sisson, whose use of the classical subject is extensive, turns

---

[35] Alec Derwent Hope, *The Wandering Islands* (Sydney, 1955), pp. 24–26.
[36] Patrick Kavanagh, *Collected Poems* (London, 1964), p. 31.
[37] C. H. Sisson, *Metamorphoses* (London, 1968), pp. 54–56.

away from Ovid at the end of the poem, rendering, instead, the twentieth-century conception of Pygmalion as a reluctant lover who wishes his wife to change back into stone.

> To his surprise the girl grew warm;
> He slobbered and she slobbered back
>
> – This is that famous mutual flame.
> The worst is yet to come.
>
> Although he often wished her back
> In silent marble, good and cold
>
> The bitch retained her human heart,
> The conquest of a stone by art.
>
> May Venus keep me from all hope
> And let me turn my love to stone.

Robert Conquest's Galatea of 1962 is regarded by Pygmalion with 'passion and reserve', and he prefers the traditional line.[38] Roy Fuller's Pygmalion (1965) is as unwilling as Sisson's, repeating the refrain: 'do not imagine I was glad she breathed'.[39] The sculptor coyly describes Galatea's naked body as a landscape which inspires his 'appetite and longing': 'the territory was deeply cleft and heathed' (Fuller, p. 50). Pygmalion's ascetic life is seen as noble in comparison with his dread of 'the unequal clash that had to be' as the statue causes him to infringe his celibate rule (Fuller, p. 50).

This negativity towards Galatea continues into the 1980s. Arthur Brestel's 'Pygmalion's second Prayer' finds Galatea 'flawed, marred flesh and bone, / A frail, and faulty, fickle, fussy wife'.[40] Pygmalion begs sympathy from Jove and asks him to 'transform my lovely one again to stone' (p. 28). The Irish poet Derek Mahon, on the other hand, stays pretty close to the original narrative, opting for poetic translation rather than interpretation. His fellow countryman, Michael Longley, reworks the tale, in the same collection, in 'Ivory and Water' (*After Ovid*, p. 240). Longley presents the story as a code for behaviour: if you are a lonely bachelor who emulates Pygmalion, then it is likely that you will find your beloved is little more than a fantasy which will dissolve into an intangibility 'until / There is nothing left of her for anyone to hug or hold' (p. 240).

---

[38] Robert Conquest, *Between Mars and Venus* (London, 1962), pp. 16–17.
[39] Roy Fuller, *Buff* (London, 1965), p. 50.
[40] Arthur L. Brestel, 'Pygmalion's Second Prayer', *The Classical Bulletin*, 59 (1983), 28.

Ted Hughes regards Ovid's popularity as a mystery, but nevertheless, finds an affinity with his work: Ovid's myths 'establish a rough register of what it feels like to live in the psychological gulf that opens at the end of an era'.[41] Hughes, who studied archaeology and anthropology at Cambridge, had a lifelong interest in myth. His 'Pygmalion' is foremost a verse translation from the *Metamorphoses*, beginning with an outline of the story of the Propoetides and the Cerastae, and Venus's displeasure at their blasphemy.[42] Hughes adds only a few details to the story: Pygmalion is sent 'slightly mad' by the spectacle of the prostituted women, but nevertheless 'adored women' (p. 145). Hughes's interest in animals is never far away from his poetry; Pygmalion's fear of women is likened to arachnophobia, and he sees 'every woman's uterus [turn] [in]to a spider' (p. 145):

> Her face, voice, gestures, hair became its web.
> Her perfume was a floating horror. Her glance
> Left a spider-bite (p. 145).

Hughes displays a post-Romantic conception of the myth in his allusion to Pygmalion's inspirational dream of the 'perfect body of a perfect woman', which is so present in his mind that it seemed as if it 'had taken possession of his body / To find herself a life' (p. 146). Like the Pygmalion of the post-Romantics, this is a Pygmalion who has little control over his talent: 'he watched his hands shaping a woman / As if he were still asleep' (p. 146). The remainder of the poem follows Ovid quite closely. The beauty of this rendering of tale lies in its simplicity. The language is plain and the pace is fast. The poem shows Hughes to be in touch with the tale's heritage.

Conclusion

The predominant interest for twentieth-century male writers is Pygmalion's creative crisis. Pygmalion's new difficulty lies in defining his attitude to idealism. As writers put into practice a Nietzschean rereading of classical myth, there is a movement away from the Apolline, affirming reason and order, and towards the Dionysian, emphasizing unattainable goals and sexual passion. Pygmalion becomes confused and anguished about how he defines his ideal, and whether he can accept her once she appears. In the late nineteenth and early twentieth century,

---

[41] Ted Hughes, *Tales From Ovid: Twenty-Four Passages from the Metamorphoses* (London, 1997), p. xi.

[42] Ten of the tales were dramatized by Tim Supple and Simon Reade for the Royal Shakespeare Company, but Pygmalion is not among them. Tim Supple and Simon Reade, *Ted Hughes's Tales From Ovid* (London, 1999).

the story is developed from being man-centred to woman-centred. The perspective of the statue is taken by many poets of the late nineteenth and early twentieth centuries, but the radical nature of the poems which adopt this viewpoint fizzles out by the 1920s. They, nevertheless, demonstrate that the name 'Galatea', made popular by W. S. Gilbert, has become so strongly associated with the myth that poems on the Pygmalion myth can stand with the statue's name as an indicator of the subject matter. On the whole, the poems of the modern age tend to be shorter, and there is a great interest in retelling the story in the confined format of the sonnet, with the transformation, or change of heart, often taking place in the volta or turning-point.

Nineteenth-century renarrations reveal male fantasies of womanhood, giving expression to ideas on the dominance, oppression, education and controlling of women. The story is about a man creating his ideal woman: she is often conceived as childlike, pure, dependent, and even animal-like in her simplicity. For some, however, her nude body inspires lust and immorality, is an emblem for Hellenic excess, has no soul, and is condemned. The revelation of gender issues is not the story's sole concern, though. Clusters of Pygmalion texts disclose other interests, such as the nature of artistic creativity, and the respectability of Greek art. The nineteenth century begins with a heavy preoccupation with the art-work as the embodiment of the artist's ideals and visions, and ends with the emasculation of the artist as the focus moves to the empowerment of the woman Galatea becomes and the overturning of the patriarchal power of Pygmalion.

The Pygmalion story between the 1940s and 1980s is largely confined to minor collections and poetry magazines. There is evidence, however, of a recent upsurge of interest in this and other tales from the *Metamorphoses* by poets at the end of the millennium. Perhaps this is because of the myths' concentration on dramatic changes. 'On the eve of the millennium', Charles Martin argues, 'no classical poet is better positioned to sustain his popular appeal than Ovid' (p. xxxiii) with his 'trenchant images of mutability, dislocation, atrocity and hope' (p. xxiv). Martin's collection of translations and renderings of Ovid, *Ovid in English* (1998), has no doubt added to the popularity of the poet's work in recent times. He notes the increasing regularity with which translations of the *Metamorphoses* have appeared since the middle of the twentieth century (p. xxxiii). His collection draws on the centuries of past interpretations of the tales. Charles Martindale's collection of essays on the influence of Ovid on from twelfth century onwards, *Ovid Renewed* (1988), likewise stresses the importance of the poet for the history of European literature. In spite of this exertion towards the popularization of Ovidian subject-matter, and the advances of feminist revisionism, the story remains the property of men in the twentieth century, and principally, these men are academics and critics. There is still something a little recherché about the classical subject, a view that the new translations and interpretations aim to dispel.

The arrival of Internet publishing and search engines has meant that new versions of the Pygmalion myth are reaching the public domain more easily than ever. The feminist agenda has been reawakened through this medium. The constant appearance of new versions of the Pygmalion story means that any study of it is by nature open-ended and provisional. I hope to have shown, however, that interpretations of the Pygmalion story are extremely diverse, and that the narrative provides a vehicle for the exploration of many very different themes. It is hoped that future renarrations continue this striking tradition, garnering imaginative insights from the original narrative and its complex heritage.

Appendix 1
The Pygmalion Story in Dictionaries and Handbooks of Classical Literature

One might expect that dictionaries of classical literature would accurately record the origins of classical stories in their earliest or most popular form or document distinct versions in such a way as to make it clear that they are separate. This, however, is not always the case with the Pygmalion story. Approaches to definition are quite diverse, with some writers conflating early versions to create a single story and others providing moralistic interpretations of the narrative. This, unfortunately, leads to confusion and occasionally contradiction.

The commonest problem with classical dictionaries is that insufficient distinction is made between Ovid's version and other early sources. William Smith's *A Classical Dictionary of Greek and Roman Biography, Mythology and Geography* (1849) combines Ovid's story of Pygmalion the sculptor and father of Paphos with Apollodorus's Pygmalion

> King of Cyprus and father of Metharme. He is said to have fallen in love with the image of a maiden which he himself had made, and therefore to have prayed to Aphrodite to breathe life into it. When the request was granted, Pygmalion, married his beloved, and became by her the father of Paphus.[1]

Apollodorus's version does not mention the statue and makes Cinyras (who, in Ovid, is Pygmalion's grandson and the man who fathered Adonis incestuously by his daughter Myrrha) Pygmalion's son-in-law and father of Adonis by Metharme. Furthermore, Smith adds something new to the story when he makes Paphos the brother (or sister) of Metharme. Ovid does not mention Metharme and Apollodorus does not refer to Paphos as a person (only as a place). It is clear that Smith has combined Apollodorus's story with Ovid's in an arbitrary fashion adding his own link to make the connection seem more plausible.

The elevation of Pygmalion the sculptor to the rank of king is a common occurrence in dictionaries and handbooks, despite there being no mention of this in Ovid. For example, Pierre Grimal's *A Concise Dictionary of Classical Mythology* calls Pygmalion 'A king of Cyprus, who fell in love with an ivory

---

[1] *A Classical Dictionary of Greek and Roman Biography, Mythology*, ed. by William Smith, 3 vols (London, 1844–1849), III (1849), 606.

statue'.² Even the recently published *Oxford Guide to Classical Mythology in the Arts* describes Pygmalion as a 'king of Cyprus' who 'carved an ivory statue'.³ Ovid's is the only source for a Pygmalion who was a sculptor of a statue, and he does not make Pygmalion royal. Arnobius's is the only account which has both a statue and a King Pygmalion, but in this version Pygmalion does not sculpt.

There are some differences of opinion concerning the statue. Many dictionaries describe it as being made of marble rather than the ivory of Ovid's version. This may be because they are using Clement of Alexandria as a source (though this is uncredited), or it may be a result of the popularity of marble in later renarrations of the story. Lemprière's *Classical Dictionary* suggests that Pygmalion 'became enamoured of a beautiful statue of marble which he had made', whilst incorrectly naming Ovid as the source of this.⁴ Marble is also suggested by Abraham Lass and Eric Smith (p. 208).⁵ Several dictionaries give the name Galatea to the statue without explaining that this is a post-classical addition to the tale. Lemprière suggests, for example, that 'the goddess of Beauty changed the favourite statue into a woman, whom the artist married, naming her Galatea' (Lemprière, 1963, p. 534). Lass's Pygmalion 'created a perfect woman of marble, naming her *Galatea*' (p. 184). Under the heading 'Galatea', Lass gives his own interpretation of the Pygmalion story, and prefers not to mention Ovid's nymph Galatea from the thirteenth book of the *Metamorphoses*:

> The sculptor *Pygmalion* scorned living women for their imperfections, and resolved to create a perfect woman. In revenge, *Aphrodite* caused him to fall in love with a cold stone statue, but finally relented and

---

² Pierre Grimal, *A Concise Dictionary of Classical Mythology*, ed. by Stephen Kershaw and trans. by A. R. Maxwell-Hyslop (Oxford, 1990), p. 380. Gail Marshall likewise assumes that Ovid's Pygmalion is king of Cyprus in 'Actresses, Statues and Speculation in *Daniel Deronda*', *Essays in Criticism*, 44 (1994), 117–139 (p. 117) and in *Actresses on the Victorian Stage* (1998), p. 17.

³ See also *Ausführliches Lexikon der Grieschischen und Römischen Mythologie*, ed. by W. H. Roscher, 6 vols (Leipzig, 1884–1937), III, 3317–3319, *Webster's New International Dictionary of the English Language*, ed. by Noah Webster (London and Springfield, Massachusetts, 1909), p. 1742, *The Oxford Companion to Classical Literature*, ed. by Paul Harvey (Oxford, 1940), p. 355, *A Handbook of Greek Mythology*, ed. by H. J. Rose (London, 1958), p. 340, *Lexikon der Grieschischen und Römischen Mythologie*, ed. by Herbert Hunger (Wien, 1959), p. 360, *Dictionary of Mythology, Folklore and Symbols*, ed. by Gertrude Jobes, 2 vols (New York, 1962), II, 1306, *A Dictionary of Classical Reference in English Poetry*, ed. by Eric Smith (Woodbridge, 1984), p. 208, *The Reader's Encyclopedia*, ed. by William Rose Benét, 3rd edn (London, 1988), p. 802, A. R. Hope Moncrieff, *Classical Mythology* (Guernsey, 1994), p. 121.

⁴ *Lemprière's Classical Dictionary*, ed. by F. A. Wright (London, 1963).

⁵ *The Facts on File Dictionary of Classical, Biblical and Literary Allusions*, ed. by Abraham Lass (New York and Oxford, 1987), p. 184.

brought it life as the mortal Galatea (Lass, p. 81).[6]

There is no evidence in the classical sources for an interpretation of the metamorphosis as a revenge story. Venus, in Ovid, punishes the Propoetides by turning them into stone at the beginning of Pygmalion's tale, but vengeance is not the link with the Pygmalion story.

Several dictionaries change the name of Ovid's Venus to her Greek counterpart Aphrodite. This is probably because a Roman goddess might seem out of place in a Greek story. There are definitions which claim that the statue is a portrait of Aphrodite. Gertrude Jobes's Pygmalion is a misogynistic King of Cyprus who sculpts a statue of Aphrodite and falls in love with it (Jobes, p. 1306). William Rose Benét's sculptor king likewise falls 'in love with his own ivory statue of *Aphrodite*' (Benét, p. 802). The substitution of Aphrodite for Venus is also made by Moncrieff, Rose and Edward Tripp.[7] Again, these are unacknowledged composite definitions which derive from multiple sources. Ovid does not include this detail, but it is a feature of both Clement of Alexandria and Arnobius of Sicca (who do not report that Pygmalion was a sculptor).

Aside from errors which derive from the conflation of sources, a manuscript difficulty in Ovid's *Metamorphoses* has also generated problems with the identification of the sex of Pygmalion's child, Paphos. Franz Bömer's commentary suggests that traditionally Paphos is thought of as having been female, but more recently, Paphos has come to be thought of as male.[8] H. J. Rose, Mark Morford, Jean Lang and Lemprière all indicate that Paphos is a man, whereas Tripp, M. A. Howatson, W. H. Roscher, Smith and *The Oxford Guide to Classical Mythology in the Arts* all note that Paphos is a woman.[9] Bömer suggests that the problem cannot be resolved due to difficulties with the text.

Occasionally, dictionaries and handbooks make references to later renarrations of the Pygmalion story. John Marston's version is listed most often in books published between 1940 and 1988. This is followed by George Bernard Shaw, William Morris and W. S. Gilbert.

---

[6] The statue is also called Galatea by A. R. Hope Moncrieff: 'Galatea was the name he gave his statue, in vain, hoping to call it to life' (p. 121).

[7] Edward Tripp, *The Collins Dictionary of Classical Mythology* (London, 1988).

[8] Franz Bömer, *P. Ovidius Naso. Metamorphosen. Kommentar 10–11* (Heidelberg, 1980), p. 110.

[9] Mark P. O. Morford and Robert J. Lenardon, *Classical Mythology* (New York, 1991), p. 144, *A Book of Myths*, ed. by Jean Lang (London and Edinburgh, 1915), pp. 11–15, *The Oxford Companion to Classical Literature*, ed. by M. C. Howatson (Oxford, 1989).

Appendix 2

Bibliography of Pygmalion References

1. References in Latin and Greek Literature[1]

3 BC (fl.)	Philostephanus, *(Cypriaca)* or *The History of Cyprus* (prose) †
AD 1–AD 8	Ovid, *Metamorphoses* (poetry)
1st/2nd cent. AD	Apollodorus, *Bibliotheca* (prose) †
c. AD 40	Philippos, *Garland* (in *Anthologia Graeca*, XI. 347) (Fragments of a collection of Greek epigrams)†
2nd/3rd cent. AD	Clement of Alexandria, *Protrepticus* or *The Exhortation of the Greeks* (prose) †
3rd cent.	Arnobius of Sicca, *Adversus Nationes* (prose)
before 207	Hyginus, *Fabulae* (prose)
c.270 AD	Porphyry, *De Abstinentia* (*On Abstinence From Animal Food*) (prose)[2]†
before 500	Nonnos Panopolitanus, *Dionysiaca* (prose)†
6th cent. AD	Lactantius Placidius, *Lactanti Placidi Qui Dicitur Narrationes Fabularum Ovidianorum* (prose)
c.1200	Arnulf of Orleans, *Allegoriae super Ovidii Metamorphosin* (prose)
1322–1323	Giovanni del Virgilio, *Epositore del Metamorphosi* (prose)

---

[1] This section lists all texts which are written in either Latin or Greek. I have provided a short description of the genre of each reference in brackets. Greek texts are indicated by the symbol '†'. I have been unable to date the brief reference to Pygmalion in the fragments of Hellanicus's *Cypriaca* (fragment 147) in *Fragmenta Historicorum Graecorum*, I, 65.

[2] Porphyry notes that Pygmalion is mentioned by Neanthes Cyzicenus and Asclepiades Cyprius. This is also noted in K. Müller, *Fragmenta Historicorum Graecorum*, III, 10 and 306.

c.1340	Petrus Berchorius (or Pierre Bersuire), *Ovidius Moralizatus* (prose)
1360–1420 (fl.)	Thomas Walsingham, *De Archana Deorum* (prose)
1493	Raphael Regius, *Ovidius Metamorphoses, cum Commento Familiari* (prose)
1555	George Sabinus, *Fabularum Ovidii Interpretatio Ethica, Physica et Historica* (prose)
1563	Johann Sprengius, *Metamorphoses Ovidii* (prose)
1630–1650	Anonymous, *Pygmalion* (playlet in verse)
1648	Richard Crashaw, 'In Pigmaliona' (poem)
1736	Thomas Gray, *Hymeneal* (short reference in Latin poem)

2. Renarrations of the Pygmalion Story in English Literature[3]

Major Renarrations

1390–1393	John Gower, 'Pygmaleon and the Statue' in *Confessio Amantis* (poem)
1557–1587	Anonymous, 'The Tale of Pigmalion' in *Tottel's Miscellany* (poem)
1566	Bernard Garter, 'A Strife Betwene Appelles and Pigmalion' (poem)
1568	William Fulwood, *The Enimie of Idlenesse* (poem)

---

[3] This section lists versions of the Pygmalion story in the English Language and is divided into two groups. The first group lists the major renarrations of the Pygmalion story. When the renarration is part of a larger poem, the title of the poem is given in addition to any subtitle which refers to the renarration. There follows a list of shorter references to Pygmalion. Where possible the references have been listed chronologically according to the year in which they were first published. Where the year of composition is known, I have listed references according to this and noted the date of the first publication.

Appendix 2: Pygmalion References

1576	George Pettie, *A Petite Pallace of Pettie and his Pleasure* (prose)
1592	Samuel Daniel, 'Sonnet XIII' in *Delia* (sonnet)
1596	Bartholemew Griffen, 'Compare me to Pygmalion' (sonnet)
1598	John Marston, *The Metamorphosis of Pigmalion's Image* (poem)
1611	John Davies, 'Against Pigmalions Indiscretion' (epigram in verse)
1657	Hugh Crompton, 'Pigmalion' (epigram)
1672	Anonymous, *Chaucer's Ghoast* (poem)
1773	James Robertson, 'To Please Pygmalion, Heav'n Inspir'd With Life' (poem)
1779	Anonymous, Rousseau's *Pygmalion* translated into English verse (poem)[4]
1790	Anonymous, 'Pygmalion, A Novel' in *The Massachusetts Magazine* (serialized novel)
1796	Anonymous, 'The New Pygmalion; An Interesting Story' in *The Philadelphia Minerva* (short story)
1820	Leigh Hunt, 'Rousseau's *Pygmalion*' (translation and commentary)
1823-1825	Thomas Lovell Beddoes, 'Pygmalion. The Cyprian Statuary' (poem)
1823	William Hazlitt, *Liber Amoris or The New Pygmalion* (prose)
1823	William Hazlitt, *Characteristics* (Maxim: CCCXIII)
1832	Arthur Henry Hallam, 'Lines spoken in the Character of Pygmalion' (charade-poem)
1853	James Payn, 'Pygmalion' (poem)

---

[4] This poem is a loose translation of Rousseau's play.

1857	William Cox Bennett, 'Pygmalion' (poem)
1858	George MacDonald, *Phantastes* (novel)
1860	John Byrne Leicester Warren, 'Pygmalion' (poem)
1863	Robert Buchanan, 'Pygmalion the Sculptor' (poem)
1865	Ernest Hartley Coleridge, 'Pygmalion's Bride' (poem)
1866	Keningale Robert Cook, 'Pygmalion' (poem)[5]
1867	William Brough, *Pygmalion or the Statue* (play in verse)[6]
1868-1870	William Morris, 'Pygmalion and the image' in *The Earthly Paradise* (poem)
1868	Algernon Charles Swinburne, Review of Frederick Watt's Pygmalion painting
1869	William Hurrell Mallock, 'Pygmalion to his statue, become his wife' (poem)
1870	James Rhoades, 'Pygmalion's Statue' (poem)
1871	W. S. Gilbert, *Pygmalion and Galatea* (play)
1871	George Barlow, 'Pygmalion's Doom Reversed' (sonnet)
1874	John Hooley, 'Pygmalion' (poem)
1875	Henry Ellison, 'Pygmalion Reversed' (sonnet)
1875	William Bell Scott, ''Pygmalion' (sonnet)
1875	J. R. S., 'A Song for Galatea' (poem)
1879	Lewis Carroll, 'Charade' (charade poem)

---

[5] This was first published in 1870.
[6] This is the first farcical treatment of the myth, in English, in the form of a play.

Appendix 2: Pygmalion References

1880	George Eric Lancaster, 'Pygmalion in Cyprus' (poem)[7]
1881	Emily Henrietta Hickey, 'Sonnet' (sonnet)
1881	Thomas Woolner, *Pygmalion* (poem)
1883	Andrew Lang, *The New Pygmalion or The Statue's Choice* (lyric drama)
1883	Ronald Ross, *Edgar or The New Pygmalion* (play)
1883	Henry Pottinger Stephens, *Galatea; or Pygmalion Reversed* (burlesque)
1883	Edward Rowland Sill, 'The Lost Magic' in *Hermione* (poem)
1885	Elizabeth Stuart Phelps, 'Galatea' (poem)
1886	Agnes Rous Howell, *Euphrosyne; or The Sculptor's Bride* (play)
1887	Sir Frank Marzials, 'Pygmalion' (sonnet)[8]
1887	Mary Nagle, 'Pygmalion'(poem)
1890	Joseph John Murphy, 'Pygmalion' (poem)
1891	Frederick Tennyson, *Cyprus, Pygmalion* (poem)
1892	Thomas Sturge Moore, 'Pygmalion' (sonnet)
1894	Ernest Dowson, 'Epigram' (poem)[9]
1895	Sara King Wiley, 'Pygmalion and Galatea' (poem)[10]
1898	William E. Hurrell, *Pygmalion* (poem)

---

[7] This author also published under the name of George Eric Mackay.

[8] This sonnet was inspired by the Pygmalion paintings of Edward Burne-Jones.

[9] A second version of this poem was given the title 'The Requital'. See *The Poetical Works of Ernest Dowson*, ed. by Desmond Flower (London, 1967), p. 87, p. 186 and p. 264.

[10] The poem was published in Britain.

1909	Ralph Hale Mottram, 'Pygmalion and the Image' (poem)
1910	Robert Whitehouse, *Pygmalion and the Statue* (poem)
1911	Benjamin Robbins Curtis Low, 'Galatea' (poem)
1912	George Bernard Shaw, *Pygmalion* (play)
1920	Benjamin Low, 'Pygmalion to Galatea' (poem)
1921	Ruth Pitter, 'Galatea' (poem)
1921	C. M. Lewis, 'Pygmalion' (poem)
1923	Elizabeth Coatsworth, 'To Poor Pygmalion' (poem)
1925–1926	Robert Graves, 'Pygmalion to Galatea' (poem)
1926	Genevieve Taggard, 'Galatea Again' (poem)
1928	Cecil Day Lewis, 'The Perverse' (poem)
1928	James Agee, 'Pygmalion' (poem)
1929	Roselle Mercier Montgomery, 'Galatea to Pygmalion' (poem)
1930	Frank Laurence Lucas, 'Pygmalion to Galatea' (poem)
1930	Alfred Julian Talbot, *The Passing of Galatea* (play in one act)[11]
1932	Fletcher Allen, 'Sequel to Galatea' (short story)
1934	Audrey Wurdemann, 'To Galatea' (poem)
1934	Lennard Gandalac, 'Galatea' (poem)
1935	Gilbert Coleridge, 'Pygmalion' (poem)
1938	Robert Graves, 'Galatea and Pygmalion' (poem)

---

[11] The play was printed in America and the author may be American.

Appendix 2: Pygmalion References

1940	Hilda Doolittle (H. D.), 'Pygmalion' (poem)
1944	Anna Hempstead Branch, 'Pygmalion' (poem)
1947	Charles J. Rowe, 'Galatea' (poem)
1948	Malcolm H. Tattersall, 'Galatea' (poem)
1950	R. P. Blackmur, 'All's the Foul Fiend's' (poem)
1951	Grace Greenwood (pseud. of Sara Jane Lippincott), 'Pygmalion' (poem)
1956	Alec Derwent Hope, 'Pygmalion' (poem)
1956	Alun Llewellyn, 'Galatea' (poem)
1958	Thomas Cruden, *Pygmalion and His Galatea* (comic play in one act)
1958–1960	Howard Levant, 'Pygmalion' (poem)
1961	C. H. Sisson, 'Metamorphoses' in *Metamorphoses* (poem)
1962	Robert Conquest, 'Galatea' (poem)
1964	Patrick Kavanagh, 'Pygmalion' (poem)
1965	Roy Fuller, 'The Truth about Pygmalion' (poem)
1967	Alan Jay Lerner, *My Fair Lady* (A musical play)[12]
1970	Richard Huggett, *The First Night of 'Pygmalion'* (comic play)
1981	Pamela Espeland, *The Story of Pygmalion* (prose)
1983	Arthur L. Brestel, 'Pygmalion's Second Prayer' (sonnet)
1986	Colin Way Reid, 'Pygmalion' (poem)

---

[12] Based on Shaw's *Pygmalion*.

1994	Derek Mahon, 'Pygmalion and Galatea' (poem)
1994	Michael Longley, 'Ivory and Water' (poem)[13]
1995	Richard Powers, *Galatea 2.2* (novel)
1997	Ted Hughes, 'Pygmalion' (poem)
1997	Laura Gene Beck, 'Pygmalion is Warned' (poem)
1999	Robert Manns, 'Pygmalion and Galatea' (a one-act play)

Shorter References

c.1375	Anonymous, *Pearl* (poem)
c.1387	Geoffrey Chaucer, *The Physician's Tale* and *The Knight's Tale* (poem)
before 1412	John Lydgate, *Reson and Sensuallyte* (poem)[14]
1412–1420	John Lydgate, *Troy Book* (poem)[15]

---

[13] The following have proved elusive: 'Pygmalion and Galatea', *Cambridge Review*, 20 (1898–1899), 299, Anna Wood Brown, 'Pygmalion', *Harper's Monthly Magazine*, 104 (1901–1902), 926, Albert Bigelow Paine, 'A Thwarted Pygmalion', *Harper's Monthly Magazine*, 136 (1917–1918), 609, L. Hulley, 'Pygmalion and Galatea' in *Fables and Myths From the Sibyl's Book* (1924), E. L. Squires, 'Galatea Awakes', *Poet Lore*, 38 (1927), 105, 'Pygmalion', *Dial*, 82 (1927), p. 170, 'Pygmalion', *Cambridge Review*, 49 (1927–1928), 76, Howard Levant, 'Pygmalion' *Epoch*, 10 (1958–1960), 158, Donald Williams, 'Pygmalion', *Western Humanities Review*, 27 (1973), 146, K. Poelitt, 'Pygmalion', *Poetry*, 134 (1979), 14, John Updike, 'Pygmalion', *Atlantic Monthly*, 284 (1981), 27, V. Drosd, 'Pygmalion', *Soviet Literature*, 2 (1984), 95, Mary Quattlebaum, 'The Statue Speaks with Pygmalion', *Poet Lore*, 85 (1990–1991), 9.

[14] This poem was 'written before 1412, the year in which the *Troy Book* was begun'. See *Lydgate's Reson and Sensuallyte*, ed. by Ernest Sieper, Early English Text Society, 84 and 89, 2 vols (London, 1901–1903), II (1903), 8.

[15] There are short references to Pygmalion in Lydgate's 'The Legend of St Gyle' and 'The Testament of Dan John Lydgate' in *The Minor Poems of John Lydgate*, ed. by Henry Noble MacCracken, Early English Text Series, extra series, 107 and 192, 2 vols (London, 1910–1934), I (1910), 171 and 355. These are not dated.

c.1550–1587	Alexander Montgomerie, 'Sang on the Lady Margaret Montgomerie' (poem)
1563	Bernard Garter, *The Tragicall [and True] Historie Which Happened Betwene Two English Lovers* (poem)
1567	George Tuberville, 'In Praise of Lady P.' (poem)
1572	Wilfrid Holme, *The Fall and Evill Successe of Rebellion from Time to Time* (poem)
1573	Lodowick Lloyd, 'Had Greek Calisthenes Silence Kept' in *The Pilgrimage of Princes Penned Out of Sundry Greeke And Latine Authors* (poem)
1575	R. B., *Apius and Virginia* (play)
1577	John Grange, *The Golden Aphroditis* (prose fiction)
1578	John Lyly, *Euphues: The Anatomy of Wit* (prose)
1580	Austen Saker, *Narbonus* (prose fiction)
1581	Barnaby Rich, *Riche His Farewell to Militarie Profession* (prose fiction)
1582	George Whetstone, *An Heptameron of Ciuill Discourses* (prose fiction)
1584	Robert Greene, *Debate Between Follie and Love* (prose)
c.1587	William Fowler, 'The Triumph of Love' (poem/translation)[16]
1587	Christopher Marlowe, *ii Tamburlaine* (play)
1590	Henry Roberts, *A Defiance to Fortune* (prose fiction)
1593	Thomas Churchyard, *A Pleasant Conceite Penned in Verse* (poem)

---

[16] This is based on Petrarch's text of the same name.

170	Pygmalion and Galatea
1592	Christopher Marlowe, *The Jew of Malta* (play)
1594	Christopher Marlowe, *Dido, Queen of Carthage* (play)
1595(?)	John Burel, *To The Richt High Lodwick Duke of Lenox* (poem)
1596	Bartholemew Griffen, 'If great Apollo offered as a dower' (sonnet)
1598	Robert Tofte, *Alba* (poem)
1598	Edward Guilpin, 'Satyra Secunda' *Skialetheia, or A Shadow of Truth* (poem)
1599	Thomas Middleton, 'Micro-Cynicon' (poem)
1600	Robert Ayton, 'Will Thow, Remorseles Fair (poem)
1602	William Basse, 'Three Pastoral Elegies; of Anander, Anetor and Muridella', elegy 2 (poem)
1603	William Muggins, *London's Mourning Garment* (poem)
1603	John Davies, *Microcosmos* (poem)
1604	William Shakespeare, *Measure For Measure* (play)
1605	Francis Bacon, *The Advancement of Learning* (prose)
1605	Anonymous, *The History of the Tryall of Cheualry* (play)
c.1605	John Davies, 'nihil tam bene dictum, quod non fuit dictum prius' (poem)
1606	John Hind, *Eliosto Libidinoso* (prose fiction)
1606	George Chapman, *Monsieur d'Olive* (play)
1607	Richard Niccols, *The Cuckow* (poem)
1607	Gervase Markham, *The English Arcadia* (prose fiction)
1607	Thomas Tomkis, *Lingva; Or The Combat of the Tongue* (play)

Appendix 2: Pygmalion References

1611	Richard Brathwait, 'The Sixth Sonet' (poem)
1612	Richard Johnson, 'A Lover's Song in Praise of His Mistresse' (poem)
1615	R. A., *The Valiant Welshman* (play)
1619	John Heath, 'To Mistris E. S.' (poem)
1621	Richard Brathwait, 'The Fift Satyre' (poem)
1621	Richard Brathwait, 'Omphale, Or The Inconstant Shephearde' (poem)
1622	George Wither, *Faire Virtue, The Mistresse of Philarete* (poem)
1622	John Hagthorpe, 'How Wretched and How Vaine' (poem)
1626	John Kennedy, *History of Calanthrop and Lucilla* (poem)
1628	Robert Gomersall, *The Levites Revenge* (poem)
1630	John Taylor, 'A Whore' (poem)
1630	Philip Massinger, *The Renegado* (play)
1631	Richard Johnson, *Tom a Lincolne* (prose fiction)
1631	James Shirley, *The Schoole of Complement* (play)
1632	Philip Massinger, *The Emperour Of the East* (play)
1633	Fulke Greville, 'A Treatie of Humane Learning' (prose)
1633	Anonymous, *The Costlie Whore* (play)
1635	Thomas Cranley, 'To the Faire Amanda' in *Amanda: Or The Reformed Whore* (poem)
1636	William Sampson, *The Vow Breaker* (play)
1637	James Shirley, *Hide Parke* (play)

1637	Nathaniel Whiting, 'Il Insonio Insonadado' (poem)[17]
1639	Samuel Pick, 'To his Deare Mistris, H. P.' (poem)
1640	Thomas Carew, 'To the Painter' (poem)
1640	Alexander Hart, *Alexto and Angelica* (prose fiction)
1644	Anna Hume, *The Triumph of Love; of Love, Chastitie, Death. Translated out of Petrarch* (translation)
1645	Edmund Waller, 'On the Discovery of a Ladies Painting' (poem)
1647	Abraham Cowley, 'Answer to the Platonicks' (poem)
1647	John Fletcher, *A Wife For a Moneth* (play)
1650	John Reynolds, *The Flower of Fidelitie* (prose fiction)
1651	Anna Weamys, *A Continuation of Sir Philip Sydney's Arcadia* (prose fiction)
1651	Leonard Willan, *Astræa, Or, True Love's Myrrour. A Pastoral* (play)
1653	Charles Sorel, *Extravagant Shepherd* (poem)
1653	John Cleveland, 'The Antiplatonick' (poem)
1656	Abraham Cowley, 'The Gazers' (poem)
1656	Samuel Holland, *Don Zara Del Fogo* (prose fiction)
1658	Sir Aston Cokayne, 'Of a Room In An Ale-House That We Call the Apollo' (poem)
1658	Sir Aston Cokayne, 'Now After Tedious Weeks of Being Mute' (poem)

---

[17] The poem is written in English.

Appendix 2: Pygmalion References

1658	Thomas Meriton, *The Wandring Lover* (play)
1659	Anonymous, *Lady Alimony* (play)
1660	John Donne, 'A Paradoxe of a Painted Face' (poem)
1661	Alexander Brome, 'The Libertine' (poem)
1661	Thomas Ross, 'A Continuation of Silus Italicus To the Death of Hannibal' in *The Second Punick War* (poem)
1662	William Rowley, *The Birth of Merlin* (play)
1664	Henry King, 'Paradox. That Fruition Destroyes Love' (poem)
1666	William Killigrew, *The Seege of Urbin* (play)
1667	Richard Flecknoe, *The Damoiselles a la Mode* (play)
1668	John Dryden, *Secret Love; Or The Maiden-Queen* (play)
1669	Robert Stapylton, *Hero and Leander* (play)
1673	Matthew Stevenson, 'To A. B.' (poem)
1674	Thomas Flatman, 'The Review. Pindarique Ode to Mr William Sancroft' (poem)
1675	Henry Nevil Payne, *The Siege Of Constantinople; A Tragedy Acted at the Duke's Theatre* (play)
1676	Nathaniel Lee, *Gloriana* (play)
1676	Robert Howard, 'A Sacred Poeme' (poem)
1682	Matthew Coppinger, 'The Lover's Jubile' (poem)
1683	Thomas Shipman, 'An Hystorick Poem' (poem)
1683	Thomas Shipman, 'New Libanus' (poem)
1688	Aphra Behn, 'To Damon' in *Lycidus* (poem)

1688	Walter Scot, *A True History Of Several Honourable Families* (poem)
1689	Charles Cotton, 'The Visit' (poem)
1689	Charles Cotton, 'The Picture' (poem)
1689	Charles Goodall, 'To Idera, Speechless' (poem)
1697	Thomas Scott, *The Unhappy Kindness* (play)
1700	John Dryden, 'The Wife of Bath Her Tale' in *Fables* (poem)
1700	John Hopkins, 'To Amasia, On Her Drawing Her Own Picture' (poem)
1707	Colley Cibber, *The Comical Lovers* (play)
1710	Mary de la Rivière Manley, *Memoirs of Europe* (novel)
1722	Samuel Whyte, 'The Nosegay' (poem)
1724	Richard Savage, 'To Mr. John Dyer, A Painter' (poem)
1727	Christopher Pitt, 'The Fable of the Young Man and his Cat' (poem)
1727	Edward Young, 'Satire I. To His Grace the Duke of Dorset' (poem)
1728	Soame Jenyns, 'The Art Of Dancing' (poem)
1729	Lady Mary Wortley Montagu, 'Continuation' (poem)
1731	Joseph Mitchell, *Three Poetical Epistles to Mr Hogarth, Mr Dandridge and Mr Lambert, Masters in the Art of Painting* (Poem)
1731	Henry Travers, 'To Dr –', *Miscellaneous Poems and Translations* (poem)
1732	George Granville, 'To Myra. Loving at First Sight' (poem)

Appendix 2: Pygmalion References

1735	Robert Dodsley, *Beauty; or The Art of Charming* (poem)
1742	Henry Fielding, *Joseph Andrews* (novel)
1744	Sarah Fielding, *David Simple* (novel)
1745	Moses Mendez, *Henry and Blanche: or The Revengeful Marriage* (poem)
1748	James Thomson, *The Castle of Indolence* (poem)
1749	Thomas Tickell, 'On a Lady's Picture: To Gilfred Lawson esq.' (poem)
1752	Soame Jenyns, 'The Choice' (poem)
1756	David Garrick, *The Tempest* (play)
1764	James Woodhouse, 'The Lessowes' (poem)
1770	Edward Thompson, 'The Demi-Rep' (poem)
1773	James Robertson, 'The Metamorphosis. A Northern Tale' (poem)
1778	George Ellis (pseud. Sir Gregory Gander), 'The Canterbury Tale' (poem)
1782	William Cowper, *The Progress of Error* (poem)
1788	John Wolcot, 'Lyric Odes For the Year MDCCLXXXV' ('Ode VIII') (poem)
1792	Robert Bage, *Man As He Is* (novel)
1792	Thomas Holcroft, *Anna St Ives* (novel)
1795	Hannah Cowley, *The Town Before You* (play)
1796	Frances Moore Brooke, *Emily Montague* (novel)
1798	Mary Wollstonecraft, *The Wrongs of Woman* (novel)

1800	William Hayley, *An Essay on Sculpture* (poem)
1801	Sydney Owenson, 'The Refutation' (poem)
1804	George Huddesford, *Wood and Stone* (poem)
1806	Lucy Hutchinson, *Memoirs of the Life of Colonel Hutchinson* (prose)
1807	Samuel William Henry Ireland, *Stultifera Navis* (poem)
1807	Thomas Dermody, 'To Athemoe' and 'On Garrick's Tomb and Inscription' (two poems)
1810	Anna Seward, 'Ode to Poetic Fancy' (poem)
1811	Amelia Opie, 'Lines for the Album at Cossey' (poem)
1813	Thomas Dibdin, 'William the Conqueror' in *A Metrical History of England* (poem)
1813	Horatio Smith, 'Ode XV. The Parthenon' (poem)
1813	Richard Cumberland, *The Eccentric Lover* (play)
1815	Samuel William Henry Ireland, 'Antiquarians' (poem)
1816	George Crabbe, 'Resentment' (poem)
1819	Charles Issac M. Dibdin, 'Young Arthur, or The Child of Mystery: A Metrical Romance' (poem)
1819	Barry Cornwall, (Bryan Waller Procter) 'The Falcon' in *A Sicilian Story* (poem)
1819–1824	Lord Byron, *Don Juan* (poem)
1819	Richard Lalor Sheil, *Evadne; Or The Statue* (play)
1820	Charles Maturin, *Melmoth the Wanderer* (novel)
1820	Percy Bysshe Shelley, 'The Witch of Atlas' (poem)

Appendix 2: Pygmalion References

1821	Charles Lloyd, 'Titus and Gisippus' in *Desultry Thoughts in London* (poem)
1822	Charles Lloyd, *The Duke D'Ormond* (play)
1822	Barry Cornwall (Bryan Waller Proctor), 'Wishes' (poem)
1822	William Combe, *History of Johnny Quae Genus* (poem)
1826	William Hazlitt, 'Notes of a Journey Through France and Italy' (prose)
1837	Anonymous, 'The New Frankenstein' (short story)
1837	Richard Henry Horne, *The Death of Marlowe* (play)
1838	Robert Southey, 'Sonnet 4: The Poet Expresses His Feelings Respecting A Portrait In Delia's Parlour' in *The Amatory Poems of Abel Shufflebottom* (sonnet)
1838	Samuel Laman Blanchard, 'Helen Faucit in "The Lady of Lyons"' (poem)
1838	John Herman Merivale, 'St. George and the Dragon' (poem)
1839	Henry Ellison, 'Genius. A Series of Thoughts' (poem)
1840	Caroline Elizabeth Sarah Norton, 'Sonnet 1: On Seeing the Bust of the Young Princess De Montfort' (sonnet)
1840	James Smith, 'The Year Twenty-Six' (poem)
1841	Lady Emmeline Charlotte Elizabeth Stuart-Wortley, *Lillia Bianca* (poem)
1844	Nathaniel Hawthorne, 'Drowne's Wooden Image' (short story)
1845	Charles Mackay, 'Prologue to The Highland Ramble' (poem)
1847	Charles Mackay, 'The Out-Comer and the In-Goer' (poem)
1849	William Mackpeace Thackeray, *The History of Pendennis* (novel)

1852	Arthur Joseph Munby, 'The Eve of Change' in *Benoni* (poem)
1854	William Mackpeace Thackeray, *The Newcomes* (novel)
1855	Martin Farquhar, Tupper 'Silence' (poem)
1856	John Maddison Morton, *Done on Both Sides* (play)
1857	Elizabeth Barrett Browning, *Aurora Leigh* (poem)
1857	Bryan Waller Proctor, *The Falcon* (play)
1861	William Bell Scott, 'Half Hour Lectures on Art' (lecture)
1870	John Abraham Heraud, 'Sonnet viii' in *The In-Gathering* (poem)
1871	William Bell Scott, *The British School of Sculpture* (prose)
1879	Francis Turner Palgrave, 'Portrait of a Child of Seven' (poem)
1884	John Evelyn Barlas, 'At Rome' (poem)
1889	Gerald Massey, 'Woman' (poem)
1893	Arthur Joseph Munby, *Susan* (poem)
1895	George du Maurier, *Trilby* (novel)
1895	John Davidson, *Earl Lavender* (novel)
1895	William James Linton, 'The Counterfeit' (poem)
1898	F. Anstey (pseud. of Thomas Anstey Guthrie), *The Tinted Venus* (novel)
1908	Samuel Gordon, *The New Galatea* (novel)
1921	George Bernard Shaw, *Back to Methuselah* (play)
1928	Margaret Rivers Larminie (afterwards Mrs R. C. Tragett), *Galatea* (novel)

1958   Andrew Young, *Out of the World and Back* (poem)

1966   Louis MacNeice, *Canto XIV* (poem)

1990   Edwin Morgan, *The Norn* (poem)

References to the Pygmalion story in French Literature[18]

c.1277   Jean de Meun, *Roman de la Rose* (poem)

c.1316–1328   *Ovide Moralisé* (poem)

c.1371   Jean Froissart, *Prison d'Amour* (poem)[19]

1373   Jean Froissart, *Joli Buisson de Jonece* (poem)

c.1400   Christine de Pisan, *Épître d'Othéa* (poem and allegory)

1412   Jean Froissart, *Paradys d'Amour* (poem)

1580   Montaigne, 'The Affection of Fathers' (essay)

1627   Charles Sorel, *Le Berger Extravagant* (prose story)[20]

1681   Bernard Le Bovier de Fontenelle, *Pigmalion, Prince de Tyr* (comedy)

1691   Jean de La Fontaine, *L'Astrée. Tragédie Lyrique* (play)

1700   Antoine Houdard de la Motte, *Le Triomphe des Artes*, cinquième entrée: *La Sculpture*

---

[18] The lists of reference to Pygmalion in languages other than English are not subdivided into short references and renarrations.

[19] See also Jean Froissart's *L'Espinette Amoureuse* (poem) and Guillaume de Machaut's *Fonteine Amoureuse* (poem), *Livre du Voir-Dit* (poem), and *Confort d'Ami* (poem). I have been unable to find dates for these texts. Pygmalion is also mentioned in the anonymously written *Echecs Amoureux* (poem). This was partly translated by Lydgate as *Reson and Sensuallyte* and is an imitation of the *Roman de la Rose*. See Katherine Heinrichs, *The Myths of Love. Classical Lovers in Medieval Literature* (Pennsylvania and London, 1990), p. 82.

[20] This is about an automaton. It was published in two parts, in 1644 and 1658. It was translated into English as *The Extravagant Shepherd*, by John Davies (London, 1653).

1721–1738	Montesquieu, *Histoire Véritable* (prose)
1727	François-Joseph de Lagrange-Chancel, *Pygmalion* (tragedy)[21]
1741	Jean Antoine Romagnesi, *Pygmalion* (comic play)[22]
1741	Anonymous, *Pigmalion* (comédie Italienne)
1741	André François Boureau-Deslandes, *Pigmalion, ou, La Statue Animée* (prose story) (prose)[23]
1743	Jean-Baptiste Josephe Villart de Grécourt, 'Pygmalion' (poem)[24]
1743	Edme Sulpice Gaubier de Barrault, *Brioché, ou L'Origine des Marionettes, Parodie de Pigmalion* (play)[25]
c.1741	Thémiseul de Sainte Hyacinthe Cordonnier, *Pygmalion* (a novel)
1760	Louis Poinsinet de Sivry, *Pygmalion* (comic play in prose)[26]
1762	Jean-Jacques Rousseau, *Pygmalion* (play)[27]
1765	Jean-Jacques Rousseau, *Confessions* (prose)[28]
1770	Voltaire, 'Pygmalion' (fable)
1774	B. Desgagniers, *Le Noueveau Pygmalion*

---

[21] De Lagrange-Chancel also wrote a comic play on the subject of Pygmalion which was both unperformed and unpublished.

[22] See J. L. Carr, 'Pygmalion and the Philosophes. The Animated Statue in Eighteenth Century France', *Journal of the Warburg and Courtauld Institutes*, 23 (1960), 239–255 (p. 242).

[23] Contains a letter to Madame le Comtesse de G–. Possibly Madame de Genlis, the author of a Pygmalion play.

[24] This poem was formerly attributed to J-J Rousseau. See Carr, p. 242.

[25] Parody of Rameau. It was first published in 1753.

[26] See Carr, p. 242.

[27] The play was written in 1762, and published in 1771. Buske notes that the music was by Coignet, and that the first performance was in 1770. Further, he adds that 'Rousseau borrowed not only the name Galatea for Pygmalion's loved one, but also, as Eric Schmidt suggests, that the alive statue recognizes her metamorphosis through the touching of a marble block' (p. 347). These were, according to Buske, taken from Sainte-Hyacinthe's novel.

[28] First published in 1781.

Appendix 2: Pygmalion References

1776	Arnaud Berquin, 'Auquel on a joint Pygmalion, de J. J. Rousseau, mis en vers' in *Recueil des Idylles* (play)
1777	J-B de Goncourt, 'La Statue de Pygmalion' (verse fable incorrectly attributed to Voltaire)
1778	Michel de Cubières-Palmézeaux, *Galathée* (comic play)
1780	Barnabé Farmian de Rosoi, *Pigmalion, drame lyrique en un acte et en prose* (prose, lyrical drama in one act)[29]
1780	François Martin Poultier d'Elmotte, *L'Antipigmalion ou L'Amour Prométhée* (lyrical scene in prose)
1800	Étienne Gosse, *Pygmalion à Saint-Maur* (comic play)
1802	Madame de Genlis, 'Pygmalion et Galathée, ou La Statue Animée depuis vingt-quatre heures' in *Nouveaux Contes Moreaux et Nouvelles Historiques* (dramatic sketch)
1823	Marquis de Saint-Lambert, 'Pigmalion' (poem)
1831	Honoré de Balzac, *Le Chef D'Oeuvre Inconnu* (prose)
1849	Gustave Le Vavasseur, 'Pygmalion dans son menage' (poem)
1851	Anonymous, *Pygmalion* (verse comedy in one act)
1853	Lambert Thiboust and Théodore Barrière, *Filles de Marbre* (play)[30]
1872	Jean Aicard, *Pygmalion* (dramatic poem in one act)
1873	Auguste Jouhaud, *Galathée et Pygmalion* (play)
1878	Baron Estournelles de Constant, *Galathée* (play)[31]

---

[29] The statue is given the name Aglaé. This is possibly a form of the name Aglaia who was one of the Graces.

[30] See Meyer Reinhold, 'The Naming of Pygmalion's Animated Statue', *Classical Journal*, 66 (1979), 316–319 (p. 319), and Allardyce Nicoll, *A History of English Drama 1660–1900*, 6 vols (Cambridge, 1952–1959), V, (1959), 136.

[31] Translation of a play by S N. Basiliades.

References to the Pygmalion Story in German and Swiss Literature

1747	Johan Jacob Bodmer, 'Pygmalion und Elise' (prose story)[32]
1756	Johann Wilhelm Gleim, *Pygmalion* (comic play)
1764	Johann Georg Jacobi, 'Der neue Pygmalion' (poem)
1766	Johann Elias Schlegel, 'Pygmalion' (poem/cantata)
c.1766	Johann Wolfgang von Goethe, 'Pygmalion, eine Romanze' in *Annette* (ballad)[33]
1767	Daniel Schiebeler, *Pygmalion* (burlesque)[34]
1776	Gustav Friedrich Grossmann, *Pygmalion* (comic play)[35]
1781	Friedrich Schiller, *Der Triumphe Der Lieb*
1786	Johann Wolfgang von Goethe, *Die Italienische Reise* (The Italian Journey) (letter)[36]
1795	Friedrich Schiller, 'Die Ideale' (poem)[37]
1797	August Wilhelm von Schlegel, 'Pygmalion' (poem)
1801	Johann Gottfried Herder, 'Pygmalion oder die wiederbelebte Kunst' (poem)
1825	Karl Immermann, 'Der neue Pygmalion' (novelle)

---

[32] Swiss author. Anthony Scenna suggests that Bodmer's source was the French version of the story by Saint Hyacinthe (*Ancient Legend and History in Bodmer* [Columbia, 1937] p. 6). Meyer Reinhold also makes this point (Reinhold, p. 317).

[33] The poems in Goethe's *Buche Annette* were written during the years 1766 and 1767.

[34] Schiebeler based his Pygmalion on Jean-Baptiste Villart de Grécourt's version (1743).

[35] The play was based on Rousseau's *Pygmalion*.

[36] There is a reference to Pygmalion in the first letter to Rome, 1 November 1786. It refers to Goethe's first impressions of Rome and compares them to Pygmalion's statue, Elise, coming to life.

[37] There are two versions of this poem. The first version was published in August 1795, the second appeared in a collection of poems in 1800.

1948 Georg Kaiser, *Pygmalion* (comic play in verse)

The Pygmalion Story in Art

c.1529–1530 Agnolo Bronzino, 'Pigmalione E "Galatea"' (painting: Palazzo Vecchio, Florence)[38]

1556 Jacopo Pontormo, 'Pygmalion' (painting: Delegazione per le Restituzioni, Rome)

1588 Paolo Veronese, 'Pygmalion' (painting: Gardner Museum, Boston, no. P17w32-s-3)[39]

1593 Hendrik Goltzius, 'Pygmalion' (engraving: Netherland Art Inst., no.14787)

1631 Angelo Caroselli, 'Pigmaleone, che fa sacrificio all 'Idoli, per far vivificar una statua di femia, della quale egli era innamorator'[40]

1665–1675 Godfried Schalcken, 'Pygmalion' (painting: Gemäldegalerie, Dresden; Uffizi, Florence)[41]

1677 Magdalena de Passe (?), 'Pygmalion and the Statue – *Metamorphoses* of Ovid' (painting: Brussels, Foppens)

17th cent. Niet Volght, Pieter Feddes van Harlingen and La Hire[42]

1717 Jean Raoux, 'Pygmalion in Love with his Statue' (painting: Musée Fabre, Montpellier)[43]

---

[38] Bonnie Ray suggests that the name Galatea may be a reference to Raphael's Galatea (p. 71). This painting has been attributed to both Bronzino and Pontormo. Vasari refers to the painting as Bronzino's (Ray, p. 71). Reinhold notes that the painting was in the Galleria Barberini in Rome.
[39] *The Oxford Guide to Classical Mythology in the Arts* notes that this painting is part of a series of eight illustrating scenes from Ovid's *Metamorphoses*.
[40] This was painted for the Marchese Guistinian. See Alfred Noir, *The Italian Flowers of Caravaggio* (Cambridge, Massachusetts, 1967), p. 133, and Ray, p. 48. The painting was later called 'Allegory of a Painting'.
[41] *The Oxford Guide* notes that there are two versions of this painting.
[42] These references are in J. L. Carr, p. 244. Carr provides no more information that this.
[43] Reinhold notes that in 1971 the drawing was at the Louvre (Reinhold, p. 318).

Pygmalion and Galatea

1717	Jean Raoux, 'Pygmalion and his Statue' (drawing: Musée Paul Dupuy, Toulouse)
1717–1724	Sebastiano Ricci, 'Pygmalion and Galatea' (painting: Heinemann collection, Ruvigliana)
1722	Adriaen van der Werff, 'Pygmalion with the Statue of Galatea' (painting)
1729	Francois Le Moyne, 'Pygmalion sees his Statue Come to Life' (painting: Exhibited 1975/6 at 'The Age of Louis XV' exhibition in Toledo, Chicago. It is presently in Musée des Beaux Artes, Tours, no. 51-5-1)
c.1742	François Boucher, 'Pygmalion in love with his Statue'(painting: Hermitage, Leningrad, no. 3683)
c.1742	François Boucher, 'Pygmalion and Galatea' (painting: Metropolitan Museum, New York, no. 07.225.310)
c.1745	Jean Restout, 'Pygmalion in love with his Statue' (fragment of a painting: Mobilier National, Paris, on deposit from Louvre, Paris, no. 7452)
c.1745	Jean Restout, 'Venus Answering the Prayer of Pygmalion' (painting: Église de Saint-Germain-des Près, Paris)[44]
1749	François Boucher, 'Pygmalion devient amoureux d'une statue qu'il avoit faite et Venus la rend animee' (book illustration for *Metamorphoses*)[45]
1762	Louis Jean-François Lagrenée, 'Pygmalion' (painting on copper)[46]

---

[44] The Warburg Photograph Collection has a reproduction of a drawing by Jean Restout which bears the title 'Pygmalion'. This picture is recorded as being in the Musée des Beaux-Artes, Orléans (cat. no. 83) in 1876. It was exhibited at the Restout Exhibition in Rouen in 1970 (no. 26).

[45] There are many illustrations of the *Metamorphoses* to be found in Medieval manuscripts and later printed books. I have only listed the illustrations of artists who have shown an interest in the Pygmalion story aside from these illustrations.

[46] On the Pygmalion paintings of this artist see Antoine Schnapper, 'Louis Lagrenée and the Theme of Pygmalion', *Bulletin of the Detroit Instititue of Arts*, 53 (1975), 112–117.

Appendix 2: Pygmalion References

1762	Charles Monnet, 'Pygmalion' (painting: Galerie de Bayser(?) 1980, no. 30)
1765	Jean-Baptiste Deshayes, 'Pygmalion and Galatea' (painting: Musée des Beaux Artes, Tours)
1765	Carle Van Loo, 'Pygmalion' (painting: Museum, Warsaw)
1767–1771	G. de Saint-Aubin, 'Pygmalion' (sketch in sanguine: Bayonne, Musée Bonnat)[47]
1772	Louis Jean-François Lagrenée, 'Pygmalion in Love with the Statue of Venus' (painting: Ateneumin Taidemuseo, Helsinki)
1777	Louis Jean-François Lagrenée, 'Pygmalion' (painting)
1784	Laurent Pécheux, 'Pygmalion and Galatea' (painting: Hermitage, Leningrad, no. 7568)
1785	Jean-Baptiste Regnault, 'Pygmalion asking Venus to bring his Statue to Life' (painting: Salon des Nobles de la Reine, Château de Versailles, on deposit from Louvres, no. 7385)
19th cent.	Philippe Parrot, 'Galathée' (painting: Musée de Luxembourg)
1806	Jean-Honoré Fragonard, 'Pygmalion and Galatea' (painting: Musée, Bourges)[48]
1819	Anne-Louis Girodet, 'Pygmalion and Galatea' (painting: Chäteau Dampierre)
1815–1820	Francisco José de Goya y Lucientes, 'Pygmalion and Galatea' (Sketch: Brush and sepia wash: J. Paul Getty Museum, Los Angeles)
1823	Pierre-Paul Prud'hon, 'Pygmalion' (2 drawings: sold 1882, private collection)

---

[47] This sketch was made for an illustrated edition of Ovid's *Metamorphoses* (1767–1771?).

[48] Reinhold notes that Fragonard 'produced four compositions on this theme', (Reinhold, p. 318).

1842	Honoré Daumier, 'Pygmalion' (comic lithograph)
1855	Octave Tassaert, 'Pygmalion' (painting: Louvre, Paris, no R. F. 2395)
1864–1878	Edward Burne-Jones, 'Pygmalion' (paintings and drawings: Birmingham City Museum and Art Gallery, England)[49]
1868	George Frederick Watts, 'The Wife of Pygmalion: A Translation from the Greek' (painting: Faringdon Collection, Buscot Park, Oxfordshire)
1873	John William Waterhouse, 'Pygmalion and the Statue' (painting)[50]
c.1875	George Howard, 'Pygmalion Novissimus' (watercolour caricature: private collection)[51]
1875	William Bell Scott, 'Pygmalion' (etching to accompany sonnet)
1878	John Tenniel, 'Pygmalion and the Statue' (watercolour: Victoria and Albert Museum, no. 53–1894)
1886	Ernest Normand, 'Pygmalion and Galatea' (painting: Atkinson Art Gallery, Southport)
1890	Jean-Léon Gérôme, 'Pygmalion and Galatea' (painting: Metropolitan Museum, New York, no. 27.200)
1891	William Henry Margetson, 'Pygmalion' (painting)

---

[49] Burne-Jones made 12 drawings for William Morris's poem 'Pygmalion and the Image' in the years 1864–1868. These were never published in conjunction with the poem. Burne-Jones also painted a cycle of pictures based on these drawings in the years 1868–1878. The titles of these are 'The Heart Desires, 'The Hand Refrains', 'The Godhead Fires', 'The Soul Attains'. *The Oxford Guide* notes that Burne-Jones' gouache picture entitled 'The Altar of Hymen', which depicts Pygmalion and Galatea embracing with Hymen looking on, was based on one of his illustrations to Morris's 'Pygmalion and the Image' (1874).

[50] *The Oxford Guide* notes that this painting has been lost. Anthony Hobson notes, in *The Art and Life of J. W. Waterhouse R. A. 1849–1917* (London, 1980), that the painting was exhibited and sold for 50 guineas (p. 179).

[51] *The Oxford Guide* notes that this is a caricature of Edward Burne-Jones in the pose of his own Pygmalion.

Appendix 2: Pygmalion References 187

1902	Herbert James Draper, 'A Deep Sea Idyll'[52]
1907	Herbert Gustave Schmalz, 'The Awakening of Galatea' (painting)
1915	Herbert Gustave Schmalz, 'Pygmalion! Pygmalion!' (painting)
1927	Pablo Picasso, illustrations for edition of Honoré de Balzac *Le Chef D'Oeuvre Inconnu* (book illustrations)
1933	Pablo Picasso, etchings[53]
1938	André Masson, 'Pygmalion' (Surrealist painting: Galerie H. Odesmott, Paris, 1988)
1939	Paul Delvaux, 'Pygmalion' (Surrealist painting)
1954	George Molnar, 'Horrible Fate of a Statue Named Pygmalion' in *Statues* (book illustration)
1959	Anonymous, 'Intoxication by D'Orsay' (cartoon perfume advertisement: in *The New Yorker*, December, 1959)[54]

The Pygmalion Story in Sculpture[55]

1772	Franz Zächerle, 'Pygmalion's Statue is Transformed to Flesh' (Bronze Bas relief: Gal. des 19 Jarh. in Ob. Belvedue, Vienna)[56]

---

[52] See Joseph Kestner, *Mythology and Misogyny. The Social Discourse of Nineteenth Century British Classical Subject Painting* (Wisconsin and London, 1989), p. 290.

[53] Kenneth Clark refers to these etchings on the subject of Pygmalion in his work *The Nude. A Study of Ideal Art* (London, 1956), pp. 353–354.

[54] Further paintings on the subject of Pygmalion which I have been unable to locate or provide a date for are: Noel-Nicolas Coypel 'Pygmalion and Galatea' (painting: Sotheby's Monaco 13.6.82, lot 83), Tour Dorée 'Pygmalion: Tout le monde en amour est tous les jours dupé. Les femmes nous en font accroire. Si vous voulez aimer et n'être pas trompé, aimez une femme d'ivoire' (painting: Chateau de Bussy-Rabutin, Côte-d'Or, 21.122.05), School of Fontainebleau 'Pygmalion', Louis Gauffier (painting: Hazlitt, Gooden and Fox, 38 Bury St., London, June 1978), Wilmon Brewer refers to a paintings by Thiry and by Rodin on the subject in *Ovid's 'Metamorphoses' in European Culture. Books 6–10* (Boston, 1941), p. 1266.

[55] These references are not arranged by country.

[56] Also attributed to G. R. Donner (1693–1741). See the Warburg Photographic Collection.

c.1745	Jean Restout, 'Pygmalion in love with his Statue' (sculpture)
1761–1763	Étienne-Maurice Falconet, 'Pygmalion and Galatea' or 'Pygmalion at the Feet of his Statue' (marble statuette: Walters Gallery, Baltimore)[57]
1767–1770	Augustin Pajou, 'Pygmalion' (wood bas relief: Salle de l'Opéra, Versailles)
1774	Charles Banks, 'Pygmalion' (sculpture: Royal Academy Gold Medal)
1889	Auguste Rodin, 'Pygmalion and Galatea' (marble sculpture)[58]
1892	Jean-Léon Gérôme, (sculpture: Hearst Castle, San Simeon state historical monument, San Simeon, California)
1957	Paul Manship, 'Galatea' and 'Pygmalion and Galatea' (gilded bronze figurines)
1963	Pietro Cascella, 'Pygmalion' (stone sculpture)

The Pygmalion Story in Music[59]

1608	Orlandi, *Galatea*; libretto: Chiabrera? (opera)
1660	A. Ziani, *Pygmalion*;, libretto: A. Draghi (opera)
1689	Antonio Draghi, *Pigmaleone in Cipro* (Pygmalion in Cyprus); libretto: Nicolò Minato (opera)

---

[57] *The Oxford Guide* notes that there are two versions. One of these is illustrated in Carr, p. 244.

[58] *The Oxford Guide* notes that there are two or three versions of this.

[59] These references are not arranged by country. Dates refer to the first performance, unless otherwise stated. I have included the names of librettists whenever that information is available.

Appendix 2: Pygmalion References

1694	Johann Georg Conradi, *Der Wunderbar-vergnüte Pygmalion* (The Wonderfully Pleased Pygmalion); libretto: Christian Heinrich Postel (opera)[60]
1700	Michel de la Barre, 'La Sculpture'; libretto: Antoine Houdart de la Motte (opera / ballet)[61]
1713	Louis-Nicolas Clérembault, *Pigmalion* (cantata)
1714	Giovanni Alberto Ristori, *Pigmalione* (opera)
1734	Jean-Joseph Mouret, *Pigmalion*; choreography: Marie Sallé (ballet)[62]
1744	Charles-François Panard and Thomas L'Affichard, *Pigmalion, ou La Statue Animée* (Pygmalion or the Animated Statue) (opera comique)
1745	Carl Heinrich Graun, *Pygmalion*; choreography: Jean-Barthélemy Lany (ballet)
1746	Michel Corrette, *Pygmalion* (scene with music)
1746	J. G. Schürer, *Galatea*; libretto: P. Metastasio (opera)
1748	Jean-Phillippe Rameau, *Pygmalion*; libretto: Antoine Houdart de la Motte, rev. by M. Ballot de Sovot (opera / ballet)
1763	Joseph Starzer, *Pygmalion, ou, La Statue Animée* (Pygmalion, or the Animated Statue); choreography: Franz Anton Hilverding (ballet)[63]
1766	Johann Elias Schlegel, 'Pygmalion' (poem/cantata)

---

[60] Hunger calls the librettist Heinrich Christian Postel.
[61] This is the last act of *Le Triomphe des Arts*.
[62] The name 'Marie de la Salle' is given for the choreographer by Annegret Dinter (p. 161). *The Oxford Guide* uses the name 'Marie Sallé'.
[63] *Dictionary Catalog of the Dance Collection. A List of Authors, Titles, and Subjects of Multi-Media Materials in the Dance Collection of the Performing Arts Research Center of the New York Public Library*, ed. by Dorothy Lourdou, 10 vols (Boston, 1974), VIII notes that there may have been a performance in Vienna in 1752.

1767	Florian Johann Deller, *Pigmalion, ou, La Statue Animée* (Pygmalion, or the Animated Statue); choreography: Étienne Lauchery
1768	Christian Gottfried Krause, *Pygmalion*; libretto: Karl Wilhelm Ramler (lyric cantata)
1770	Antoine Bailleux, *Pigmalion* (cantata)[64]
1772	Anton Schweitzer, *Pygmalion*; libretto: J. F. Schmidt (lyric scene / melodrama)[65]
1773	Giambattista Cimador, *Pigmalione*; libretto: Antonio Simeone Sografi (opera)[66]
1776	Franz Asplmayr, *Pygmalion*; libretto: J. G. von Laude (lyric scene / melodrama)[67]
1779	Georg Benda, *Pygmalion*; libretto: Rousseau (monodrama for a speaker and piano)
1780	Bonesi, *Pygmalion*; libretto: Du Rozoy (comic opera / caricature)
1794	Karl A. Herklots, *Pigmalion oder die Reformation der Liebe* (lyrical drama)
1795	Antonio Bartolomeo Bruni, *Galathée*; libretto: François Martin Poultier d'Elmolte (lyric scene)[68]

---

[64] The date of the first publication.

[65] Translation of Rousseau.

[66] After Rousseau. There is some confusion over the date of this work. The opera was first performed in 1773 (according to *The Oxford Guide*). Grove's Dictionary, however, dates the opera 1790. This might have something to do with the opera's unusual history. According to Grove, Cimador was dissatisfied with this work: 'he burnt the score and renounced composition; however the work survived (parts of it were even published later in London) and achieved considerable popularity throughout Europe as a concert piece for both male and female singers, being revived as late as 1836'. *The New Grove Dictionary of Music and Musicians*, ed. by Stanley Sadie, 20 vols (London, 1980), IV, 398.

[67] This text is a translation of Rousseau's *Pygmalion* into German. Note that Hunger calls the composer Franz Aspelmeyer and suggests the date 1772.

[68] Performed as a sequel to Rousseau's *Pygmalion*.

Appendix 2: Pygmalion References

1795	Johann Christoph Friedrich Bach, *Pygmalion*; libretto: Ramler (cantata)
1797	G. Liverati, *Pimmalione*; libretto: Şografi (opera)
1800	F. C. Lefebvre, *Pygmalion*; choreography: Louis-Jacques Jessé Milon (ballet / pantomime)
1809	Luigi Cherubini, *Pigmalion*; libretto: A. S. Sografi and S. Vestris (opera)
1812	Volkert, *Pigmalion oder die Musen bey der Prüfung*; libretto: F. X. Gewey (parody)
1835	H. Schmidt, *Pygmalion*; libretto: F. and Th. Elßler (opera)
1852	Victor Massé, *Galathée*; libretto: Jules Barbier and Michel Carré (comic opera)
1863	Frédéric-Étienne Barbier, *Madame Pygmalion*; libretto: Jules Adenis and Francis Tourte (comic operetta)
1865	Francis Tourte, *Monsieur Pygmalion* (operetta)
1865	Franz von Suppé, *Die Schöne Galathée* (The Lovely Galatea); libretto: Poly Henrion and Leopold Karl Dittmar Kohl von Kohlenegg (comic opera).[69]
1875	Caroline de Sainte-Croix, *Pygmalion*; libretto: Eugène Hugot (operette bouffe in one act)
1887?	Dionyssios Lavrangas, *Galatea*; libretto: Guidi (opera)[70]
1888	Ambroise Thomas, *Pygmalion and Galatea* (opera)
1896	Julian Edwards, *The Goddess of Truth*; libretto: Stanislaus Stange (musical comedy)

---

[69] This was produced in Berlin in 1865, and in London in June 1872 under the title *Ganymede and Galatea* (Reinhold, p. 319). English version by Willard G. Day (Boston, 1884).

[70] Libretto after S. Vassiliades. The composer studied under Delibes and later under Massenet (*Grove*).

	Pygmalion and Galatea
1911	Francis Thomé, *Mademoiselle Pygmalion* (ballet / pantomime)
1923	Henry Houseley, (Mrs Frances Houseley) *Pygmalion* (opera)
1930	Radie Britain, *Overture to Pygmalion* (orchestral composition)
1946?	William Thayer Ames, 'Pygmalion'; libretto: Hilda Doolittle [H. D.] (Song cycle)
1949	Herbert Bliss (choreography), *Pygmalion and Galatea*; music by Maurice Ravel (ballet / Pas de deux)
1956	Frederick Loewe, *My Fair Lady*; libretto: Alan Jay Lerner (musical comedy)[71]
1981	M. Zur, *Pygmalion* (an operatic scene for soprano and piano)
1984	Wai On Ho, *Pygmalion and Galatea* (composition for piano)
1992	Frederick Goossen, *Pygmalion* (a choreographic poem)[72]

---

[71] After Bernard Shaw.

[72] Further references to Pygmalion in music which I could not date are: Luigi Cherubini *Pigmalion* (opera), Giovanni Battista Gordigiani *Pygmalione* (drama with music), Francis Sirotti *Il Pimmaglione* (drama with music), Rolande Falcinelli (b. 1920) *Pygmalion Delivre* opus 14. See Aaron I. Cohen, *International Encyclopedia of Woman Composers* (New York, 1987), I, 228 for reference.

Bibliography

Primary Sources

Manuscripts

MS letter from W. S. Gilbert to Clement Scott, 10 December 1883. Pierpont Morgan Library, New York, The Gilbert and Sullivan Collection
MS letter from Moy Thomas to Clement Scott, 11 December, 1883 (Copy in Theatre Museum Library, Covent Garden, Lyceum, 1883)

Published Literature

Aldington, Richard, *The Complete Poems* (London, 1948)
Anonymous, *Tottel's Miscellany (1557–1587)*, ed. by Hyder Edward Rollins, 2 vols (Cambridge, Massachusetts, 1965)
Anonymous, *Chaucer's Ghoast. Or, A Piece of Antiquity. Containing twelve pleasant Fables of Ovid penn'd after the ancient manner of writing in England. Which makes them prove Mock-Poems to the present Poetry* (London, 1672)
Anonymous, *Pygmalion, A Poem* (London, 1779)
Anonymous, 'The New Frankenstein', *Frasers Magazine*, 17 (1838), 21–30
Anonymous, *The Puzzler. Being a Collection of 238 Original Charades, Enigmas, Rebuses, Anagrams, Conundrums, Transpositions etc With Solutions* (London, 1845)
Anonymous, *The Poems of the Pearl Manuscript: 'Pearl', 'Cleanness', 'Sir Gawain and the Green Knight'*, ed. by Malcolm Andrew and Ronald Waldron (Exeter, 1989)
Asclepiades Cyprius, in *Fragmenta Historicorum Graecorum*, ed. by Karl Müller, 5 vols (Paris, 1841–1870) III (1849), 306
Baker, Henry, *Medulla Poetarum Romanorum; or The Most Beautiful and Instructive Passages of the Roman Poets*, 2 vols (London, 1737), II
Barlow, George, *Poems and Sonnets*, 2 vols (London, 1871)
Basse, William, *The Poetical Works of William Basse (1602–1653)*, ed. by R. Warwick Bond (London, 1893)
Beddoes, Thomas Lovell, *The Works of Thomas Lovell Beddoes*, ed. by Henry Wolfgang Donner (Oxford, 1935)
Beddoes, Thomas Lovell, *Plays and Poems of Thomas Lovell Beddoes*, ed. by Henry Wolfgang Donner (London, 1950)
Bennett, William Cox, *Poems* (London, 1862)
Blackmur, R. P., *Poems of R. P. Blackmur*, ed. by Denis Donoghue (Princeton, New Jersey, 1977)

Blake, William, *The Complete Works of William Blake*, ed. by Geoffrey Keynes (London, 1966)
Boucicault, Dion, *Grimaldi; Or the Life of An Actress. A Drama, in Five Acts*, in *Dion Boucicault: 35 Plays*, Popular Nineteenth Century Drama on Microfilm (Canterbury, 1982)
Branch, Anna Hempstead, *Last Poems*, ed. by Ridgeley Torrence (New York and Toronto, 1944)
Brathwait, Richard, *Natures Embassie; or The Wilde-Mans Measures: Danced Naked By Twelve Satyres, With Sundry Others Continued in the Next Section* (London, 1621)
Brestel, Arthur L., 'Pygmalion's Second Prayer', *The Classical Bulletin*, 59 (1983), 28
Brontë, Charlotte, *Jane Eyre*, ed. by Margaret Smith (Oxford, 1986)
Brough, William, *Pygmalion; Or, the Statue Fair: An Original Burlesque* (London, 1867)
Buchanan, Robert, *Undertones* (London, 1863)
Buchanan, Robert, 'The Fleshly School of Poetry: Mr D. G. Rossetti', *The Contemporary Review* (1871), 334–350
Buchanan, Robert, *The Fleshly School of Poetry and Other Phenomenon of the Day* (London, 1872)
Byron, George Gordon Noel, *Byron's Don Juan: A Variorum Edition*, ed. by Truman Guy Steffan and Willis W. Pratt, 4 vols (Austin, Texas, 1957)
Carroll, Lewis, *The Magic of Lewis Carroll*, ed. by John Fisher (Harmondsworth, 1975)
Chaucer, Geoffrey, *The Complete Works of Geoffrey Chaucer*, ed. by F. N. Robinson (Oxford, 1933)
Chaucer, Geoffrey, *The Riverside Chaucer*, ed. by Larry D. Benson (Oxford, 1988)
Churchyard, Thomas, *A Pleasant Conceite Penned in Verse. Collourably Sette Out, and Humblie Presented on New Year's Day Last to the Queenes Maiestie at Hampton Court* (London, 1593)
Coatsworth, Elizabeth, *The Creaking Stair* (New York, 1923)
Cokayne, Aston, *Small Poems of Divers Sorts* (London, 1658)
Coleridge, Ernest Hartley, *Poems* (Chertsey, 1881)
Coleridge, G. D. J., *Pygmalion and Other Poems* (London, 1935)
Coleridge, Samuel Taylor, *The Complete Works of Samuel Taylor Coleridge*, ed. by Ernest Hartley Coleridge (Oxford, 1912)
Coleridge, Samuel Taylor, *Coleridge, Poems and Prose*, ed. by Kathleen Raine (Harmondsworth, 1986)
Conquest, Robert, *Between Mars and Venus* (London, 1962)
Cook, Keningale Robert, *Purpose and Passion: Pygmalion and Other Poems* (London, 1870)

Cowley, Abraham, *The Collected Works of Abraham Cowley*, ed. by Thomas O. Calhoun, Laurence Heyworth and J. Robert King, 2 vols (London and Toronto, 1993)

Crashaw, Richard, *The Poems English, Latin and Greek of Richard Crashaw*, ed. by L. C. Martin (Oxford, 1957)

Crompton, Hugh, *Poems* (London, 1672)

Cruden, Thomas, *Pygmalion and His Galatea* (London, 1635)

Daniel, Samuel, *The Complete Works in Verse and Prose of Samuel Daniel*, ed. by Alexander B. Grosart (London, 1885)

Davies, John, *Microcosmos. The Discovery of the Little World, With the Government Thereof* (Oxford, 1603)

Davies, John, *Wittes Pilgrimage* (London, 1605)

Davies, John, *The Scourge of Folly* (London, 1611)

Dionysius Periegetes, *Geographi Graeci Minores*, ed. by Karl Müller, 2 vols (Paris, 1855–1861)

Donne, John, *The Complete Poems of John Donne*, ed. by Alexander B. Grosart, 2 vols (London, 1872)

Donne, John, *The Poems of John Donne Edited from the Old Editions and Numerous Manuscripts*, ed. by Herbert J. C. Grierson, 2 vols (London, 1912)

Dowson, Ernest, *The Poetical Works of Ernest Dowson*, ed. by Desmond Flower (London, 1967)

Eliot, George, *Daniel Deronda*, ed. by Barbara Hardy (London, 1986)

Ellis, George, *Poetical Tales By Sir Gregory Gander* (Bath, 1778)

Ellison, Henry, *Stones from the Quarry; or Moods of Mind. By Henry Browne* (London, 1875)

Espeland, Pamela, *The Story of Pygmalion* (Minneapolis, 1981)

Fuller, Roy, *Buff* (London, 1965)

Fulwood, William, *The Enemie of Idlenesse* (London, 1568)

Gandalac, Lennard, 'Galatea', *Canadian Forum*, 14 (1934), 268

Garter, Bernard, *A Strife Betweene Appelles and Pigmalion. The Other Ditty, Of Trust and Trial* (London, 1566)

Gilbert, W. S., *Pygmalion and Galatea* (London, 1872)

Gilbert, W. S., *Letter Addressed to the Members of the Dramatic Profession in Reply to Miss Henrietta Hodson's Pamphlet* (London, 1877).

Glassford, James, *Sphinx Incruenta; or 212 Original Enigmas and Charades* (Edinburgh, 1835)

Godwin, William, *Things as They Are; Or The Adventures of Caleb Williams*, ed. by Maurice Hindle (London, 1988)

Gomersall, Robert, *The Levites Revenge* (London, 1628)

Gower, John, *The English Works of John Gower*, ed. by G. C. Macaulay, Early English Text Society, 81, 2 vols (London, 1900)

Granville, George, *The Genuine Works in Verse and Prose of the Right*

Honourable George Granville, Lord Lansdown, 2 vols (London, 1732)
Graves, Robert, *Poems (1914–1926)* (London, 1927)
Graves, Robert, *Collected Poems* (London, 1938)
Greenwood, Grace, *Poems* (Boston, 1951)
Guilpin, Edward, *Skialetheia; or A Shadowe of Truth, In Certaine Epigrams and Satyres*, ed. by Alexander B. Grosart (Manchester, 1878)
Hallam, Arthur Henry, *The Writings of Arthur Henry Hallam*, ed. by T. H. Vail Motter (New York and London, 1943)
Hazlitt, William, *The Complete Works of William Hazlitt*, ed. by P. P. Howe, 21 vols (London and Toronto, 1932)
Heath, John, *The House of Correction; or Certayne Satyricall Epigrams. Written by J. H. Gent. Together With a Few Characters, Called Par Pari: or, Like to the Like, Quoth the Devill to the Collier* (London, 1619)
Henrietta Hodson, *A Letter from Miss Henrietta Hodson, an Actress, to the Members of the Dramatic Profession, Being a Relation of the Persecution which She has Suffered from Mr William Schwenck Gilbert, a Dramatic Author* (London, 1877)
Hickey, Emily H., *A Sculptor and Other Poems* (London, 1881)
Hoffmann, Michael and James Lasdun, eds., *After Ovid: New Metamorphoses* (London, 1994)
Hooley, John, *Pygmalion and Other Poems* (Calcutta, 1874)
Hope, Alec Derwent, *The Wandering Islands* (Sydney, 1955)
Hopkins, John, *Amasia, or The Work of the Muses*, 3 vols (London, 1700)
Howell, Agnes Rous, *Euphrosyne; or The Sculptor's Bride. Being the Story of Pygmalion, With a Sequel. A Libretto in Three Acts* (Norwich, 1886)
Huggett, Richard, *The First Night of Pygmalion. A Comedy For Two People* (London, 1970)
Hughes, Ted, *Tales From Ovid: Twenty-Four Passages from the Metamorphoses* (London, 1997)
Hunt, Leigh, 'Rousseau's *Pygmalion*', *The Indicator*, 1 (1820), 241–246
Hunt, Leigh, *Leigh Hunt's Literary Criticism*, ed. by L. H. Houtchens and C. W. Houtchens (New York, 1956)
Hurrell, William E., *The Passionate Painter and Other Verse* (London, 1918)
Hyginus, *Fabulae*, ed. by P. K. Marshall (Stuttgart, 1993)
Jenyns, Soame, *The Works of Soame Jenyns*, 4 vols (London, 1790)
Johnson, Richard, *A Crowne-Garland of Goulden Roses. Gathered Out of Englands Royall Garden. Being the Lives and Strange Fortunes of Many Great Personages of this Land* (Landon, 1612)
Kavanagh, Patrick, *Collected Poems* (London, 1964)
Keats, John, *Letters of John Keats*, ed. by Robert Gittings (Oxford, 1987)
Lactantius (Placidius), *P. Ovidi Metamorphoseon Libri XV. Lactanti Placidi qui dicitur narrationes fabularum Ovidianarum*, ed. by Hugo Magnus (Berlin,

1914)
Lancaster, George Eric, *Pygmalion in Cyprus* (London, 1880)
Lang, Andrew, 'The New Pygmalion; or The Statue's Choice', *Longman's Magazine*, 1 (1883), 299–302
Levant, Howard, 'Pygmalion', *Epoch*, 10 (1958–60), 158
Lewis, Cecil Day, *Country Comets* (London, 1928)
Lewis, Charlton M., 'Pygmalion', *Yale Review*, 10 (1921), 726–728
Llewellyn, Alun, 'Galatea', *Poetry Review*, 47 (1956), 19
Low, Benjamin R. C., *Broken Music, Selected Verse* (New York, 1920)
Lucas, Frank Laurence, *Marionettes* (Cambridge, 1930)
Lydgate, John, *Reson and Sensuallyte*, ed. by Ernest Sieper, Early English Text Society, 2 vols (London, 1901–1903)
Lydgate, John, *Lydgate's Troy Book*, ed. by Henry Bergen, Early English Text Society, 97, 103 and 106, 3 vols (London, 1906–1910)
Lyly, John, *Euphues: The Anatomy of Wit, Euphues and his England*, ed. by Morris William-Croll and Harry Clemons (London, 1916)
Lytton, Edward Bulwer, *Money* (London, 1840)
MacDonald, George, *Poems* (London, 1857)
MacDonald, George, *The Poetical Works of George MacDonald*, 2 vols (London, 1893)
MacDonald, George, *The Visionary Novels of George MacDonald: Lilith, Phantastes*, ed. by Anne Freemantle (New York, 1954)
MacDonald, George, *Phantastes and Lilith*, ed. by C. S. Lewis (London, 1962)
MacDonald, George, *Phantastes*, ed. by Derek Brewer (Woodbridge, 1982)
Mallock, William Hurrell, *Poems* (London, 1880)
Marlowe, Christopher, *The Second Part of the Bloody Conquests of Mighty Tamberlaine*, ed. by Fredson Bowers, 2 vols (Cambridge, 1981)
Marston, John, *The Poems of John Marston*, ed. by Arnold Davenport (Liverpool, 1961)
Marzials, Frank, *Death's Disguises and Other Sonnets* (London, 1887)
Mason, William, *The Works of William Mason*, 4 vols (London, 1811)
Maugham, W. S., *Liza of Lambeth* (London, 1897)
Middleton, Thomas, *The Works of Thomas Middleton*, ed. by A. H. Bullen, 8 vols (London, 1886)
Miles, Geoffrey (ed.), *Classical Mythology in English Literature: A Critical Anthology* (London, 1999)
Milton, John, *The Poems of John Milton*, ed. by John Carey and Alistair Fowler (London, 1968)
Mitchell, Joseph, *Three Poetic Epistles to Mr Hogarth, Mr Dandridge, and Mr Lambert, Masters in the Art of Painting* (London, 1731)
Montgomery, Roselle Mercier, *Many Devices* (New York and London, 1929)
Moore, Thomas Sturge, *The Vinedresser and Other Poems* (London, 1899)

Mottram, Ralph Hale, *New Poems* (London, 1909)
Munby, Arthur, *Susan* (London, 1893)
Murphy, Joseph John, *Sonnets and Other Poems Chiefly Religious* (London, 1890)
Nagle, Mary, *Pygmalion, Child of the Lake, The Three Rings, and Other Poems*, ed. by May Cross (Watertown, New York, 1887)
Neanthes Cyzicenus, in *Fragmenta Historicorum Graecorum*, ed. by Karl Müller, 5 vols (Paris, 1841–1870)
Ogle, George, *The Canterbury Tales of Chaucer, Modernis'd By Several Hands* (London, 1741)
Pater, Walter, *The Renaissance: Studies in Art and Poetry*, New Library Edition (London, 1910)
Pater, Walter, *Greek Studies: A Series of Essays*, New Library Edition (London, 1910)
Pater, Walter, *Walter Pater. Selected Works*, ed. by Richard Aldington (London, 1948)
Payn, James, *Poems* (Cambridge, 1853)
Payn, James, *Some Private Views* (London, 1881)
Pettie, George, *A Petite Pallace of Pettie and His Pleasure* (London, 1576)
Phelps, Elizabeth Stuart, *Songs of the Silent World and Other Poems* (Boston, 1885)
Philippos, *Anthologie Grecque*, ed. by Robert Aubreton, 13 vols (Paris, 1928–1980) X (1972), 193
Philostephanus, in *Fragmenta Historicorum Graecorum*, ed. by Karl Müller, 5 vols (Paris, 1841–1870) III (1849), 31
Pick, Samuel, *Festum Voluptatis; or The Banquet of Pleasure; Furnished With Much Variety of Speculations, Wittie, Plesant, and Delightful. Containing Divers Choyce Love-Poesies, Songs, Sonnets, Odes, Madrigals, Satyres* (London, 1639)
Pitt, Christopher, *Poems and Translations* (London, 1727)
Pitter, Ruth, *First and Second Poems 1912–1925* (London, 1927)
Poseidippus, in *Fragmenta Historicorum Graecorum*, ed. by Karl Müller, 5 vols (Paris, 1841–1870) IV (1851), 482
Reid, Colin Way, *Open Secret* (Gerrards Cross, Buckinghamshire, 1986)
Rhoades, James, *Poems* (London, 1870)
Rigmerole, Tobias, *A Treatise on the Charade, Translated from the French of the Sieur Rondeaulet, Member of the Academy of Belles Lettres, at Paris, with Alterations Adapted to the English Language* (London, 1777)
Robertson, James, *Poems on Several Occasions* (London, 1773)
Robertson, T. W., *T. W. Robertson; Six Plays*, ed. by Michael Booth (Ashover, Derbyshire, 1980)
Ross, Ronald, *Edgar; or The New Pygmalion and The Judgement of Tithonus* (Madras, 1883), p. 123.

Rossetti, Dante Gabriel, 'The Stealthy School of Criticism', *The Athenaeum*, 16 December (1871), 792–794
Rossetti, Dante Gabriel, *The Poetical Works*, ed. by William Michael Rossetti (London, 1898)
Rossetti, William Michael, *The Diary of William Michael Rossetti 1870–1873*, ed. by Odette Bornand (Oxford, 1977)
Rousseau, Jean-Jacques, *Pygmalion. Scène Lyrique* (London, 1799)
Rowe, Charles J., 'Galatea', *Poetry Review*, 38 (1947), 414
S., J. R., 'A Song for Galatea', *Blackwood's Edinburgh Magazine*, 118 (1875), 608–609
Savage, Richard, *The Works of Richard Savage, Esq. Son of the Earl Rivers. With an Account of the Life and Writing of the Author by Samuel Johnson*, 2 vols (London, 1777)
Scot, Walter, *A True History of Several Honourable Families of the Right Honourable Name of Scot. In the Shires of Roxburgh and Selkirk, and Others Adjacent* (Edinburgh, 1688)
Scott, William Bell, *Half-Hour Lectures on the History and Practice of the Fine and Ornamental Arts* (London, 1861)
Scott, William Bell, *The British School of Sculpture* (London, 1872)
Scott, William Bell, *Poems* (London, 1875)
Seward, Anna, *The Poetical Works of Anna Seward*, 3 vols (Edinburgh, 1810)
Shakespeare, William, *Measure for Measure*, ed. by S. Nagarajan, The Signet Classic Shakespeare (New York and London, 1964)
Shakespeare, William, *Measure for Measure*, ed. by J. W. Lever, The Arden Edition (London, 1965)
Shaw, George Bernard, *The Works of Bernard Shaw*, 33 vols (London, 1930–1938), XVI (1930)
Shaw, George Bernard, *The Bodley Head Bernard Shaw. Collected Plays With Their Prefaces*, ed. by Dan H. Laurence, 7 vols (London, 1970–1974), IV (1972)
Shelley, Mary, *Frankenstein*, ed. by M. K. Joseph (Oxford, 1971)
Shelley, Percy Bysshe, *The Complete Poetical Works of Percy Bysshe Shelley*, ed. by Thomas Hutchinson (London, 1965)
Sill, Edward Rowland, *The Poetical Works of Edward Rowland Sill* (Boston and New York, 1906)
Sisson, C. H., *Metamorphoses* (London, 1968)
Southey, Robert, *The Poetical Works of Robert Southey*, 10 vols (London, 1837–8)
Stephens, Henry Pottinger and W. Webster, *Galatea; or Pygmalion Re-versed* (London, 1883)
Stevenson, Matthew, *Poems; or A Miscellany of Sonnets, Satyrs etc* (London, 1673)

Swinburne, Algernon Charles, *The Complete Works of Algernon Charles Swinburne*, ed. by Edmund Gosse and Thomas James Wise, The Bonchurch Edition, 20 vols (London and New York, 1925–1927)
Taggard, Genevieve, *Words for the Chisel* (New York, 1926)
Talbot, A. J., *The Passing of Galatea. A Fantasy in One Act* (London, 1930)
Tattersall, Michael H., 'Galatea', *Poetry Review*, 39 (1948), 383
Taylor, John, *All The Workes of John Taylor The Water-Poet* (London, 1630)
Taylor, Tom, *An Unequal Match* (Manchester, 1874)
Tennyson, Alfred, *The Poems of Tennyson*, ed. by Christopher Ricks (London, 1969)
Tennyson, Frederick, *Daphne and Other Poems* (London and New York, 1891)
Tennyson, Frederick, *The Shorter Poems of Frederick Tennyson*, ed. by Charles Tennyson (London, 1913)
Tennyson, Frederick, *Letters to Frederick Tennyson*, ed. by Hugh J. Schonfield (London, 1930)
Travers, Henry, *Miscellaneous Poems and Translations* (London, 1731)
Walsingham, Thomas, *De Archana Deorum*, ed. by Robert A. Van Kluyve (Durham, North Carolina, 1968)
Warren, John Byrne Leicester, *Ballads and Metrical Sketches. By George F. Preston* (London, 1860)
Westmacott, Richard, *A Lecture on Sculpture Delivered in the Town-Hall, Cambridge, Before the Cambridge School of Art, on Tuesday Evening, March 17th, 1863* (Cambridge, 1863)
Whitehouse, Robert, *Pygmalion and the Statue* (London, 1910)
Wiley, Sara King, *Poems Lyrical and Dramatic, To Which is Added Cromwell, An Historical Play* (New York and London, 1900)
Wither, George, *Faire Virtue, The Mistresse of Philarete* (London, 1622)
Wollstonecraft, Mary, *Mary and The Wrongs of Woman* (Oxford, 1998)
Woolner, Thomas, *Pygmalion* (London, 1881)
Wurdemann, Audrey, *Bright Ambush* (New York, 1934)

Translations

Anonymous, *Pygmalion, A Poem* (London, 1779)
Apollodorus, *The Library*, trans. by Sir James George Frazer, The Loeb Classical Library, 2 vols (London, 1921)
Arnobius of Sicca, *The Case Against the Pagans*, trans. by George E. McCracken, 2 vols (Westminster, Maryland and London, 1949)
Christine de Pisan, *The Epistle of Othea: Translated From The French Text of Christine de Pisan by Stephen Scrope*, ed. by Curt Ferdinand Bühler, Early English Text Society, 264 (Oxford, 1970)
Clement of Alexandria, *The Exhortation to the Greeks*, trans. by G. W.

Butterworth (London, and Cambridge, Massachusetts, 1960)
Gower, John, *Confessio Amantis*, trans. by Terence Tiller (Baltimore, Maryland, 1963)
Hyginus, *The Myths of Hyginus*, trans. by Mary Grant (Kansas, 1960)
Lorris, Guillaume de and Jean de Meun, *The Romance of the Rose*, trans. by Charles Dahlberg (Hanover and London, 1983)
Nonnos (Panopolitanus), *Dionysiaca*, trans. by W. H. D. Rouse, notes by H. J. Rose, The Loeb Classical Library, 3 vols (London and Cambridge, Massachusetts, 1940)
Porphyry, *Selected Works of Porphyry*, trans. by Thomas Taylor (London, 1823)
Swedenborg, Emanuel, *Emanuel Swedenborg: Essential Readings*, ed. and trans. by Michael Stanley (Northamptonshire, 1988)
Winckelmann, Johann Joachim, *Writings on Art*, ed. by David Irwin (London, 1972)

Translations and Commentaries on Ovid's Metamorphoses

Bömer, Franz, ed., *P. Ovidius Naso. Metamorphosen. Kommentar Books 10–11* (Heidelberg, 1980)
Caxton, William, *Ovyde, Hys Booke of Metamorphose*, ed. by S. Gaselee and H. F. B. Brett-Smith (Oxford, 1924)
Coulson, Frank T., *Vulgate Commentary on Ovid's 'Metamorphoses' Book 10* (Toronto, 1991)
Golding, Arthur, *The XV Books of P. Ovidius Naso, Entytuled 'Metamorphoses', Translated Out of Latin Into English Meeter By Arthur Golding Gentleman* (London, 1567)
Ovid, *Ovid's Metamorphoses*, trans. by A. D. Melville (Oxford and New York, 1986)
Ovid, *Metamorphoses*, trans. by Mary M. Innes (Harmondsworth, 1986)
Regius, Raphael, *Ovidius Metamorphoseos, cum commento familiari* (Venice, 1493)
Sabinus, George, *Fabularum Ovidii Interpretatio Ethica, Physica, et Historica* (Cambridge, 1584)
Sprengius, Johann, *Metamorphoses Ovidii, Argumentis Quidem Solua Oratione, Enarrationibus Autem et Allegorijs Elegiaco Versu Accuratissime Expositae, Sumaque* (Frankfurt am Main, 1563)

Secondary Literature

Books

Abrams, M. H., *The Mirror and the Lamp. Romantic Theory and the Critical Tradition* (London, Oxford and New York, 1971)
Allen, Morse S., *The Satire of John Marston* (Columbus, Ohio, 1920)
Anonymous, *The Stage Life of Miss Mary Anderson, With Tragic and Comic Recitations from the Répertoire of this Favourite Actress* (London, 1884)
Baldick, Chris, *In Frankenstein's Shadow: Myth and Monstrosity in Nineteenth Century Writing* (Oxford, 1990)
Benét, William Rose, ed., *The Reader's Encyclopedia*, 3rd edn (London, 1988)
Bennett, J. A. W., *Middle English Literature*, ed. by Douglas Gray (Oxford, 1986)
Berst, Charles A., *Pygmalion: Shaw's Spin on Myth and Cinderella* (New York, 1995)
Bloom, Harold, *The Visionary Company* (London, 1961)
Brewer, Wilmon, *Ovid's 'Metamorphoses' in European Culture: Books 6–10* (Boston, 1941)
Brown, Sarah Annes, *The Metamorphosis of Ovid: From Chaucer to Ted Hughes* (London, 1999)
Bush, Douglas, *Mythology and the Romantic Tradition in English Poetry* (New York, 1963)
Bush, Douglas, *Mythology and the Renaissance Tradition in English Poetry* (New York, 1963)
Chance, Jane, *The Mythographic Art: Classical Fable and the Rise of the Vernacular in Early France and England* (Gainesville, Florida, 1990)
Dabundo, Laura, ed., *Encyclopedia of Romanticism. Culture in Britain, 1780s-1830s* (London, 1992)
Day, Martin, *The Many Meanings of Myth* (Lanham, Maryland, 1984)
De Man, Paul, *Allegories of Reading. Figural Language in Rousseau, Nietzsche, Rilke, and Proust* (New Haven and London, 1979)
Dent, Alan, *Mrs Patrick Campbell* (London, 1961)
Dinnis, Enid, *Emily Hickey: Poet, Essayist – Pilgrim. A Memoir* (London, 1927)
Donno, Elizabeth Story, *Elizabethan Minor Epics* (London, 1963)
Duffy, Edward, *Rousseau in England. The Context of Shelley's Critique of the Enlightenment* (California, 1979)
Evans, T. F., ed. *George Bernard Shaw: The Critical Heritage* (London, 1997)
Frye, Northrop, *Anatomy of Criticism: Four Essays* (London, 1957)
Furst, Lilian, *Romanticism*, The Critical Idiom Series (London, 1969)
Grimal, Pierre, *A Concise Dictionary of Classical Mythology*, ed. by Stephen Kershaw and trans. by A. R. Maxwell-Hyslop (Oxford, 1990)
Gunn, Alan, *The Mirror of Love: A Reinterpretation of the Romance of the Rose*

(Lubbock Texas, 1952)
Gwynn, Frederick Landis, *Sturge Moore and the Life of Art* (Kansas, 1952)
Harvey, Paul, ed., *The Oxford Companion to Classical Literature* (Oxford, 1940)
Hein, Rolland, *The Harmony Within. The Spiritual Vision of George MacDonald* (Michigan, 1982)
Heinrichs, Katherine, *The Myths of Love: Classical Lovers in Medieval Literature* (Pennsylvania, 1990)
Holroyd, Michael, *Bernard Shaw: The One Volume Definitive Edition* (London, 1997)
Honey, John, *Does Accent Matter? The Pygmalion Factor* (London, 1991)
Hönnighausen, Lothar, *The Symbolist Tradition in English Literature. A Study of Pre-Raphaelitism and 'Fin de Siècle'*, European Studies in English Literature (Cambridge, 1988)
Hooton, Joy, *A. D. Hope*, Australian Bibliographies (Melbourne, 1979)
Howatson, M. C., ed., *The Oxford Companion to Classical Literature* (Oxford, 1989)
Humm, Maggie, *Practising Feminist Criticism: An Introduction* (London, 1995)
Hunger, Herbert, ed., *Lexikon der Grieschischen und Römischen Mythologie* (Wien, 1959)
Hyder, Clyde K., ed., *Swinburne, The Critical Heritage* (London, 1970)
Jenkyns, Richard, *Dignity and Decadence. Victorian Art and the Classical Inheritance* (London, 1991), 115–142
Jobes, Gertrude, ed., *Dictionary of Mythology, Folklore and Symbols*, 2 vols (New York, 1962)
Kelly, Lori Duin, *The Life and Works of Elizabeth Stuart Phelps: Victorian Feminist Writer* (Troy, New York, 1983)
Ketterer, David, *Frankenstein's Creation: The Book, The Monster and Human Reality*, English Literary Studies Monograph Series, 16 (Victoria, Canada, 1979)
Lang, Jean, ed., *A Book of Myths* (London and Edinburgh, 1915)
Larryngton, Caroline, ed., *The Woman's Companion to Mythology* (London, 1997)
Lass, Abraham, ed., *The Facts on File Dictionary of Classical, Biblical and Literary Allusions*, (New York and Oxford, 1987)
Lee, Alvin A. and Robert D. Denham, eds, *The Legacy of Northrop Frye* (Toronto, 1994)
Lesky, Albin, *A History of Greek Literature*, trans. by James Willis and Cornelis de Heer (London, 1966)
Makaryk, Irena R., ed., *Encyclopedia of Contemporary Literary Theory: Approaches, Scholars, Terms* (Toronto, 1993)
Marshall, Gail, *Actresses on the Victorian Stage: Feminine Performance and the Galatea Myth* (Cambridge, 1998)
Martin, Charles, *Ovid in English* (London, 1998)

Martindale, Charles, *Ovid Renewed: Ovidian Influences on Literature and Art from the Middle Ages to the Twentieth Century* (Cambridge, 1988)
McGillis, Roderick, ed., *For the Childlike. George MacDonald's Fantasies for Children* (New Jersey and London, 1992)
Meisel, Martin, *Shaw and the Nineteenth Century Theater* (London, 1963)
Miles, Alfred, ed., *The Poets of the Century*, 10 vols (London, 1879)
Miles, Geoffrey, ed., *Classical Mythology in English Literature: A Critical Anthology* (London, 1999)
Miller, J. Hillis, *Versions of Pygmalion* (Cambridge, Massachusetts, 1990)
Moncrieff, A. R. Hope, ed., *Classical Mythology* (Guernsey, 1994)
Moss, Ann, *Ovid in Renaissance France. A Survey of Latin Editions of Ovid and Commentaries Printed in France Before 1600*, Warburg Institute Surveys, 8 (London, 1982)
Munich, Adrienne Auslander, *Andromeda's Chains. Gender and Interpretation in Victorian Literature and Art* (New York, 1989)
Nicoll, Allardyce, *A History of English Drama 1660–1900*, 6 vols (Cambridge, 1952–1959)
Nietzsche, Friedrich, *The Birth of Tragedy And Other Writings*, ed. by Raymond Guess and Ronald Speirs, trans. by Ronald Speirs (Cambridge, 1999)
Propp, Vladimir, *Morphology of the Folktale*, transl. by Laurence Scott (Austin, Texas and London, 1968)
Quinn, Vincent, *Hilda Doolittle* (New York, 1967)
Reade, Benedict, and Joanna Barnes eds., *Pre-Raphaelite Sculpture. Nature and Imagination in British Sculpture 1848–1914* (London, 1991)
Reynolds, L. D., ed., *Texts and Transmission. A Survey of the Latin Classics* (Oxford, 1983)
Richer, Louis, *L'Ovide Bouffon; ou Les Metamorphoses Burlesques* (Paris, 1650).
Robertson, D. W., *A Preface to Chaucer. Studies in Medieval Perspectives* (Princeton, New Jersey, 1969)
Robinson, Philip E. J., *Jean-Jacques Rousseau's Doctrine of the Arts*, European University Studies, 90 (Berne, 1984)
Rose, H. J., ed., *A Handbook of Greek Mythology* (London, 1958)
Rosenthal, Robert and Lenore Jacobson, *Pygmalion in the Classroom: Teacher Expectation and Pupils' Intellectual Development* (New York, 1968)
Rowell, George, *The Victorian Theatre 1792–1914: A Survey*, 2nd edn (Cambridge, 1978)
Schlobin, Roger, ed., *The Aesthetics of Fantasy Literature and Art* (Notre Dame, 1982)
Secker, Martin, *The Eighteen-Nineties: A Period Anthology in Prose and Verse* (London, 1948)
Small, Christopher, *Ariel Like a Harpy: Shelley, Mary and Frankenstein* (London, 1972)

Smith, Eric, ed., *A Dictionary of Classical Reference in English Poetry* (Woodbridge, 1984)
Smith, William, ed., *A Classical Dictionary of Greek and Roman Biography, Mythology*, 3 vols (London, 1844–1849)
Solodow, Joseph B. *The World of Ovid's Metamorphoses* (Chapel Hill, North Carolina and London, 1988)
Steadman, John M., *Nature Into Myth. Medieval and Renaissance Moral Symbols* (Pittsburgh, 1980)
Stedman, Jane, *W. S. Gilbert: A Classic Victorian and His Theatre* (Oxford, 1996)
Swann, Thomas Burnett, *The Classical World of H. D.* (Nebraska, 1962)
Taylor, Edward William, *Nature and Art in Renaissance Literature* (New York and London, 1964)
Thomas, Donald, *The Post Romantics* (London, 1990)
Tripp, Edward, *The Collins Dictionary of Classical Mythology* (London and Glasgow, 1988)
Valency, Maurice, *The Cart and the Trumpet: The Plays of George Bernard Shaw* (New York, 1973)
Vinge, Louise, *The Narcissus Theme in Western Literature up to the Early Nineteenth Century* (Lund, 1967)
Wall, Kathleen, *The Callisto Myth From Ovid To Atwood* (Kingston, 1988)
Ward, A. W., and A. R. Waller, *The Cambridge History of English Literature*, 15 vols (Cambridge, 1907–1916)
Warner, Marina, *Monuments and Maidens: The Allegory of the Female Form* (London, 1985)
Winter, William, *Shadows of the Stage*, 3 vols (New York and London, 1892–1893)
Wood, Christopher, *The Pre-Raphaelites* (London, 1981)
Woolner, Amy, *Thomas Woolner. R. A. His Life in Letters* (London, 1917)
Yenal, Edith, *Christine de Pisan. A Bibliography of Writings by Her and About Her* (Metuchen, New Jersey and London, 1982)
Ziolkowski, Theodore, *Varieties of Literary Thematics* (Princeton, 1983)

Articles in Books and Journals

Barkan, Leonard, '"Living Sculptures": Ovid, Michelangelo, and *The Winter's Tale*', *English Literary History*, 48 (1981), 639–667
Bauer, Douglas, 'The Function of Pygmalion in the *Metamorphoses* of Ovid', *Transactions of the American Philological Association*, 93 (1962), 1–21 (p. 2)
Bowers, R. H., 'An Anonymous Renaissance Pygmalion Playlet', *Modern Philology*, 47 (1949), 73–81
Buske, Walter, 'Pigmaliondichtungen des 18. Jahrhunderts', *Germanisch-*

Romanische Monatschrift, 7 (1915), 345-354

Caputi, Jane, 'On Psychic Activism: Feminist Mythmaking', in *The Woman's Companion to Mythology*, ed. by Caroline Larryngton, pp. 425-440

Carr, J. L., 'Pygmalion and the Philosophes. The Animated Statue in Eighteenth Century France', *Journal of the Warburg and Courtauld Institutes*, 23 (1960), 239-255

Cassidy, John A., 'Robert Buchanan and the Fleshly Controversy', *PMLA*, 67 (1952), 65-93

Cooper, Helen, 'Chaucer and Ovid: A Question of Authority' in *Ovid Renewed*, ed. by Charles Martindale, pp. 71-81

Cox, John F., 'Some Letters of Thomas Woolner to Mr and Mrs Henry Adams (I)', *Journal of Pre-Raphaelite and Aesthetic Studies*, 1 (1981), 1-27

Cox, John F., 'Thomas Woolner's Letters to Mr and Mrs Henry Adams (II)', *Journal of Pre-Raphaelite and Aesthetic Studies*, 2 (1981), 1-21

Cross, Gustav, 'Marston's "Metamorphosis of Pigmalion's Image": A Mock Epyllion', *Études Anglaises*, 17 (1960), 331-336

Durbach, Errol, 'Pygmalion: Myth and Anti-Myth in the Plays of Ibsen and Shaw', in *George Bernard Shaw's 'Pygmalion'*, ed. by Harold Bloom (New Haven, 1988), pp. 87-98

Egbert, Virginia Wylie, 'Pygmalion as Sculptor', *Princeton University Library Chronicle*, 28 (1966), 20-33

Fairchild, Arthur H. R., 'Shakespeare and the Arts of Design', *University of Missouri Studies*, 12 (1937), 71-89

Finkelpearl, Philip J., 'From Petrarch to Ovid: Metamorphoses in John Marston's "Metamorphosis of Pigmalion's Image"', *A Journal of English Literary History*, 32 (1965), 333-348

Ghisalberti, Fausto, 'Arnulfo d'Orléans, un cultore di Ovidio ne secolo XII', in *Memorie del Reale Istituto Lombardo di Scienze e Lettere*, 24 (1932), 157-234

Gresseth, Gerald K. 'The Pygmalion Tale', *Journal of the Pacific Northwest Council on Foreign Languages*, 2 (1981), 15-19

Harbert, Bruce, 'Lessons From the Great Clerk: Ovid and John Gower', in *Ovid Renewed*, ed. by Charles Martindale, pp. 83-97

Harris, Edward P. 'The Liberation of Flesh from Stone: Pygmalion in Frank Wederkind's *Erdgeist*', *The Germanic Review*, 52 (1977), 44-56

Hayes, Elizabeth T., '"Like Seeing You Buried": Persephone in *The Bluest Eye*, *Their Eyes Were Watching God*, and *The Color Purple*', in *Images of Persephone: Feminist Readings in Western Literature*, ed. by Elizabeth T. Hayes (Gainesville, Florida, 1994), pp. 170-194

Hill, Thomas D., 'Narcissus, Pygmalion, and the Castration of Saturn: Two Mythographic Themes in the *Roman de la Rose*', *Studies in Philology*, 71 (1974), 404-426

Hoffman, Richard, 'Pygmalion in the "Physician's Tale"', *American Notes and Queries*, 5 (1967), 83–4
Hummel, John H., 'Rousseau's *Pygmalion* and the *Confessions*', *Neophilogus*, 56 (1972), 273–284
Jackson, Russell, 'The Lyceum in Irving's Absence: G. E. Terry's Letters to Bram Stoker', *Nineteenth Century Theatre Research*, 6 (1978), 25–33
Johnson, Hiram Kellogg, 'Thomas Lovell Beddoes' *The Psychiatric Quarterly* (New York, 1943)
Joshua, Essaka, 'The Mythographic Context of Shaw's *Pygmalion*', *Nineteenth Century Theatre*, 26 (1998), 112–137
Kramer, Victor A., 'Agee's Early Poem, "Pygmalion" and his Aesthetic', *Mississippi Quarterly*, 29 (1976), 191–196
Law, Helen H., 'The Name Galatea in the Pygmalion Myth', *Classical Journal*, 27 (1932), 337–342
Lee, Alvin A., 'Archetype', in *Encyclopedia of Contemporary Literary Theory: Approaches, Scholars, Terms*, ed. by Irena R. Makaryk (Toronto, 1993), p. 508
Lerner, Laurence, 'Ovid and the Elizabethans', in *Ovid Renewed*, ed. by Charles Martindale, pp. 121–135
Lévi-Strauss, Claude, 'The Structural Study of Myth', in Thomas A. Sebeok, *Myth. A Symposium* (Bloomington, Indiana and London, 1965), 81–106
Lyon, Judson S., 'Romantic Psychology and the Inner Senses: Coleridge', *PMLA*, 81 (1966), 246–260
MacDonald, Christine V., 'The Animation of Writing', in *The Dialogue of Writing: Essays in Eighteenth-Century French Literature*, ed. by Christine V. MacDonald (Waterloo, Ontario, 1984), pp. 47–60
Marshall, Gail, 'Actresses, Statues and Speculation in *Daniel Deronda*', *Essays in Criticism*, 44 (1994), 117–139
Maxwell, Catherine, 'Browning's Pygmalion and the Revenge of Galatea', *English Literary History*, 60 (1993), 989–1013
Miller, Jane M., 'Some Versions of Pygmalion', in *Ovid Renewed*, ed. by Charles Martindale, pp. 205–214
Pollin, Burton R., 'Philosophical and Literary Sources of *Frankenstein*', *Comparative Literature*, 17 (1965), 97–108
Purkiss, Diane, 'Women's Rewriting of Myth', in *The Woman's Companion to Mythology*, ed. by Caroline Larryngton, pp. 441–457
Reade, Benedict, 'Was There Pre-Raphaelite Sculpture?', in *The Pre-Raphaelite Papers*, ed. by Leslie Parris (London, 1984), pp. 97–110
Reinhold, Meyer, 'The Naming of Pygmalion's Animated Statue', *Classical Journal*, 66 (1979), 316–319
Reynolds, William D., 'Sources, Nature, and Influence of the *Ovidus Moralizatus* of Pierre Bersuire', in Jane Chance, *The Mythographic Art*, pp. 83–99

Rico, Barbara Roche, 'From "Speechless Dialect" to "Prosperous Art": Shakespeare's Recasting of the Pygmalion Image', *Huntingdon Library Quarterly, A Journal For the History and Interpretation of English and American Civilization*, 48 (1985), 285–295

Riga, Frank, P., 'From Time to Eternity: MacDonald's Doorway Between', in *Essays on C. S. Lewis and George MacDonald. Truth, Fiction and the Power of the Imagination*, ed. by Cynthia Marshall, Studies in British Literature, 11 (Lewistown, Queenstown, Lampeter, 1991), 83–100

Rudd, Niall, 'Daedalus and Icarus (ii). From the Renaissance to the Present Day', in *Ovid Renewed*, ed. by Charles Martindale, pp. 37–53

Spell, Jefferson R., 'Pygmalion in Spain', *Romanic Review*, 25 (1934), 395–401

Tarrant, R. J., 'Ovid', in L. D. Reynolds, *Texts and Transmission*, pp. 257–284

Vesonder, Timothy, 'Eliza's Choice: Transformation Myth and the Ending of *Pygmalion*', in *Fabian Feminist: Bernard Shaw and Women*, ed. by Rodelle Weintraub (London, 1977), pp. 39–45

Weber, Shierry M., 'The Aesthetics of Rousseau's *Pygmalion*', *Modern Language Notes*, 83 (1968), 900–918

Unpublished Theses

Butler, Stephen Henry, 'The Pygmalion Motif and Crisis of the Creative Process in Modern Fiction' (unpublished doctoral dissertation, University of Brandeis, 1984)

Marshall, Gail S., 'Artful Galateas: Gender and the Arts of Writing and Acting in Novels, 1876–1900' (unpublished doctoral thesis, University of Cambridge, 1992)

Ray, Bonnie MacDougall, 'The Metamorphoses of Pygmalion: A Study of the Treatment of the Myth from the Third Century BC to the Early Seventeenth Century' (unpublished doctoral dissertation, University of Columbia, 1981)

Reynolds, William D., 'The *Ovidius Moralizatus* of Petrus Berchorius: An Introduction and Translation' (unpublished doctoral dissertation, University of Illinois, Urbana-Champaign, 1971)

Index

Abrams, M. H., 56n
Acis, 34
Adonis, 3, 5, 69, 145, 148, 157
Aldington, Richard, 143-4
Allegory, xv, 8, 9, 10, 12, 13, 14, 21, 27, 72, 82, 121
Allen, Fletcher, 150
Anderson, Mary, 110-111, 112, 113-4
Antinomy, 49
Apelles, 15, 19, 19n, 22, 29
Aphrodite, 1, 2, 63, 66, 67, 94, 120, 130, 145, 148, 157, 158, 159 (*see also* Venus)
Apollo 19, 70, 85, 86, 91 (*see also* Pygmalion Story: Apolline art)
Apollodorus, 5, 6, 157
Archetype. *See* Myth: as archetype; *Metamorphoses*: as archetype
Ariadne, 69, 131, 136
Ariel, 73
Arnobius of Sicca, 1-2, 6, 9, 24, 158
Arnulf of Orléans, 8-9, 9n, 11, 14, 20
Athene, 145
Atropos, 131
Auden, W. H., 70
Augustine, Saint, 43

Baker, Henry, 34
Baldick, Chris, 63-4
Barnes, Joanna, 95
Basse, William, 30
Bauer, Douglas, 4
Beddoes, Thomas, 40
Beddoes, Thomas Lovell, xx, 37-51 *passim*, 73, 135
Benét, William Rose, 159
Bennett, J. A. W., 20, 20n
Bennett, William Cox, 68-70, 136
Berchorius, Petrus. *See* Pierre Bersuire
Berst, Charles A., 122, 122n
Bersuire, Pierre (or Petrus Berchorius), 8, 10, 11-12, 13, 20, 110
Blackmur, Richard Palmer, 151
Blake, William, 48, 56-7, 76
Bloom, Harold, 48
Bömer, Franz, 159
Boucher, François, 33
Boucicault, Dion, 124-5, 126

Boureau-Deslandes, André François, 35n
Brathwait, Richard, 28, 29
Brestel, Arthur, 153
Brewer, Wilmon, 6
Brontë, Charlotte, 60, 142
Brough, William, 104, 105, 117, 133
Brown, Sarah Annes, 41-2, 48, 147
Browning, Robert, xv, xvi, 53, 139
Buchanan, Robert, 66, 81-2, 83, 84, 85, 86-7, 135, 136
Bulwer Lytton. *See* Lytton, Edward Bulwer
Burgam, E. B., 53
Burke, Edmund, 37
Burlesque, 103-4, 105, 114, 115, 130, 133, 137
Burne-Jones, Edward, 88, 88n, 89, 94
Bush, Douglas, 31, 76
Buske, Walter, xvn
Butler, Stephen, xiv-xv, xviii
Byron, Lord, 37, 40

Campbell, Mrs Patrick, 107, 117
Caputi, Jane, 137
Carr, J. L., 33, 50
Carroll, Lewis, 62
Catholicism. *See* Pygmalion Story: anti-Catholic polemic
Caxton, William, 10
Charade, 60-62
Charon, 48
Chaucer, Geoffrey, 13, 18-19, 32, 33
Chester Mystery Plays, 55
Christian interpretations. *See* Pygmalion Story: Christian interpretations
Christine de Pisan, 13-14, 20
Churchyard, Thomas, 18
Cinderella, 97, 98, 99, 118, 121-9, 132, 133
Cinyras, 3, 5, 10, 157
Classical Dictionaries, 35, 104, 157-9 (*see also* Lemprière's *Classical Dictionary* and under individual editors)
Clement of Alexandria, 1-2, 6, 9, 24, 159
Clough, Arthur Hugh, 53
Cnidus, 1-2
Cockayne, Aston, 30
Coleridge, Ernest Hartley,

Coleridge, Gilbert, 23
Coleridge, G. J. D., 150-1
Coleridge, Samuel Taylor, 37, 40, 57, 58, 59, 64, 65, 67, 68, 145
Conquest, Robert, 153
Cordonnier, Thémiseul de Sainte Hyacinthe, xvn
Cowley, Abraham, 29-30
Crashaw, Richard, 27
Crompton, Hugh, 28
Cubières-Palmézeaux, Michel de, 34
Cullwick, Hannah, 118
Cyprus, 1, 2, 5, 6, 16, 50, 66, 69, 77, 135n, 145

D., H. (Hilda Doolittle), 139, 144-7
Daniel, Samuel, 39
Darnford, Henry, 39, 46 (*see also* Wollstonecraft, Mary)
Davenport, Arnold, 24
Davies, John, 28, 29, 30
Day, Martin, xi
Decadents, The, 119
Dickens, Charles, 66
Dickinson, Emily, 142
Dictionaries. *See* Classical Dictionaries
Dido, 6, 13, 50
Dionysius, 136 (*see also* Pygmalion Story: Dionysian art)
Donne, John, 31
Donno, Elizabeth Story, 10
Doolittle, Hilda. *See* D., H.
Dryden, John, 33, 34, 34n
Durbach, Errol, 4

Educating Rita. See Russell, Willy
Edwardes George, 114
Eliot, George, 60
Eliot, T. S., 144
Elizabeth I, 24, 27
Ellis, George, 32-3
Elysium, 48
Enigma, 61
Eros, 144
Euphrosyne, 129, 130, 131

Feminist Criticism, xii-xiii, xxi
Finckelpearl, Philip J., 24
Fleshly Controversy, 81-96 *passim*
Fontenelle, 34, 50

Formalism, xiv
Francis, Saint, 21
Frankenstein. See Shelley, Mary
Frankenstein, Victor, 44, 64 (*see also* Shelley, Mary)
Frye, Northrop, xii-xiii
Fuller, Roy, 153
Fulwood, William, 23

Gaiety Theatre, 114
Galatea (statue/woman)
  animal-like, 86, 136, 154, 155
  beauty of, xi, 11, 12, 13, 14, 16, 18, 19, 27, 29, 31, 38, 39, 40, 61, 69, 74, 77, 78, 83, 84, 85, 86, 87, 88, 91, 101, 107, 118, 122, 132, 135, 136, 140, 147, 148, 150, 158
  blush, 3, 16, 50, 99, 140
  body of, xi, xxi, 38, 72, 81, 83, 84, 85, 87, 88, 91, 93, 95, 96, 136, 147, 153, 154, 155
  chained, 136
  chastity of, 11, 12, 16, 17, 18, 21, 81, 87, 91
  child-like, 68, 100, 106, 113, 130, 131, 132, 133, 135-6, 137, 155
  chryselephantine, 23, 130
  clay, 23, 152
  death of, 49, 129, 140, 150
  deceiver, 21, 23, 101
  as embodiment of a dream, xxi, 18, 53-79 *passim*
  as dreamer, 108, 139, 143
  education of. *See* Pygmalion Story: education theme
  flower-like, 67, 86, 135, 136
  'Galatea-aesthetic', xvi, 115
  hair of, 69, 86, 135, 136, 154
  ideal, xxi, 16, 18, 23, 38, 42, 45, 46, 73, 76, 77, 79, 81, 85, 87, 107, 118, 119, 120, 121, 135, 147, 148, 149, 150, 152, 154, 155
  immortality as a statue, 20, 140, 150
  independence of, xvi, 100, 101, 116, 117, 127, 142
  innocence of, xvi, 3, 8, 18, 63, 100, 101, 102, 104, 105-6, 107, 108, 114, 115, 116, 117, 124, 127, 130, 132, 133, 135, 137, 155
  ivory, xi, 1, 2, 3, 6, 9, 11, 14, 15, 16,

21, 22, 23, 25, 28, 33, 39, 76, 81, 140, 153, 157, 158
  as a man, 38, 115
  marble, 2, 20, 20n, 23, 39, 40, 46, 49, 64, 68, 69, 72, 73, 74, 78, 83, 86, 88, 91, 94, 111, 113, 117, 119, 131, 132, 135, 136, 142, 143, 146, 149, 150, 153, 158
  name, xi, xiv, xvn, 34-5, 35n, 50, 63, 104, 129, 130, 131, 152, 155
  as narcissistic reflection. *See* Pygmalion: narcissist
  nude, 1, 10, 17, 81, 86, 88, 120, 121, 138, 153, 155
  painted statue, 18, 25-6, 27, 29, 30, 31, 91
  passion of, 12, 45, 81, 87, 105, 106, 108, 110, 114, 115, 133, 136, 138
  as a picture, 28
  as property, 24, 117
  prostitute, 26, 27
  created as a punishment for Pygmalion's behaviour, 104, 159
  rejection of Pygmalion, xvii, 46, 142
  reluctant to come to life, 141
  selective knowledge or vocabulary of, 106, 115, 131, 136
  as servant, 9, 10, 11, 118-119
  sexual violation of statue, 1, 14
  as silent, xxi, 68, 99, 152, 153
  soul of, xxi, 16, 32, 65, 67, 68, 69, 70, 81, 82, 83, 85, 87, 88, 93, 95, 96, 108, 131
  as soulless, 65, 78, 81, 86
  as statue of Venus or Aphrodite, 1, 2, 38, 91, 159
  stone, 4, 15, 23, 24, 25, 28, 29, 30, 41, 49, 131, 147, 149, 153, 158
  as temptress, xxi, 135
  transformation of, xi, xvii, 3-4, 8, 9, 10, 12, 13, 14, 15, 16, 19, 22, 23, 24, 25, 27, 32, 39, 46, 47, 48, 49, 50, 51, 62, 63, 64, 69, 73, 74, 75, 81, 86, 87, 91, 93, 95, 97, 98, 99, 101, 103, 104, 110, 111, 116, 121, 122, 123, 125, 127, 128, 129, 130, 131, 137, 139, 140, 146, 147, 150, 151, 155
  vanity of, 28, 105, 130 (*see also* Pygmalion, Pygmalion Story)
Gall, Franz Joseph, 58, 64

Gallienne, Richard le, 95
Gandalac, Lennard, 150
Garter, Bernard, 22
Garth, Samuel, 34n
Genlis, Madame de, 63
Gilbert, W. S., xxi, 50, 62, 97, 102-133 *passim*, 155, 159
Gillman, Charlotte Perkins, 142
Giovanni del Virgilio, 9n
Gladstone, W. E., 94
Glassford, James, 61
Godwin, William, 44, 44n
Goethe, Johann Wolfgang von, 64, 65
Golding, Arthur, 20-21
Gomersall, Robert, 29, 30-31
Gower, John, 12-13, 20, 83
Granville, George, 32n
Granville-Barker, Harley, 103, 104
Graves, Robert, 137-8, 137n, 148, 149
Greek sculpture, 81, 82, 83, 84, 85, 86, 87, 88, 91, 95, 111, 113, 155
Gresseth, Gerald K., xiv
Grimal, Pierre, 157
Grotesque, 53
Guillaume de Lorris. *See Roman de la Rose*
Guillaume de Machaut, 18-19
Guilpin, Edward, 25-6, 27, 30
Gunn, Alan, 17
Gwynn, Frederick Landis, 119, 120

H. D. *See* D., H.
Haggard, Henry Rider, 130
Hallam, Arthur, 59-62, 68
Hardy, Thomas, xv
Harris, Edward P., 35n
Hay, F., 104
Hayes, Elizabeth, xiii
Haymarket Theatre, 102, 103, 107n, 108n, 114, 116n
Hazlitt, William, 37, 39-40, 45, 46, 58, 59, 135
Heath, John, 30-31
Hector, 13
Hecuba, 13
Hegel, George Wilhelm Friedrich, 147
Hein, Rolland, 73
Heinrichs, Katherine, 14-15
Helios, 145
Hellanicus, 2

Hermaphroditus, 84
Hephaestos (Vulcan), 145, 146
Hickey, Emily Henrietta, 138, 139, 140, 142
Hill, Thomas D., 9n, 10, 15, 17
Hodson, Henrietta, 108
Hoffman, E. T. A., 71
Hoffman, Michael, 151, 151n
Hoffman, Richard, 19n
Hollingshead, John, 114
Holman Hunt, William, 95
Hooley, John, 136
Hope, Alec Derwent, 151-2
Hopkins, John, 34
Howatson, M. A., 159
Howell, Agnes Rous, 129, 130-131
Hughes, Ted, 151, 154
Hulse, Clarke, 10
Humm, Maggie, xii
Hummel, John, 43
Hunt, J. H., Leigh, xx, 37, 39, 39n, 40, 42, 43, 46, 50
Hurrell, William E., 118, 119, 121
Hurston, Zora Neal, xiii
Hyacinthus, 69
Hyginus, 2

Imagination, 18, 38, 39, 42, 44n, 45, 48, 49, 53, 54, 145-6, 147, 151
Imagism, 143

James, Henry, xv
Jenkyns, Richard, xvn, 93-4
Jenyns, Soame, 31-32
Jean de Meun. *See Roman de la Rose*
Jobes, Gertrude, 159
John of Garland, 9
Johnson, Hiram Kellogg, 46, 48
Johnson, Richard, 29
Jove. *See* Zeus
Joyce, James, 144
Jupiter. *See* Zeus

Kant, Immanuel, 65
Kavanagh, Patrick, 152
Keats, John, 51, 53, 54, 55, 56, 57, 143
Kelsall, Thomas Forbes, 41, 51
Kenny, J., 104
Ketterer, David, 63
King, Henry, 30

Kleist, Heinrich von, xv
Kunstmärchen, 71, 72

Lancaster, George Eric, 135, 136
Landow, George, P., 71
Lang, Andrew, 23, 129-130, 135
Lang, Jean, 159
Langtry, Lily, 101, 102
Larkin, Philip, 151
Lasdun, James, 151, 151n
Lass, Abraham, 158
Law, Helen H., xvn
Lemprière's Classical Dictionary, 145, 158, 159
Lerner, Laurence, 21
Lévi-Strauss, Claude, xix
Lewis, Cecil Day, 147
Lewis, Charlton M., 148
Lewis, C. S., 70
Llewellyn, Alun, 151
Longley, Michael, 153
Lucas, Frank Laurence, 149
Lucretius, 55
Lyceum Theatre, 114
Lydgate, John, 15, 18-19, 20
Lyly, John, 26
Lytton, Edward Bulwer, 126-7

Macdonald, George, 70-75, 78
Mahon, Derek, 153
'Maitland, Thomas' (*pseud.*). *See* Buchanan, Robert
Mallock, W. H., 75-6
Man, Paul de, 49
Mann, Thomas, xv
Marsh, Edward, 119
Marshall, Gail, xv, xvn, xvi-xviii, 48, 107n, 115, 158n
Marston, John, 24-5, 159
Martin, Charles, 137n, 155
Martindale, Charles, 7, 155
Mason, William, 34, 37, 50
Massingham, H. W., 97
Maugham W. Somerset, 128-9
Maurier, George du, 123-4
Maxwell, Catherine, xv-xvi, xviii
McGillis, Roderick, 71
Medusa, 142
Meisel, Martin, 122
Metamorphoses: passim

as archetype, xiv-xv, xviii, xix, 95
   (for translations and interpretations see
   under individual authors)
Metharme, 5, 157
Midas, 70
Middleton, Thomas, 26-7
Miles, Geoffrey, xviin, 10, 10n, 21-2, 32n
Miller, J. Hillis, xv, xviii
Miller, Jane M., 3, 4, 9
Milton, John, 55, 56, 57, 58
Mitchell, Joseph, 32, 32n
Modernism, 139, 143, 151
Moncrieff, A. R. Hope, 159
Montgomery, Roselle Mercier, 139, 142-3
Moore, G. E., 119
Moore, Thomas Sturge, 118, 119
Morford, Mark, 159
Morris, William, 87-8, 91, 93, 94, 159
Morrison, Toni, xiii
Morton, John Madison, 125
Morton, Thomas, 125
Moss, Ann, 21
Motte-Fouqué, La, 71
Munby, A. J., 118
Munich, Adrienne Auslander, xviii-xix
Murphy, Joseph John, 135, 136
Myrrha, 3, 4, 20, 148, 157
Myth, xi, xii, xix, xxi, 8, 34
   'archaic myth', xi, xvi
   as archetype, xii-xvi, xviii-xx, 95
   'derivative myth', xi, xv, xix
   and gender, xii, 137, 137n
   'intermediate myth', xi, xvii, xix
   social function, xii
   (*see also* Metamorphoses: as
   archetype)

Nabokov, Vladimir, xv
Narcissism, xx, 37, 38, 42, 43 (*see also*
   Pygmalion: narcissist)
Narcissus, 14, 15
New Frankenstein, The, 62-6
Newman, John Henry, 94
Neilson, Julia, 111
Nietzsche, Friedrich, 55, 72, 79, 154 (*see
   also* Pygmalion Story: Apolline Art;
   Pygmalion Story: Dionysian Art)
Niobe, 73
Niobelle, 131
Nonnos (Panopolitanus), 6

Novalis, 71
Ogle, George, 33
Orpheus, 14
O'Shaugnessy, Arthur, 59
Osiris, 65
Ovid. *See Metamorphoses*
   'aetas Ovidiana', 7, 27
   Ovide Moralisé, 8, 9, 10, 19

Pan, 70
Pandora, 69, 145
Pantheism, 78
Paphos
   person, 3, 5, 9n, 10, 12, 29, 99, 150,
      157, 159
   place, 5, 6, 157
Pater, Walter, 53-4, 82
Patmore, Coventry, 94
Payn, James, 66-8, 135, 136
Pearl, 18
Persephone, xiii
Pettie, George, 23, 24, 25
Phaethon, 7
Phelps, Elizabeth Stuart, 138, 140-2, 143
Phidias, 29
Philostephanus, 1, 2
Pick, Samuel, 30
Pigmalion (1741), 34
Pitt, Christopher, 32n
Planché, James Robinson, 103
Platonism, 72, 75, 78, 84
Pollin, Burton R., 33, 63
Pollock, W. H., 130
Porphyry, 5, 6, 145
Port Folio, 38
Poseidippus, 1
Post-Romanticism, xxi, 53-79 *passim*, 81,
   120, 148, 154 (*see also* Romanticism)
Potter, Paul, 123
Pound, Ezra, 144
Pre-Raphaelites, 81-96 *passim*
Priam, 13, 19
Prometheus, 32-3, 63, 67, 68, 130, 146
Propoetides, 3, 12, 16, 22, 44, 154, 159
Propp, Vladimir, xiv
Psyche, 71, 77, 86, 105, 117, 144
Prosopopoeia, xv, xvii
Pygmalion, *passim*
   artistic crisis of, xiv-xv, xviii, xxi, 139,
      143-4, 146, 147, 154, 155

blindness of, 30, 116
chastity of, 13, 17, 20, 86
child-like, 67, 142
chivalry of, 17
death of, 41, 47, 51, 73, 74
and dominance, 8, 155
father-figure, 116, 125, 131
as fool, 10, 17, 20, 26, 30
gentleman, 23
god-like, 20, 69, 121
as hard-worker, 60, 69, 119, 120
idolatory of, 1, 12, 16-17, 22, 23, 24, 25, 28-9, 30-31, 85, 87 (*see also* Pygmalion Story: anti-Catholic polemic)
as imitator, 18, 19, 23
as king of Cyprus, 1, 5, 6, 50, 145, 157, 158, 159
as lecher, 13, 17, 20, 21, 29
as lover of someone other than Galatea, xvii, 23, 86, 94, 105, 116, 116n, 147
madness of, 1, 16, 19, 21, 48, 87, 150, 154
melancholy of, 12, 24
as misogynist, xvi, 11, 23, 24, 25, 104, 147, 159
not a misogynist, 12, 22, 66, 154
as narcissist, xx, 37, 38, 42, 43, 46, 135 (*see also* Narcissism)
as nobleman, 9, 131
as painter, 18
as Phoenician, 5, 13, 50
from Piedmont, 23
piety of, 3, 4, 20
rejection of human Galatea, xvii, 76, 79, 87, 116n, 132, 150, 153
rejection of statue, 17, 116, 153, 147
as sculptor, xi, xxi, 2, 9, 10, 12, 13, 14, 15, 16, 17, 19, 19n, 20, 22, 23, 27, 28, 37, 50, 55, 60, 64, 66, 67, 68, 69, 71, 72, 74, 76, 79, 81, 82, 86, 91, 93, 95, 97, 99, 103, 104, 115, 117, 131, 132, 135, 136, 139, 141, 142, 144, 145, 146, 147, 148, 150, 152, 158
soul of, 1, 59, 60, 68, 70, 72, 77, 79
as statue, 131, 152
suicidal, 47
vanity of, 37, 43, 115
as a woman, 115, 114, 152
as young man, 12, 66, 138

(*see also* under individual authors; Galatea; Pygmalion Story)
Pygmalion (1630–50), 27
Pygmalion, A Poem (1779), 34, 50
Pygmalion Story
and anti-Catholic polemic, 23, 24, 26, 27
and anti-myth, 4
and Apolline art, 55, 56, 69, 75, 76, 79
as archetype. *See Metamorphoses*: as archetype
as birth myth, 4
Christian interpretations of, 1-20 *passim* (*see also* anti-Catholic polemic)
and class, 99, 101, 105, 118, 123-133 *passim*
and comedy, 34, 64, 102, 105, 113, 114, 132, 137
and Dionysian art, 55, 59, 67, 68, 69, 73, 75, 76, 79, 84, 138, 148, 154
and dream, xxi, 53-79 *passim*, 87, 130, 131, 147, 148, 154
and education theme, xiv, xx, 8, 9, 10, 11, 78, 99-133 *passim*, 155
and Fleshly Controversy, xxi, 81-96 *passim*
and marriage, 3, 13, 21, 23, 28, 97, 98, 100, 117, 118, 122, 126, 131
and morality of art, 81-96 *passim*
narrator in, 22-3, 25, 44, 67, 94, 137, 138
and presentation of gifts scene, 3, 16, 97, 123
and satire, 24, 25, 27, 28, 107, 110
separation from *Metamorphoses*, 3, 14, 15, 22, 27
transformation scene. *See* Galatea: transformation
and unrequited love, 25, 27, 30, 31, 39, 45, 73, 116
(*see also* under individual authors; Galatea; Pygmalion)

Ray, Bonnie MacDougall, 12-13, 28n
Reade, Benedict, 95
Reade, Simon, 154n
Reid, Jane Davidson, 88n
Reinhold, Meyer, xvn, 2
Restout, Jean, 33

Index

Reynolds, L. D., 7,
Reynolds, W. D., 10-11, 12
Richer, Louis, 34
Ricketts, Charles, 119, 120
Riga, Frank P., 71-2
Rigmerole, Tobias, 60-61
Robertson, D. W., 11n, 17
Robertson, Madge (Mrs Kendal), 107, 107n, 111
Robertson, T. W., 125
Romagnesi, Jean-Antoine, 34
Roman de la Rose, 9, 10, 15, 16, 17, 18, 19, 19n, 20
Romanticism, xxi, 32, 33, 35, 37-51 *passim*, 53, 55, 64, 68, 73, 76, 79, 146, 147 (*see also* Post-Romanticism)
Roscher, W. H., 159
Rose, H. J., 159
Ross, Ronald, 129, 131-132, 135
Rossetti, Dante Gabriel, 54, 82, 83, 91n
Rossetti, William Michael, 91n
Rousseau, Jean-Jacques, xii, xiii, xvn, xx, 33-4, 35, 37-51 *passim*, 53, 61, 79, 130, 135, 146, 147
Rowe, Charles J., 139, 151
Rowell, George, 102, 103, 104, 114
Russell, Willy, xiv

Sabinus, George, 21
Sandys, George, 27
Savage, Richard, 32, 32n
Savoy Theatre, 114
Scot, Walter, 30n
Scott, Clement, 106n, 114
Scott, William Bell, 85, 86, 87, 88, 91, 91n, 92, 93, 94
Secker, Martin, 119-120
Seward, Anna, 32
Shakespeare, William
  Measure for Measure, 26
  The Winter's Tale, xiv, 28n, 48, 60, 74
Shannon, Charles Hazlewood, 119, 120
Shaw, George Bernard, xvi, xix, xx, xxi, 9, 97-133 *passim*, 136, 159
Shelley, Mary, xiv, 32, 44, 48, 57, 58, 62, 63, 65, 67, 121, 138 (*see also* Victor Frankenstein)
Shelley, Percy Bysshe, 37, 40, 42, 44, 56, 58, 64, 71
Sisiphus, 23

Sisson, C. H., 151, 152-3
Sivry, Louis Poinsinet de, 34
Sleeping Beauty, 73
Small, Christopher, 63
Smith, Eric, 158
Smith, William, 157, 159
Smyrna, 148
Sotheby, Charlotte, 59
Solodow, Joseph, 2
Southey, Robert, 39, 40
Sprengius, Johannes, 21
Spurzheim, Johann Gaspar, 58, 64
Statue. *See* Galatea
Stedman, Jane, 102n
Stephens, Henry Pottinger, 114-115, 130, 133
Stevenson, Matthew, 30
Strand Theatre, 104, 114
Sublime, 46, 47, 53
Sullivan, Sir Arthur, 102
Supple, Tim, 154n
Svengali, 123, 124, 128
Swann, Thomas, Burnett, 145
Swedenborg, Emanuel, 76, 77, 78, 79
Swinburne, Algernon Charles, 82, 83-4, 85, 88, 91

Taggard, Genevieve, 139, 142
Talbot, A. J., 116n
Tattersall, Malcolm H., 151
Taylor, John, 29-30, 30n
Taylor, Tom, 125, 127
Tennyson, Alfred Lord, 53, 59, 76
Tennyson, Charles, 77, 76n
Tennyson, Emily, 59, 62
Tennyson, Frederick, 76-9, 76n, 136
Terry, G. E., 102
Terry, Marion, 62, 107-8, 110
Thomas, Donald, 53
Thomas, Moy, 114
Tottel's Miscellany, 22-3
Travers, Henry, 32
Tree, Herbert Beerbohm, 117, 123-4
Tripp, Edward, 159

Urania (Venus), 77, 78, 130

Valency, Maurice, 97, 122, 124
Vegetarianism, 5, 145
Venus, xi, 3, 11, 12, 13, 14, 15, 16, 17, 23,

28, 32, 33, 34, 38, 41, 44, 45, 48, 49,
50, 60, 61, 67, 68, 69, 77, 82, 85, 86,
91, 93, 104, 121, 122, 123, 146, 153,
154, 159
Vesonder, Timothy, 98, 99, 121, 122
Vinge, Louise, 7, 9, 27, 34, 35
Vulcan. *See* Hephaestos

Walker, Alice, xiii
Wall, Kathleen, 11
Waller, Edmund, 30
Walsingham, Thomas, 14
Waterhouse, John William, 88, 88n
Watts, George Frederic, 88, 91
Wedmore, Frederick, 111
Westmacott, Richard, 84-5

Whitehouse, Robert, 136
Wilde, Oscar, xv, 119
Winckelmann, Johann Joachim, 85, 86
Wither, George, 18
Wollstonecraft, Mary, 37, 38, 46
Woodhouse, James, 32
Woolner, Thomas, 93-5
Wurdemann, Audrey, 150

Yenal, Edith, 13

Zeus, 31, 130, 145, 153
Zeuxes, 15, 18, 19n, 29, 32
Ziolkowski, Theodore, xx

For Product Safety Concerns and Information please contact our EU
representative GPSR@taylorandfrancis.com
Taylor & Francis Verlag GmbH, Kaufingerstraße 24, 80331 München, Germany

www.ingramcontent.com/pod-product-compliance
Lightning Source LLC
Chambersburg PA
CBHW071353290426
44108CB00014B/1527